Book of Personal Technology

The Wall Street Journal Book of Personal Technology

Walter S. Mossberg

RANDOM HOUSE

 Published in the United States by Times Books, a division of Random House, Inc., New York, and simultaneously in Canada by Random House of Canada Limited, Toronto.

All of the columns that appear in this work are by Walter Mossberg and were originally published in *The Wall Street Journal.*

Grateful acknowledgment is made to Nurit Karlin for permission to reprint 8 illustrations.

Library of Congress Cataloging-in-Publication Data

Mossberg, Walter S.
The Wall Street journal book of personal technology / Walter S. Mossberg.—1st ed.
p. cm.
Includes index.
ISBN 0-8129-2602-1 (trade paper)
1. Microcomputers. 2. Computer networks. I. Title.
QA76.5.M6487 1995
004.16—dc20 95-12196

Manufactured in the United States of America on acid-free paper
98765432
FIRST EDITION
Book design by Laura Hammond Hough

To Edie, Steve, and Jon,

and for my parents,

Rhoda and Jack

Preface

It's been fifteen years since the mass-market personal computer made its appearance, and by now it is a common feature in most businesses and schools, and in nearly a third of American homes. It is unquestionably a wonderful invention that has placed vast new power into the hands of average people, and promises to link us all together in one great information-sharing society.

Yet, unlike any other consumer product that has enjoyed great commercial success, the PC remains remarkably difficult for most people to use skillfully. Even if they master its basic operation, or learn one computer program well, casual computer users can quickly get lost again if they try to add a new piece of hardware or adopt new software. The computer makes smart people feel stupid, and conscientious people feel guilty for not becoming more technically literate. It seems to demand that you either become an expert, or be consigned to the role of a bumbling bystander as everyone else joins the technology revolution.

Some of this is no doubt due to the unusual nature of the computer. Unlike a microwave oven or the automatic transmission in your car, the PC has a constantly varying look and feel, depending on what software it's running. Conquering a spreadsheet program on Monday doesn't necessarily make you the master of the machine on Tuesday, when you use graphics software to turn the same computer into a digital easel. In addition, the technologies behind computers and software are improving so rapidly that it's hard even for experts to keep up.

But a lot of the problems with computers stem from something much more prosaic, and less forgivable. They are made and designed by members of a technology-oriented class which knows little about average users and often assumes that those who struggle with PCs are either too dumb or too lazy to get it right. A favorite expression in the industry is "RTFM!"—which means "Read the F——— Manual!" Too bad that manual is often as dense and unintelligible as the product it's supposed to explain. The industry has finally latched onto the buzzword of "usability," and products are slowly improving. A few companies have made good strides, but most just talk, and the user continues to feel confused and abandoned.

That's why we launched the Personal Technology column in *The Wall Street Journal* in 1991. Our idea was to take the consumer's side in the struggle to master the machine, to deliver a weekly dose of useful information in plain English, but in a way that never condescends to our readers just because they can't tell one chip from another. What's more, we were determined to deviate sharply from the reverent, worshipful, gee-whiz tone that permeated most reviews of computers and software. If computers and software were a mystery to many smart, but nontechnical, users, we reasoned, maybe it was the fault of their designers and manufacturers, not the users.

And that's why the very first sentence of the very first Personal Technology column, on October 17, 1991, read, "Personal computers are just too hard to use, and it isn't your fault."

The idea for such a column came to me the year before, in 1990, while I was serving as the *Journal*'s national security correspondent, covering the final stages of the cold war and the opening stages of the Persian Gulf War. I spent many days that year jetting around the world with Secretary of State James Baker, wedged into a narrow rear press seat in his ancient government jet with a dozen or so other journalists. By that time, computers had been my hobby for nearly a decade, and I knew enough about them to find myself serving as a kind of answer man for friends and colleagues who found the PC confusing, a role played out by other aficionados in offices and neighborhoods everywhere. Even on Baker's plane, where there was no shortage of brains and talent, two or three of us who were computer savvy spent a lot of time helping the others cope with their laptop machines.

One problem, I found, was that these smart folks had no good place to read about how to use their computers. The computer magazines had long ago abandoned casual users like them, and become hard for the uninitiated to understand. Most computer coverage in the general press was either news-oriented, or consisted of columns that suffered from many of the same flaws as the trade magazines. I wondered if it would be possible to do a regular column that would explain and review computers and software in the same way I was doing it personally for my friends and colleagues—in English, but always bearing in mind that my audience consisted of smart people and that consumers had a right to expect products they could use more easily.

That year, I took the idea to the *Journal*'s managing editor, who snapped it up in a brief conversation, and said I could do it once my foreign policy assignment was over. In mid-1991, after the Gulf War, I returned with a detailed written plan for the column, and won formal approval from the top editors, who had the guts to try something new and different. In several respects, they were taking a big risk, breaking from the traditional *Journal* style. This would be a personal, subjective feature with a strong voice—almost unheard of in the *Journal*'s news pages. It would be likely to criticize products sold by some of the paper's largest advertisers. It would run weekly in a prominent place where no column at that time had weekly status. And it would take the form of a single essay each week, rather than a series of short news items like most other *Journal* columns.

So unusual was this computer column that it was given a different logo and typeface from other columns, and its launch was watched over by a half dozen top editors. The unstated condition was that, if readers found the tone too strong or the topics too narrow, Personal Technology would be killed after six months or so. But by the end of 1991, after only about ten weeks, the column was drawing more positive reader mail and phone calls than any new *Journal* feature since the paper had instituted an index years before. We've never looked back. The column has now been imitated in a half-dozen other publications, and has inspired the creation of several other weekly *Journal* columns with strong voices, on health, careers, and work and the family.

This volume contains 88 of the best of these Personal Technology columns, from that maiden entry in 1991 through the end of 1994. I have organized them into seven parts, ranging from general consumer advice to specific reviews or primers on PC hardware and software, going on-line, multimedia and CD-ROMs, kids and games, and a handful of columns about fax machines and other noncomputer topics. One entry, the only one penned by a guest author while I was on vacation, even concerns the lowly typewriter.

Because of the rapid changes in the computer business, it made sense to tilt the column selections toward newer entries. Thus, more than half of these columns are from 1994. But every column here, even if it was written in 1992 and didn't mention more recent developments like Pentium chips or Power Macs, was selected because the advice it gives holds true today, despite the advent of new models or versions. Where appropriate, I have added notes at the end of some columns to update the topics they covered, and reflect changes in the market since they were written.

Acknowledgments

So many people—in journalism, the computer industry, and elsewhere—have helped me with these columns that it would be impossible to name them all. But a few must be acknowledged.

First and foremost are the two managing editors of the *Journal* under whom the Personal Technology column has flourished. Norm Pearlstine, who has since moved on to Time, Inc., had the guts and foresight to approve the idea instantly, to help shape it, and to make sure it happened despite some doubts elsewhere in the paper's hierarchy. He is the father of these columns. The current managing editor, Paul Steiger, was present at the column's creation as Norm's deputy and has been a strong supporter from the first meeting when I presented a detailed plan for the project. He continues to advise and support me in every way. Barney Calame, the deputy managing editor, and Cynthia Crossen, editor of the Marketplace page, have also been generous with encouragment and advice. Cathy Panagoulias, the *Journal*'s technology editor, has been another strong source of inspiration and feedback. Peter Kann, the *Journal*'s publisher, has lent me maximum support, and even pinch-hit for a week in 1994 with a wonderful ode to that low-tech favorite, the typewriter (reprinted herein).

I have also been blessed with three strong yet subtle column editors during the period covered by this collection—first Don Arbour, then Bob Muller, and lastly Rose Ellen D'Angelo. They have made each week's installment more succinct and literate, improving my prose without intruding on the personal style and subjective views so necessary to give the column a voice. They also wrote all those clever headlines. Another talented person who has made me look better is

Nurit Karlin, an independent artist whose humorous weekly illustrations have helped humanize a sometimes forbidding topic. (Samples of her work appear throughout this book.) My administrative assistant, Carrie Kent, a journalist herself, helped organize the material for this book and has managed my office and my work schedule and thus saved me from disappearing under a towering stack of review software.

Many colleagues in journalism offered moral support and practical advice about launching the column and about making the unusual transition from covering national and world affairs to writing on technology. Among them were the *Journal*'s own Gerald Seib, Robert Greenberger and Gregg Zachary; David Hoffman of *The Washington Post*; Thomas Friedman and Peter Lewis of *The New York Times*; John McWethy of ABC News; and Margaret Warner of public television.

Inside the computer industry, I have gained valuable insights from a host of people who speak to me periodically and candidly about their products and businesses, and offer feedback on the columns, positive and negative. Some of my more spirited—and valuable—discussions have been with Bill Gates, Chris Peters, and Patty Stonesifer of Microsoft; Dave Nagel, Don Norman, and Brodie Keast of Apple; Jim Manzi and Jeffrey Beir of Lotus; Philippe Kahn of Borland; Steve Case and Jean Villanueva of America Online; Barry Berkov of CompuServe; and Scott Kurnit, formerly of Prodigy. I have also benefited from insights provided by some veteran public relations people, including Pam Alexander of Alexander Communications, and Matt Mirapaul, formerly of Zenith.

The notion of turning the columns into this book was hatched by Peter Osnos, publisher of Times Books, and Dick Tofel, the *Journal*'s assistant managing editor. Karl Weber, managing director of Times Business Books, edited this volume deftly and helped define and design it. There would simply be no book without these three people, and I am in debt to all of them.

Finally, I could never have carried off the column and this anthology without the love and support of my wife, Edie, and my teenage sons, Steve and Jon. They have all contributed ideas and feedback to the columns over the years. And they have tolerated my erratic work schedule, whether in the office or locked away in my study at home, staring at computer screens for long periods at odd hours. Whatever creativity or energy I have been able to put into these columns I owe to them.

—Walter S. Mossberg
April 1995

Contents

Part II: Hardware

Part III: Productivity Software

Part VII: Other Stuff

Part I
The Computing Consumer

Many of my columns over the years have been about the broad, cross-cutting issues affecting computer owners as consumers; how to read a computer ad, buy computers via mail order, or choose the right beginners' book or magazine. Others have been warnings about, or critiques of, industry practices. These include charging for telephone support, issuing bug-ridden first versions of software, or equipping new machines with too little memory to run popular programs well. Among my favorites here are the two-part series on pet peeves about computers, which included input from readers, and the broadside against Intel's initial refusal to replace defective Pentium chips for every owner, regardless of occupation.

1
How to Stop Worrying and Get the Most from Your Computer

Personal computers are just too hard to use, and it isn't your fault.

The computer industry boasts that its products can help everyone become more productive. Maybe so. But many people can't afford the time and money needed to get the most out of PCs. Sure, there are exceptions. Everyone knows a PC addict who gives advice all around. But these wizards often spend hours on their hobby to hone their skills. And there are those who use a specific program like the Lotus 1-2-3 spreadsheet all day and can make it sing. But even these people tend to conquer only one package.

For most people, getting the fullest use out of computer products means training classes, books, and the like. This is an unusual phenomenon in the history of consumer technology. There are no user groups or seminars for owners of, say, televisions or toaster ovens.

You can speed the learning process, but it may require a greater initial investment. If you buy Apple Computer's Macintosh, you'll find that powerful software can be relatively easy to master because even complex functions are controlled by manipulating pictures on the screen, or through "menus" listing commands that vary little from program to program. But the powerful Macintosh models often are costlier than heavily discounted International Business Machines clones.

Some of the Macintosh's simplicity and consistency can be obtained on IBM-compatible computers by using Microsoft Windows, special software that lets you control the computer using Macintosh-type screens and commands. But despite the hype in many computer magazines, Windows runs poorly on millions of older PCs. And it requires lots of memory and large hard-disk drives to operate at its best, even on newer computers.

What about those who would like to get more out of their computers without breaking the bank? Here's a sampling of relatively inexpensive products that can increase productivity by demystifying common tasks, organizing your work or juicing up your hardware. Each is readily available for around $100 or less at popular mail-order houses or discount stores.

To be sure, each of these items has good and useful competitors. But I've found these six to be reliable and easy to master.

Menu Works: This versatile program for IBM-compatible machines displays a menu whenever you turn on your computer. The menu lists all of the programs on your hard-disk drive and lets you run them with a single keystroke, without forcing you to remember file names and locations. When you're done with a program, you bounce back to the Menu Works menu, ready to launch another or perform such tasks as locating or copying files. Menu Works is easy to install, and it will even scan your disk and build a menu for you. The manual is brief and clear on how to alter menus. (PC Dynamics, $14.95.)

XTreeGold: This program presents the entire contents of your IBM-compatible machine's hard disk and floppy disks in clear diagrams and lists, and then makes it easy to copy, delete, move, rename, or launch programs. The program is easy to install and customize. It allows you to view documents, including pictures, created by other programs. It presents commands clearly on the screen. (XTree, $92.)

Stacker: A software program that compresses all the files on your IBM-compatible PC's hard disk. The result is to effectively expand the size of your hard disk by as much as 100 percent. The process is complex, but you don't have to understand it. The installation program guides you step by step. (Stac Electronics, $99.)

Adobe Type Manager: A small program that permits a Macintosh or IBM-compatible PC running Windows to produce handsome fonts made for costly industry-standard PostScript printers even on less expensive printers that lack Adobe's proprietary PostScript circuitry. It operates "in the background," meaning you don't have to enter repeated instructions to get it to work. (Adobe Systems, $59.)

Access PC: Another program that works in the background on a Macintosh. This one automatically permits the current line of Macs to read and write files directly from and to 3½-inch disks formatted on IBM-compatible PCs, greatly simplifying the exchange of data between the two kinds of machines. All you do is put the Access PC file into a special directory, or folder, on your hard disk, and you automatically gain the ability to use—and even to format—IBM-compatible disks. (Insignia Solutions, $62.)

Super Boomerang: This one lets Mac users leap quickly to their most-used folders, or directories, and summon their most-used files from any program's standard "open" or "save" command. The program remembers your frequently-used files and folders. It's bundled as part of a package called Now Utilities. (Now Software, $89.)

10/17/91

2
A Buyer's Guide for Translating PC into English

For a lot of people—even smart, successful people—the process of shopping for a PC ranks right up there with car-buying as a vision of Consumer Hell. It's true that computer sales clerks aren't likely to offer to throw in free floor mats if you'll take the lime-green model with fake wood trim. But at least car salespeople mainly exaggerate in terms you can understand. Everybody knows what power windows are—the kind made at glass factories, not at Microsoft. Plus, with a car, you can usually eyeball most of the features. And you can take it for a test drive.

Walk into a computer store, however, and you instantly feel stupid, even if you're known to the rest of the world as a genius at whatever else you do. All the machines pretty much look the same: gray boxes of various sizes with a lot of very important-looking stuff displayed on their screens. Their distinguishing features are hidden from view and identified only by a cascade of technobabble terminology. There's little chance to test-drive the computers, and you're gripped with the fear that whatever you buy will be obsolete within weeks, unable even to run the next version of electronic solitaire.

So it seems sensible to offer up a couple of columns to help computer shoppers—a sort of "Guide to the PC Perplexed." First, I'll present a brief glossary of some common computer terms and acronyms. In the next column, I'll lay out my recommendations on how much computer power and capacity you should buy for personal and small-business use.

The most confusing computer concepts for many people are memory and disk storage. Both describe the capacity of a computer to retain data—whether that data is a software program you buy or something you create, such as a memo, picture, or mailing list. And both are measured in the same tongue-twisting units: kilobytes, or KB—roughly equal to 1,000 typed characters, or 150 to 200 words; and megabytes, MB or "megs"—equal to 1,000 kilobytes, or roughly a million typed characters. By way of example, the text of this chapter is about six kilobytes in size, while you could fit a pretty hefty novel into a single megabyte.

Memory and storage are different things entirely. Memory—or RAM, for random access memory—is the temporary capacity of a computer to store data at any given moment. It is located on chips deep inside the machine, but the data stored in them are erased once you turn the computer off. And it usually totals a relatively small number of megabytes—say, four or eight.

Disk storage is usually much larger—at least 200 megabytes these days—and, as the term implies, it doesn't use chips but instead encodes data on spinning platters coated with magnetic materials similar to what's used on audio or video tapes. These disks record the same kind of information held in memory chips, but they retain it when the power goes off. Without enough memory and disk storage, a PC can be crippled no matter how new it is. The latest software requires generous amounts of both.

Think of memory as being roughly analogous to the temporary assembly of documents on your desk for completing a project. Disk storage, in contrast, is more like a file cabinet in which you permanently store the documents. When you open a word-processor file, you are transferring it from a disk into the computer's memory chips, where it resides as you edit, read, or print it. When you save a file you've created, you're copying it from the memory chips to long-term disk storage.

To add to the confusion, there are different kinds of disk storage. A hard-disk drive is a PC's principal long-term data repository. It contains one or more fast-spinning platters sealed in a box tucked away in the machine. A floppy disk is actually a fairly rigid 3½-inch plastic square (the floppy, circular part is inside the plastic shell) that holds up to 1.44 megabytes of data. The computer reads these portable disks via a floppy-disk drive—the slot into which you pop the disks.

The hottest form of disk storage is called CD-ROM, for compact disc–read only memory. These removable disks are small, shiny platters that look exactly like music CDs, but can store a whopping six hundred megabytes or more of computer data for far less cost than a hard disk. The catch is that you can't save any of your own data to a CD-ROM disk. Your PC can only read the data that came on it—thus the ROM, or "read only," part of the title. Most PCs now come with CD-ROM drives for reading these disks. The standard type of CD-ROM drive today is called double speed (2X), which only means it's twice as fast as the first generation in certain ways.

A computer's main chip, its central brain, is usually called a CPU, or central processing unit. These come in too many varieties to list here, but on IBM-compatible PCs, the mainstream type is a 486 and the fastest current CPU is a Pentium. On Apple's Macintosh machines, the mainstream CPU is a 68040 and the speed demon is a PowerPC.

Even a PC's video has its own terminology. VGA (video graphics array) is the basic standard type, while Super VGA, or SVGA, offers greater resolution. Local bus video means the video is driven by special high-speed circuitry inside.

These terms, of course, hardly exhaust the technobabble arsenal of a skilled PC peddler. But learning them will give you a start when you head to the dealership to kick the tires on that '94 Compaq with power Windows.

8/25/94

3
Before You Shop, Arm Yourself

This column is devoted to my recommendations for the essential features an average buyer should look for in a new desktop computer. This compact buyer's guide is meant for a typical family or small business that needs a robust, versatile PC. It's not for big corporations, specialized users like graphic designers, or computer freaks who want the latest, fastest and biggest of everything.

Even so, I find myself recommending a significantly more powerful configuration than in the past, for several reasons.

First, software applications like word processing and even games are demanding more and more machine to run adequately. (See "Dense Software Strains the Memory of the Average PC," page 24.) Second, PC operating systems, the underlying programs that control a computer, are due for fundamental revisions in 1995. Both Microsoft's new operating system for IBM-compatibles, code-named Chicago, and Apple's new Macintosh operating system, code-named Copland, will require more muscular machines than those typical today. And third, the explosion in multimedia software and in sophisticated on-line services puts heavy new demands on hardware.

The good news is that the heftier machine outlined below won't cost you any more than a lesser PC from a couple of years ago, because of the constant decline in hardware prices.

Memory and disk storage: Nothing is more important to a satisfying computer experience than having enough memory (RAM) and hard-disk storage capacity. These factors matter more than small differences in the main processor chip or the computer's brand name. An extra $300 or $400 invested here will pay huge dividends.

Do not buy a PC with less than eight megabytes (8MB) of memory. If the model you like has only four megabytes of memory, pay extra on the spot to have it expanded to eight megabytes, or add memory chips yourself. Adding four megabytes of memory should cost around $200.

Your hard disk should be at least 300 megabytes in size; 500 megabytes would be better. It's much cheaper to buy extra hard-disk capacity at purchase time than it is later; often another 100 megabytes can be had for $50 or $75. (On a Mac, you might get away with 250 megabytes of hard disk, because Mac programs tend to take up less room.)

Central Processing Unit (CPU): This is the main brain of the computer. On an IBM-compatible, I prefer at least a 486 chip running at a speed of 66 MHz. On a Mac, you want at least a 68040 chip running at 33 MHz. The top-of-the-line CPU chips are Pentium chips on IBM-compatibles and PowerPC chips on Macs. They are so new that few software programs take full advantage of them, and the chips are quirky in some situations. Most good computers now can be upgraded with these speed-demon chips later, though the upgraded machines won't likely be as fast as a Pentium or PowerPC model built from the ground up.

Video: Get a monitor with a "dot-pitch" rating of 0.28 mm or less—a smaller number means a sharper image. Make sure the computer's internal video system has at least one megabyte of VRAM, which is special video memory that makes the screen display faster, and that it can display sixty-five thousand colors or more on the screen, which makes for more realistic images. On a PC, make sure it can handle a resolution of 800 × 600 or better and is "local bus video."

Sound: Macs come with good sound. Make sure an IBM-compatible has a built-in sound system that is compatible with the popular Sound Blaster card, and that it comes with stereo speakers.

CD-ROM drive: Even if you don't care about multimedia software, get a CD-ROM drive. You'll need it, because all kinds of software will soon be distributed mainly on CD-ROM. Make sure the drive is rated at "double-speed," with an "access time" of 350 milliseconds or less (less is faster).

Modem: Another essential, especially if you ever hope to ride the information highway. Make sure it has the ability both to send and to receive faxes, and that it can send data at a speed of 14,400 bits per second (BPS) or higher. Stay away from the new 28,800 BPS models unless they meet a standard called V.34, or can be upgraded cheaply and easily to that standard. A good model in that latter category is the Sportster from U.S. Robotics.

Expandability: Make sure your computer can be upgraded to the next-level CPU chip, has at least one free slot for add-on circuitry inside and can accept at least 32 megabytes of memory.

Brand names: Unless you are a techie, don't buy a superstore's unknown house brand, or a no-name computer from your brother-in-law or from that little local shop where a socially challenged guy builds his own. Stick with established names that offer good warranties and service plans, like Compaq, Apple, IBM, AST, and Dell. Gateway 2000 and Packard Bell are generally okay, but I consider their quality and customer service to be a bit below that of the first five brands.

Finally, whatever you do, don't let yourself get flustered by some fast-talking salesperson. Stick to your guns on the key features above and you'll be a happy camper, at least until the thing crashes on you and the telephone help line puts you on hold. But that's another column.

9/1/94

4
For PC Shoppers Who Know What They Want: Mail Order Delivers

Back in the early days of personal computing—a whole dozen years ago—buying a computer and software was something like purchasing a delicate scientific instrument, or maybe rare and expensive audio equipment. You went to a small, specialized store where people steeped in technical knowledge advised you at length and then sold you costly components, which you carted to home or office with great care.

Today, such shops are increasingly rare, replaced by a few scattered computer "superstores" the size of Kmarts where the clerks usually know little and customers casually pile computers and software into shopping carts as if they were cans of soup.

For many people and businesses, however, the quickest and cheapest way to buy computer hardware and software is by mail order. You just dial a toll-free number, make your choices, and the stuff is delivered to you pronto, often overnight.

To those who haven't tried it, let me assure you it works. So long as you have a fair idea of what you want before you call, pick a reputable company to deal with, and follow a few basic precautions, mail order is as effective for buying powerful computers as for ordering that new cassette of great Beatles hits performed by a polka band.

There are two main types of PC mail-order companies. One sells mainly computers and related hardware. These companies largely market their own brands, so your choice among them depends heavily on an advance evaluation of each company's product line. The other main type of mail-order company handles products from a large number of suppliers and mostly sells software and "peripherals"—equipment like printers and monitors.

If you're looking for a complete PC, there are scores of mail-order companies to choose from. But the vast majority are no-name brands, difficult to judge for quality or even to distinguish from one another. The safest course is to pick a mail-order brand used successfully by people you know, or one that has been repeatedly praised by the leading computer magazines. These magazines aren't exactly investigative journals, and the mail-order companies are among their biggest advertisers. But brands that consistently "win" the magazine reviews are likely to be generally reliable.

Among the top mail-order brands are Dell Computer (800-348-8342), Gateway 2000 (800-846-2000) and Zeos International (800-554-7172). Each has had a few problems here and there, but on the whole they sell good systems with quality components at low prices. International Business Machines (800-426-2968) also sells some of its PCs over the phone, as does Compaq Computer (800-888-5858).

The profusion of features, and technical distinctions among them, can be very confusing, even for people familiar with computers. The ads are studded with terms like "local bus video" (a faster mechanism for displaying things).

So, before calling, try to settle on roughly the features you want (by talking to friends or reading the magazines) and how much you want to spend. Call several vendors and make specific comparisons. Above all, don't be afraid to ask a lot of questions, even if you worry they may be dumb ones. Make the salesperson speak English.

All of the above applies mainly to IBM-compatible PCs. Apple Computer's Macintosh machines aren't sold as much by mail, because the company discourages the practice. Apple sells a few models through a catalog it issues (800-795-1000).

For software and peripherals, two companies stand out, in my experience. Each has separate arms specializing in products for IBM-compatibles and Macs. One pair is PC Connection (800-800-0004) and MacConnection (800-800-3333). The other is Micro Warehouse (800-367-7080) and Mac Warehouse (800-255-6227).

These catalogs contain not only software, but memory chips, hard-disk drives, CD-ROM drives, cables, modems, and more. Micro Warehouse even sells a $239 complete do-it-yourself replacement "motherboard," the main internal component in a computer (I, for one, won't be doing-it-myself).

Again, it's sensible before calling these places to know what software or add-ons you want, or at least to have it narrowed down to a few choices. You can't browse by phone.

Some general tips apply to both kinds of mail-order dealers. Always use a credit card to order; that gives you more leverage to cancel or contest the sale, and some credit-card companies offer added warranties. Always confirm the price; ads and catalogs are frequently revised, and the fine print may contain extra fees. See whether the company offers "price protection"—a rebate if the price drops within a short period after you buy. Make sure the dealer you choose offers a money-back guarantee (usually good for thirty days), and try out your purchases within the allotted time. Avoid companies that require a "restocking fee" on returns or charge extra for credit-card sales. For software, make sure you're getting the latest version, and check to see whether it's in stock. Software publishers often advertise their new releases months before they are available.

But, on the whole, if you stick to well-known companies and follow these basic rules, mail order can be an excellent way to buy computer hardware and software. Not to mention your own copy of the "Penny Lane Polka."

3/25/93

5
In PC Product Names, Zero Often Carries Negative Connotations

Computer users can benefit from what hobbyists sometimes call "the rule of zero": *Never buy any new software, or major new revision of software, whose version number ends in a zero.*

That's because the first version shipped of a new program—say, Version 1.0—or of a major new edition of an existing program almost always seems to be afflicted with bugs and other flaws, such as incompatibilities with other software and hardware. It's smart to wait a few months for Version 1.1, or whatever the publisher calls the cleaned-up version, especially in the case of software that has a big impact on your work or business, such as word processors, spreadsheets, and accounting packages.

And the concept extends beyond software. Major new pieces of hardware, including PCs, often come to market with kinks that are ironed out only in subsequent production runs. Though hardware products usually don't have version numbers, their builders make repeated small design and manufacturing changes to fix things, especially in the early months after a model's introduction. To avoid headaches, it makes sense to wait a little while.

That's truer now than ever. In today's highly competitive market, with consumers demanding bare-bones pricing and rapid introduction of new models, hardware makers have less time and money than ever for field testing. So, the first buyers, the "early adopters" who can't wait to get their hands on a new product, too often find that they are guinea pigs for the vendors.

Even the biggest and best companies run into problems with "zero" versions of their products. Lotus Development issued version

1.1 of its 1-2-3 spreadsheet for IBM-compatible PCs running Windows after users complained that version 1.0 was sluggish. Microsoft has brought out version 5.0a of its market-leading Microsoft Word for the Macintosh computer to fix a problem that afflicted version 5.0.

Such fixes are usually free, but early adopters must suffer until they're available, and in many cases publishers don't send them out automatically; users must somehow hear about them and then request them.

There's no standard naming system for new versions that fix mistakes. Embarrassed companies may label them version 1.1, or 1.01, or 1.0a, and call them "maintenance releases" or "updates" or some other euphemism. A few try to put one over on their customers by fixing bugs in mid-production without issuing a new version, a practice called slipstreaming. That helps future buyers but stiffs early adopters.

Things can be even trickier in the case of hardware, depending on the problem and the manufacturer. Some early buyers of Apple Computer's PowerBook notebook computers wound up with faulty disk drives, though the machine had undergone field testing and is widely regarded as one of the best-designed computers on the market. Apple offered to fix the faulty computers free, then changed the disk drive's design, and the PowerBooks have gone on to sell like $3,000 hotcakes. But users had to know they had the problem, and how to resolve it, to get it fixed.

With lower-margin mail-order companies, the process may not be so smooth. One Fortune 500 company president told me recently that a major mail-order computer company had been unable to fix a notebook computer he had bought from them that was getting only a fraction of the promised battery life. The company was prompt and polite in repeatedly trying different solutions and even sending him replacement machines. But he said a company representative admitted that the technicians were stumped and that the model hadn't undergone much field testing before being released.

It isn't supposed to be this way. The software industry uses a practice called "beta testing," in which experienced users are asked to confidentially try out new programs, or major revisions of old ones, usually for a period of months. As the testers report the bugs and problems in the prerelease versions, the publisher tries to fix them and ships back a series of revised versions for further testing. Sometimes the process gets gargantuan. Microsoft used thirteen thousand beta testers to help develop the latest big revision of Windows, and set up a special electronic bulletin board to receive their daily reports.

But even the best beta testing can't account for every possible combination of computer, printer, monitor, and software that users may try to hook up, or every odd use they may make of a program. So bugs and conflicts still occur.

There's great temptation to become an early adopter. Computer companies often advertise a new product or model for months before it's available, and buyers are salivating for it. Such ad campaigns also put immense pressure on engineering and production people inside the companies to get the goods out the door despite any last-minute glitches.

But my advice to potential early adopters is to keep cool. If you must be first on your block to have new computer stuff, you might volunteer to be a beta tester. (The reward for such testing is usually a free copy of the software.) Otherwise, unless you have money and time to burn, at least try to avoid being an involuntary beta tester for computer companies. A little patience up front can save a lot of hassles later.

7/30/92

Version numbers now are higher, but the "rule of zero" still holds. In early 1995, for instance, Microsoft had to announce a free upgrade for Word for Macintosh 6.0, because the program was so sluggish.

6
PC Users Can Benefit and Foster Innovation by Buying "Shareware"

Now that you've bought that new computer, you've probably learned a fact of life with PCs: Software can be expensive. Even with price wars and discounts, leading word-processing and spreadsheet packages can top $200, and games and utility packages, designed to make computing fun or easy, can approach $100 a pop.

But there's an alternative source of good software that costs much less than commercial companies' products. It's called "shareware," and dedicated computer users have relied on it for years.

Most shareware programs are written by talented individuals in their spare time and made available on the honor system. If you try one for a week or so and decide to use it regularly, you are asked to mail the author a check for a relatively small sum, typically $10 to $50. In return, the author may send you a printed manual for the program, agree to provide updates as he or she improves it, tell you how to activate additional features, or deactivate notices the program displays reminding you to pay up.

Shareware isn't free unless it's specifically labeled as such (and thus becomes "freeware"), and it isn't in the public domain unless its author explicitly places it there. It is also not to be confused with free "demo" versions of commercial programs, which usually are passed out in crippled form—for instance, without the ability to save or print files.

In most cases, shareware programs are full-featured copyrighted products whose authors expect to be paid. They are merely offered on a try-before-you-buy basis, and are distributed through bulletin boards, on-line services, and other unconventional means. Authors encourage copying of the software, so it can be tried by more people. But if you make a shareware program part of your regular repertoire of software, you're supposed to pay for it.

Paying for shareware not only is the right thing to do, it's in the self-interest of computer users. It encourages innovation and helps maintain a broad base of programming talent that can give rise to great products the big companies overlook. ProComm Plus, a communications package, and Kid Pix, a children's art program, both began as shareware but found big retail audiences.

Many people assume that shareware is inferior to commercial software or consists mainly of oddball or technical applications. It's true that these programs often have fewer bells and whistles than commercial competitors. The shareware precursors of ProComm and Kid Pix—which can still be found—have fewer features than the retail versions. But I've tried hundreds of shareware programs over the years, and overall, have found them to be good, practical products.

Some people fear shareware will introduce a virus into their PC. But many well-known sources of shareware screen the programs for viruses before making them available.

There are three main ways to acquire shareware. Each entails some up-front costs, in addition to the shareware fees themselves. But they buy you access to a cornucopia of software, including word processors, spreadsheets, personal-finance programs, games, utilities and many more types than can be listed here.

The most common way to get shareware is by modem, through logging onto a local bulletin board or commercial on-line service that maintains libraries of such programs. The big services, especially CompuServe and America Online, have tens of thousands of shareware programs for IBM-compatible and Macintosh computers. You can also get shareware collections on disks, for modest amounts, from either computer user groups or a few commercial distribution companies.

The third method is to buy one of the growing number of books about shareware, which often come with disks containing programs the author has selected. Two such volumes that I like are *The Windows Shareware 500* and *The Mac Shareware 500*, both published by Ventana

Press, Chapel Hill, North Carolina. The books cost $40 and come with free membership and free time on America Online, where additional and updated programs can be found.

Many shareware subcategories have emerged, mainly based on how the authors get compensated. I've seen "beerware," in which you're asked to toast the author with a brew; and "charityware," in which you're asked to send a check to a designated good cause. Some shareware authors produce "nagware," in which the typical payment-reminder notices are so obnoxious and intrusive you might pay just to avoid seeing them. One shareware program I used would put up a nag screen at random moments while the software was in use, requiring users to acknowledge the reminder before they could resume work.

Other authors appeal to the user's conscience and sympathy. I recently came upon this appeal in an impressive Macintosh shareware color drawing program written by Sean Bergin of County Kerry, Ireland: "StudioCraft was written by an individual to be used by individuals. I have a wife and two young children who would, I am sure, be delighted if StudioCraft turned out to be a success. That success depends on you, and people like you, trying it, liking it, and sending me a paltry $35."

I have sent payments over the years for many shareware programs I've used heavily. But writing this column has prompted me to look over my hard disk and identify a few I never paid for. I'll be sending several checks in coming days. Maybe you should do the same.

5/27/93

7
Talk Is Cheap? Not If You're Calling for Software Support

Hold on to your wallets. Free unlimited telephone support, long the safety net for computer users trying to figure out complicated software programs, is being eliminated by the major software companies on at least some of their products. Instead, the companies will force customers seeking help on those programs to pay for it, after a brief initial period, at rates as high as two dollars a minute—kind of like calling one of those telephone psychics.

The new pay-for-help policies vary from company to company and product to product, but the bottom line for consumers is that there are more hidden costs built into the price of some software, including off-the-shelf copies of Microsoft's popular Windows 3.1 program. And the hardest-hit users are likely to be those least able to pay and most in need of technical support: individuals and small businesses and organizations.

These new support charges aren't the result of caprice or sheer avarice. The costs of phone support have surged in recent years, as products have become more numerous and powerful, and more individuals and small businesses without in-house support staffs have started buying them. Companies such as Microsoft and WordPerfect have built expensive support centers and devote a large share of their work forces to staffing them.

At the same time, the retail prices of software programs have drifted downward. Word processors and spreadsheets that once fetched $300 or so at discount now bring in less than half of that, on average. And another big plunge may be in the offing, as Borland International has started selling a top-of-the-line Windows spreadsheet, Quattro Pro, for just $49.95.

In addition, many top programs are being increasingly sold as part of combined packages called "offices" or "suites," and others—including Windows itself—are mainly delivered pre-installed on the hard disks of new PCs. These sales methods lower costs but also yield less revenue per individual product.

If you're a shareholder in a software company, the new pay-for-help policies may be good news. But if you're a software consumer, they mean all these new lower prices aren't really the bargains they seem. (Those of you who are both will have to figure it out for yourselves.)

Some industry officials have tried to cloak the end of free unlimited support in press releases that tout new, multitiered pay-for-help plans, ranging from $2-a-minute phone calls, through $129 or $195 annual fees, to $20,000-a-year retainers for big businesses. They say they're adding more features, such as twenty-four-hour service and toll-free lines, in the new pay-for-help plans.

Most companies stress they will still offer free, unlimited canned help in the form of taped tips played over the phone or automated systems that fax canned answers to common questions. But those services don't feature personalized help from a human. Most firms also offer help via bulletin boards on on-line services, but of course using those services costs money.

The companies even claim that many of the changes were made at "customer request." Maybe so, but I doubt that even the most confused customers flooded the companies with requests to please, please let them pay $2 a minute to get their questions answered.

Here's a rundown of the new policies for small users at some leading software companies.

At Microsoft, if you buy Windows off the shelf, free support (via a toll call) is now limited to ninety days from the date of your first call, the period when the company says most questions come in. After that, it'll cost you either $2 a minute, up to $25 a call, or $195 a year for unlimited toll-free calls. If you get Windows pre-installed on your computer, Microsoft won't help at all, in most cases. It will usually direct you to the computer's builder for help on Windows. Such support may still be free, but I've found it can be pretty bad.

It's important to note, however, that this new pay-for-help plan applies only to Windows itself. In the U.S., Microsoft is still offering free unlimited phone support, via a toll call, for its most popular software programs designed for Windows users, such as Word and Excel.

For Borland's Quattro Pro spreadsheet, free support covers installation questions. Other questions will cost $2 a minute to get answered, or $129 a year for unlimited calls. That's a hefty price on a $50 product, and may make it costlier than Excel, depending on your need for support.

Since 1991, users of Lotus Development's 1-2-3 spreadsheet, the Ami Pro word processor, and other mainstream Lotus products have been stuck with pay-for-help policies. Free toll-free support is limited to ninety days from the first call. After that, it's $2 a minute, or $129 a year combined for all products.

These changes make it imperative for customers to investigate support costs before buying software. Lean toward the easiest-to-use programs, and to those still offering free support for the life of the product. Don't buy products with complicated features you don't need, and don't upgrade to new versions that add nonessential features you'll have to learn. Otherwise, you might find yourself on the phone, with the meter ticking away.

10/14/93

Lotus later corrected an erroneous press statement and said it wasn't charging for Ami Pro support. Since then, however, it has in fact decided to make users pay for it.

8
Dense Software Strains the Memory of the Average PC

Leave it to the computer industry. Just as the hardware makers have started selling fairly powerful personal computers at prices that put them in reach of many more families and small businesses, the software publishers have begun to require more memory for new programs than those popular computers typically offer.

Average consumers are caught in the middle. Many people buying heavily advertised, high-powered mass-market machines from leading companies—like Compaq, IBM, Apple, and Dell—will wind up mighty frustrated. When they try to use the latest versions of some popular business software from the likes of Microsoft, Borland, and WordPerfect—or even many elaborate games and multimedia offerings—they'll find some of it runs slowly and poorly in the four megabytes of memory commonly installed on popular PCs that sell for under $2,000. And the mismatch is likely to spread to more and more programs.

The hardware companies, caught in a price war, are reluctant to boost the cost of their machines by upping the standard memory capacity. The software companies, racing to cram scores of often marginal features into their programs, conveniently overlook today's typical configuration. What's more, people on both sides of the industry live in a sort of dream world. They too often work on machines with two, three or four times the usual memory. They rely too much on feedback from customers in big business who equip their own machines lavishly. And many falsely assume that average people will find it just as trivial as they do—in money, time, and skill—to pop open their machines and add more memory.

As a result, small-business and individual owners soon will find themselves either settling for less capable software (like the basic all-in-one programs often bundled with their machines) or shelling out a couple of hundred dollars for memory chips and trying to install them. It's happened before—every few years, in fact. But that's no excuse for selling customers products that work badly together.

Here's a brief explanation of what's involved in this memory mess, and a little advice on what to do.

When I refer here to "memory," I'm not talking about the computer's long-term storage capacity, which is the size of the hard-disk drive inside—though that aspect of the hardware also is under pressure from fatter and fatter software.

Instead, the real crisis for average buyers lies in the machine's short-term capacity, the total size of the programs and data files it can work on at any one moment. This is what the industry means by "memory," or RAM (for random access memory), as opposed to disk storage. The size of memory is governed by how many and what type of memory chips a computer holds. Most mainstream machines being sold in large computer, electronics, and office-products stores come with four megabytes of such memory, or enough to hold about four million characters of text at once.

The best way to cope with the memory squeeze is to buy more memory in the first place. I used to advise getting four megabytes with new computers, and more if you could afford it. I now must reluctantly boost that recommendation. If you expect to use your computer with the most capable business and entertainment software, you should pick a computer with at least eight megabytes of memory. This is especially crucial if you're buying a multimedia machine. An extra four megabytes should add $200 or less to a machine's price. If you can afford even more, get it. You can never have too much.

What if you own a four-megabyte machine? First, you can just stick with the all-in-one packages that ship with many machines, such as Microsoft Works, or ClarisWorks. These take far less memory than highly touted stand-alone word processors, spreadsheets, and art programs, but they are probably good enough for most people.

Second, you can favor those major programs that run well on

four-megabyte machines. If you're running Windows with four megabytes, pass up the latest Windows version of WordPerfect in favor of Microsoft Word, or Lotus's Ami Pro word processor. Avoid Borland's Quattro Pro for Windows spreadsheet and skip Microsoft's Excel as well, except for light-duty spreadsheet work. For writing on a Macintosh, you can choose WriteNow from WordStar or Claris's MacWrite Pro.

Third, don't believe the memory requirements listed on boxes of software. They often are understated, so assume it'll take a megabyte or two more to run the program optimally.

Finally, you can add memory chips, which come embedded on plastic sticks called SIMMs (for single in-line memory module) and pop into special little slots in your computer. At about $50 a megabyte, they are pretty cheap. But they can be tricky to install, because different computer models—even from the same maker—accept extra memory in different combinations and steps. Some may not permit you to add small increments like one or two megabytes, or even force you to pull out and waste the memory chips you have before adding larger ones.

In my view, this is just another case of the computer industry overpromising and making things harder than necessary for nontechnical users. It's time for either leaner software or a change in the standard under-$2,000 machine so it offers more memory. Something's got to give.

2/17/94

By the end of 1994, eight-megabyte machines were slowly gaining ground, but most consumer models still had just four megabytes. Meanwhile, even some children's software offered during the 1994 Christmas season required eight megabytes.

9

Gentle Guides to Cracking Open Computers' Mysteries

When folks settle down with their first computer, or with a new type or new generation of computer, they instinctively grab for a book to tell them what to do. Computers make even smart people feel dumb. So the computer-book section of every bookstore groans with fat, costly volumes that promise to make people the masters of their machines.

Of all these books, there are a couple I'd recommend for beginners. For new or prospective IBM-compatible owners, the class of the field, in my view, is a new volume called *The Little PC Book* by veteran computer columnist Lawrence J. Magid. The $17.95 guide, published by little Peachpit Press of Berkeley, California, bills itself as "a gentle introduction" to PCs, and that's exactly what it is. Instead of overwhelming the reader with explanations of complicated commands and the like, Mr. Magid takes a rock-bottom-basic approach, explaining the difference between hardware and software, between Apple's Macintosh models and IBM-compatibles, between the DOS operating system and the Windows interface software that makes it more friendly. He doesn't even discuss turning on the machines till page 88.

The Little PC Book never talks down to its readers, never makes them feel stupid or inadequate just because they know little about computers. There are copious tips about buying a computer, which parts of the thing do what, which software to choose—even how to plug it into the wall and how to avoid computer-related health problems.

Mr. Magid does explain the main DOS and Windows commands, but these are relegated to different colored "cookbook" sections at the back of the volume and are organized by English-language topic (e.g., "To Copy a Floppy Disk").

For new or prospective Macintosh owners, I recommend *The Little Mac Book* by prolific computer writer Robin Williams, also from Peachpit. This slender $16 book, which preceded the companion PC volume, isn't organized the same way, but it's just as gentle and helpful. Ms. Williams even includes a chapter called, simply, "Typing," and another that explains in one place all the little visual cues that the Macintosh uses.

These aren't the only good books for novices, of course. The best-selling such volumes are known collectively as the *Dummies* books and are published by IDG Books Worldwide, San Mateo, California. They include *PCs for Dummies* by Dan Gookin and Andy Rathbone, *Macs for Dummies* by David Pogue, and *DOS for Dummies*, also by Mr. Gookin. I hate the titles, which I believe play on the low self-esteem and feelings of inadequacy that computers engender. But the text is clear, funny, and irreverent, and you won't go wrong buying them.

PCs for Dummies is more focused on explaining technical things and less on making practical brand-name product recommendations than is *The Little PC Book*. Mr. Magid even recommends other books you can buy. That kind of hard-headed, nontechnical content is one reason I prefer *The Little PC Book*.

12/16/93

10
Three Magazines Put an Everyday Perspective on Computers

It has taken me years of fiddling with computers to get to the point where I can understand most, though certainly not all, of the articles in the leading computer magazines. If you haven't put in all those years, wading through a typical 300-page computer magazine packed with technobabble is about as inviting an experience as having a hernia repaired (a procedure you may need after carrying a few of these tomes around).

Recently, though, three slick computer magazines have been launched with a mission to cover the topic in plain English for nontechnical people at home, who constitute a juicy advertising target for computer companies. The three monthlies are *Family PC*, *Home PC*, and *Computer Life*. After poring over their initial issues, I think they are generally off to a good start, but each has a different approach, with its own strengths and weaknesses.

Family PC is the most visually inviting. It's designed to put parents at ease and help them figure out what their kids can get out of computers, not merely to tell them what to buy. Thus, the premiere issue featured articles on getting and using computerized weather information, finding homework help on line and writing a family newsletter. *Family PC* also reviews PC hardware and software, but it doesn't use techies and test labs to evaluate the products. Instead, it uses panels of real kids and parents. I thought their reviews in the first issue were clear and generally on the mark, based on my own evaluation of the same products.

But in many cases, I thought *Family PC* stretched to find topics combining computers and families. Several articles seemed to be about drawing things on computers and then printing them out to use as decorations—a rather obvious idea that doesn't require multiple pages to explain. The magazine completely ignores families without children and in which the children are grown and gone. And it is focused way too heavily on very young kids.

Perhaps that's why the magazine seems to assume that kids can learn from parents how to use the computers, and that kids want their parents sitting with them when they're at the computer. In my experience, kids over the age of five or six zoom past their parents in computer proficiency and don't want adults joining them at the keyboard.

Home PC looks and feels more like a traditional computer magazine and is more product-oriented than *Family PC*. But I like the fact that it's aimed at every kind of home, whether children live there or not. In addition to articles on kids' software, *Home PC*'s October 1994 issue covered software on investment, art, and wine.

Home PC also seemed more gender-neutral than *Family PC*. There was an article on software specifically for girls and an unusual and interesting piece on furnishing and decorating your computer room that had the look and feel of a traditional woman's magazine article.

Unfortunately, the main reviews were mostly done by adult "experts," and the few reviews by actual kids are relegated to a separate section. I also thought *Home PC* had too much technical stuff. For instance, even a lighthearted advice column called "Ask Dr. PC" insisted on explaining obscure PC files like "io.sys" and "command.com." Worse, in a couple of places the magazine encouraged people to perform do-it-yourself multimedia upgrades, a practice that is so onerous and frustrating it has actually created something of a consumer backlash.

Computer Life has staked out a different territory altogether. It's aimed at people who really, really like their computers but regard themselves as nontechnical. In some ways, *Computer Life* carries off its mission well. The writing is sprightly and often personal. I liked a satire on "Hit CDs of Tomorrow" (example: *Little Teeny Wormlet's Busy ABC Day*). But the editors seemed to be stretching when they devoted four pages to explaining how to plug a laptop PC into your car's electrical system and use special software to do an auto tune-up.

Overall, the first issue had a jumbled, confused look and feel, and seemed to be trying too hard to be hip. The front section was laid out in a jarring, reader-unfriendly style that seemed obviously derivative of *Wired* magazine, a niche journal for computer-industry insiders, not users. I think the concept behind *Computer Life* is strong and many of the articles well done, but the package needs work.

All three magazines also appeared timid about tackling the big picture and consumer issues, like repetitive-stress injuries, the lack of computers available to poor children, and the new practice of computer companies charging for technical support.

One last thing. These magazines aim to be trusted by consumers, but the early issues of two of them displayed sloppy ethical practices that could undermine that trust. *Family PC* anointed an Apple Macintosh model as the best home PC—a sound choice. But in the same issue it announced it would conduct a promotional tour through shopping malls across the country that would be partly financed by Apple. The magazine protests that the Apple promotion didn't affect its PC review, but it sure raises the appearance of a conflict. *Computer Life* ran an unusual triangular ad in its first issue for a video game called "Under a Killing Moon" that was placed in such a way that it resembled an illustration for an article. There was no label saying it was an ad. The magazine says it was a simple rookie error that won't recur. Let's hope not.

9/22/94

Each of the magazines has improved in subsequent editions—especially Family PC.

11
Six Little Things That Drive This PC User Nuts

Using a personal computer can be an enjoyable, empowering experience—even if you're just doing office work on it. There's still something magical about being able to manipulate words, numbers, and pictures on a screen in a million interesting ways. It can be exhilarating to dial into an on-line service and retrieve news and information, or carry on discussions with people all over the world.

But digital delight can quickly turn to frustration and anger because of a host of irritating quirks and obstacles that plague computers and software programs. I'm not referring here to the big, overarching shortcomings of PCs that I've attacked with some regularity—the complex and creaky DOS operating system, the painful process of configuring or expanding an IBM-compatible PC, the miserable state of instruction manuals, and the difficulty of getting a lot of today's multimedia software to run properly on your computer without disabling other programs.

Sometimes it's the little things that get you, the minor design flaws that seem trivial by themselves but add up to make you feel stupid and clumsy on the PC. Many of them could be corrected easily by the computer companies, and some companies are fixing some of them. But too often these little glitches are hard for users to articulate, and don't make it onto companies' priority lists.

So here's my personal list of the little things that drive me nuts about computers, in no particular order.

Mystery icons: Most modern computer programs use icons, or little pictures on the screen, to let users control key features. You click with a mouse on an icon, and a program is launched or a file is saved or printed. But the trend has run amok, and too many of the icons are indecipherable or inconsistent. What does that little paint brush do in your word processor—redecorate? Or maybe it's a little broom? It's hard to tell. If I click on a pencil or a little running man or a rocket, it isn't obvious what will happen. It's gotten so bad that software publishers now attach explanations to the pictures, but the whole idea was that icons would replace words, not require more of them.

Messages from hell: When something goes wrong, you can rarely figure out why. Even Apple's supposedly cuddly Macintosh machines frequently report things like this: "The application (Unknown) has unexpectedly quit because an error of Type 1 occurred." Gee, that sure clears things up. Microsoft's Windows software occasionally shuts down a program I'm using and tells me something like "This application has violated system integrity and will be terminated." Sounds like a press release from a death squad.

In the dark: It's useful to have little lights on computers so you can tell whether the disk drives are working or how much life is left in a laptop battery. But Apple must think they're uncool, because it rarely uses them. And on other machines, there are so many lights you can't figure them out. My favorite light is one called "turbo," which tells you how fast the microprocessor inside is running—hardly vital information when you're designing the invitations for your kid's birthday party. And only a techno-geek could love the little lights on modems, which seem to be labeled in secret code.

Hide and seek: Hard disks are divided into sections called "directories" or "folders," and computer experts encourage users to create and use directories to organize logically the files they create. The idea is to put all your budget files in a "budget" directory, and so forth. But most users just dump everything into the same pile, or even think they've "lost" files because they wind up in the wrong section of the disk. That's because the "save" command in most programs automatically brings up the same directory every time, usually the directory where the program is stored, not one where documents might logically go. Can't Microsoft and others fix this so the "save" feature jumps to a directory the user chooses, or at least to the last directory used?

Laptop contortions: Most of the mice, or cursor-control devices, built into portable computers are just plain awful. Compaq uses a little "trackball" in the corner of the lid that forces your hands off the keyboard and gets gummed up too easily with dust. Others hang a trackball off the side of the computer that gets in the way and can snap off. IBM's "pointing stick" and Apple's original centered trackball worked pretty well, but most imitators have come up short. And Apple has now dumped its trackball in favor of a new gizmo—a flat little square that you just touch with a finger. It may be great, but you'd think by now a clear, solid standard would have emerged.

Turn it down: Now that computers come equipped with stereo sound and elaborate video, it can be really frustrating to do simple things such as turning the volume up and down. The little speakers that come with multimedia machines often have volume dials, but in many cases they're useless because the software program controls the sound.

I could spin out five or ten more of these pet peeves. But, in an effort to pander to you readers and get an easy source of material for another column, I invite you to send me your own lists of little things about computers that make you crazy. If I get enough good ones, I'll print them.

And now, this column will terminate. Please reboot your system.

7/14/94

12 Readers Vent over THAT 123*%#@! PC

Boy, are you a cranky group. After I invited readers to send in their lists of maddening computer quirks, more than three hundred electronic-mail messages poured in, most bearing tales of woe. And the U.S. snail mail has started delivering a plethora of high-tech gripes.

The writers ranged from know-it-all teenagers to baffled retirees and even included a number of sympathetic people from inside major software and computer companies, some of whom asked that their names not be used. A handful of those writing—mainly folks for whom it seems computers are a passion or a profession—were angry at me, not their machines (more on that later). Here's a sampling.

Many writers apologized for "venting my spleen" or "ranting," suggesting some strain in the bond between human and machine. The best of this genre was, "My greatest frustration is that my PC cannot understand one *#!!&%$ word when I scream at it." Another choice entry was, "I can't tell you how many times this PC has almost left the office for a trip through the window onto the street below."

Two of my personal complaints drew a lot of reaction. Many people wrote to explain various techniques that make it easier to save files to a favorite directory, or section, of your hard disk. I know about such methods, but my point was that this sort of intelligence ought to be an automatic, built-in feature of software, requiring no extra measures on the user's part. Others wrote to defend the little lights on modems, saying they are a useful way to monitor data transmissions. I agree, but was merely saying that the labels identifying their functions are written in useless technobabble.

To my surprise, some of the most frequent complaints concerned the most basic operations of the computer and its keyboard. Many people hate the fact that, in some cases, the on/off switch is at or near the rear of the machine.

Another big issue is that many machines start up with the Num Lock key turned on, which activates the numeric keypad used for math operations, but disables shortcut commands that make use of those same keys. A related gripe is that it's way too easy to hit the Caps Lock key, which capitalizes every letter you type, so YOU SEEM TO BE SHOUTING. Still another is that, in Macintosh software and in Microsoft Windows software, you have to click twice with a mouse to invoke many commands. One click should be enough, several writers said.

Numerous writers cited conflicts between software programs, or between software and hardware. Others wondered why, even in supposedly standard Windows programs, identical commands do different things. Another big issue was that many programs, during installation, change key system files on your machine in ways that may render other software unusable. And lots of people griped that you can't easily remove a Windows program from your machine, because of the many special files it creates in varied locations on the hard disk.

There were bitter charges that computer companies lie to their customers about the amounts of memory and disk space new programs really require to run smoothly, and about how long a laptop PC will run on battery power. There were multiple complaints about the proliferation of software upgrades, which often cost a lot and appear just to fix bugs in earlier releases.

Writers were down on telephone technical support, citing long waits for vague answers. "Comments offered by the experts were downright vaudevillian," said one. But a PC "expert" declared: "I get aggravated when all my friends and relatives call up and describe a screen on their computer and want to know what it means—what am I, psychic?"

A few proposed "laws" of computing. The gist of one: "Every time you buy a faster machine, the software companies come out with new versions that make your new machine run as slow as your old one." Another entry: "The productivity gains we get from computers we eventually give back in the time we spend screwing around with them."

A generation gap was evident in some replies. My teenage correspondents were incredulous that anyone would be frustrated by some of the things I cited. But one suffering mother wrote in to complain that her computer-savvy kids had reprogrammed her Mac so, instead of beeping at her when she makes an error, it says, "You silly billy!" This, she reports, is "not what I want to hear as my frustration mounts," but she can't figure out how to restore the machine to normal.

And then there were those who angrily dissented from the whole gripe fest, apparently because the machines are modern miracles for which we should be grateful. One self-described "techno-geek" wrote, "I'm sorry to see that you're out of new ideas for your column. It's time to ask for a new assignment!" Another writer added, "Mr. Mossberg, here is my little contribution to what drives some computer users nuts. It is YOU. It is scandalous that you can persuade the *WSJ* into publishing your crybaby story."

I'd reply strongly to these cutting attacks, but I can't get this 1238*7 Num Lock key unstuck 4561++, I keep hitting THE STUPID CAPS LOCK key, and my computerized thesaurus can't locate a good synonym for "silly billy."

7/21/94

13
Intel Misserved the Millions Who Bought Its Pentium Campaign

Intel doesn't seem to want us nontechnical computer users, the computer-buying rabble, to get the idea that we might want to demand replacements for the Pentium chips in PCs millions of us have bought, even though the company admits they're defective. But you might want to demand a new chip anyway.

Intel has spent the past few years running a massive consumer advertising campaign designed to make its name and the name of its high-powered Pentium computer chip household words. But over the past month, when it was forced to disclose a defect in the Pentium chip that causes it to do some math calculations wrong, Intel has done virtually nothing to reach out directly to that same mass audience of garden-variety computer owners in homes and small businesses. It has directly contacted technical and scientific users, big companies, computer retailers. It has issued press releases and held telephone conferences with Wall Street analysts. But as of this date, it hasn't run any mass-market print or TV ads explaining the situation or publicizing the toll-free phone number it has set up for concerned Pentium users.

Worse, Intel has taken the position that, for the kind of computing most of us plain folks do, a defective Pentium is good enough. Before Intel will routinely agree to replace the chip with one that does math right, the company has said, you must prove you do work on your computer that's mathematically complex enough to meet Intel's self-defined rules about who needs accuracy. Intel defends this policy on grounds that the bug occurs so rarely it's only likely to affect people doing the most sophisticated math operations.

From my point of view, this is outrageous. Computers do math all the time behind the scenes, even in programs like graphics software where it isn't obvious to the average user. The kind of math the Pentium gets wrong, called "floating point" math, is relatively uncommon, and the Pentium only stumbles on certain combinations of numbers. But that's not the point. Why should an average user have to worry that some program he buys next year might—just might—be trying to divide, in the background, two numbers the Pentium can't divide correctly?

If you have a spreadsheet program, you can make a Pentium goof up by entering a fairly simple calculation that has no decimal points, uses no complex math functions and is in fact easier than my teenagers' homework problems. Just enter this formula: 4,195,835 – ((4,195,835/3,145,727) * 3,145,727). The correct answer is zero, because the formula amounts to subtracting a number from itself. My Apple Macintosh (which doesn't use Intel chips) gets it right, as does a PC using an older Intel chip. But my costly new Pentium machine generates a bogus answer of 256. It's a rare case, contrived by critics to highlight the defect, but it's not rocket science.

If you want a new, nondefective Pentium chip, you can get one by calling Intel's toll-free number (800-628-8686), even if you're not an MIT professor. Intel doesn't make it easy. But in a test I conducted over the past week, I managed to get Intel to agree to send me a new Pentium even though I refused to tell Intel what I did for a living or what software I used. The company said I'd have it within thirty days. "If you insist on a new chip, we'll supply a new chip," Intel Senior Vice President Carl Everett reluctantly conceded in an interview before I called the 800 number.

But it isn't a consumer-friendly process. I had to go through multiple conversations (it took me three phone calls over six days). When I was asked if I wanted to talk to an expert or receive a "white paper" about the nature of the defect in the chip, I said no thank you, that I just wanted a new chip.

The Intel person then wanted to know what software I used. I replied that it was none of his business, and I wanted a new chip, period. I had to give Intel a credit-card number and agree to a potential charge of $1,000 if I failed to return my old Pentium within twenty-nine days after receiving my new one—an ironic requirement from a company that delayed for months even disclosing the defect. Intel pays for shipping both the new chip to you and the old one back, but not for any labor costs you may incur in hiring somebody to swap the chips.

I'm not saying you should definitely get a new chip. I can't say how likely it is that the Pentium math defect will strike you. And it's no trivial matter to swap chips. Depending on your computer, the Pentium may be tough to pull out or hidden behind other components you'll have to remove. One Pentium machine I've seen even has a little fan stuck on top of the chip, to dissipate heat.

But if you want to feel confident that your Pentium can do math right every time, don't hesitate to demand a new chip, despite the hassles Intel throws in your path and the $50 or so it might cost to get a computer shop to do the job for you.

Just don't assume that junking a defective Pentium will solve all your math woes. It turns out that other math screwups lurk inside our IBM-compatible PCs, whether they use a Pentium chip or not. The calculator program that Microsoft includes with each copy of Windows makes math errors too, no matter what chip your computer uses. If you try to subtract 2.00 from 2.01, it gives an answer of 0.00. And it mishandles other numbers ending in .01. Microsoft knows of the problem, but doesn't plan to fix it until the next version of Windows ships next year (unless consumers raise a hue and cry).

Maybe you ought to consider a Macintosh.

12/15/94

The day after this column ran, Microsoft announced it would release a new, repaired calculator program and make it available for free. It attributed the new policy to this column. A few days later, Intel capitulated and took national newspaper ads offering free no-questions-asked replacements, with labor included, to all Pentium users.

14

Personal Computing Is Too Dumb to Know Easy Is Smart

In 1991, this column was launched with the contention that personal computers are too hard to use, and that the blame lies not with the people trying to use them but with the supposed geniuses who design the machines and the software that runs on them. Since then, steady progress has been made on the margins, but it's slow going. The fundamental complexity and limitations of the IBM-compatible PC design still haunt us, well into its second decade of existence.

Things are moving in the right direction but at a snail's pace. Computers are shipping with many more features built in, eliminating the need for users to poke around inside to add things. But anyone who tries to add more, especially to install one of those much-touted multimedia upgrade kits, quickly finds himself in trouble.

The same is true of software. Programs have lots more built-in help and colorful icons to click on, but they can still be hellishly confusing to use. Many of the new multimedia programs are nearly impossible even to install correctly.

Recently in *The Washington Post*, columnist Tony Kornheiser wrote that he went out and bought a home computer but can't use it. "I sit there staring at a blank screen," he wrote, "waiting for it to do something magical on its own, like it's the Oracle at Delphi. The only thing I can do on that screen is Windex it."

Mr. Kornheiser is no doubt exaggerating a bit (columnists do that). But even rocket scientists are baffled by personal computers. I once got e-mail from a scientist at NASA who works on giant supercomputers all day with aplomb but goes home at night and finds to his great frustration that he can't get the family IBM-compatible PC to run multimedia software correctly.

Two big computing advances that were supposed to cure a lot of these woes have been put off until 1995. One is Microsoft's new Windows 95 operating system, which will fix most of the dumb features in its Windows program and finally kill off the dreadful DOS operating system. The other is a new hardware standard called Plug and Play, which is supposed to make it simple to configure and expand IBM-compatible PCs.

These are great ideas. But even if they work as promised, they will mainly bring IBM-compatibles up to the ease-of-use standard set by Apple with its Macintosh models starting in 1984. And even the Mac isn't as easy as it could be for novices to grasp. It's hard to believe the industry can't do better than that in 1995.

Apple has a secret project to radically redesign the Mac's main software, to make it simpler and smarter. And it's been talking to IBM about a new compatible computer design. But what's needed is much more: a fundamental redesign of the whole concept of the PC, with ease of use and integration as the guiding principles. The last machine built from the ground up with those goals in mind was the Mac, and that was eons ago in computer time. I wonder if any company out there now has the courage to break the mold again.

Meanwhile, the news isn't all bad. While changes in the basic box and its underlying control software are on hold, a few software designers are trying out a new style of computer program that I call active software.

Active software programs don't work in rigid ways but try to tailor the way they work to the context of what's going on at the moment, and to the habits and preferences of the user. They learn these either by intelligently observing what's happening at the computer or by conducting interviews with users to determine how they work and what they want. The essence of these programs is that they match up a user's personal profile and habits with expert tools or expert content and then intelligently propose a solution to the problem at hand.

These active computing features can be subtle. For instance, Microsoft Word can learn the words you misspell most often and correct them automatically without requiring you to run the spellchecker. The new version of WordPerfect for Windows has a smart search-and-replace feature that will replace every form and tense of a given word with the appropriate form and tense of a word you choose to replace it. Thus, if you want to replace "purchase" with "buy," the program is smart enough to replace "purchased" with "bought."

Or active computing can be more obvious. The new 3D Landscape program from Books That Work proposes plantings for your yard based on the actual design and geographic location of your property. Rand McNally's new TripMaker software proposes a driving plan, with map, for any journey across the country after interviewing you to learn your preferences about where and how often to stop, how fast and long you like to drive each day, and so forth.

There are more examples already, and I expect the trend to spread. Within a year or two, I bet many programs will conduct an interview with users up front to determine how they want to work and to learn any other information or characteristics that are appropriate to the purpose of the software. Then the software will work and act accordingly.

For now, we'll just struggle along with PCs and software too dumb to be easy. Please pass the Windex.

10/20/94

Part II
Hardware

How do you know what computer or printer to buy? What are the potential problems? Can IBM-compatibles and Apple's Macintoshes be used together? These columns tackle those questions and more. And, as always, the emphasis is on simple, cheap solutions that don't require lots of technical support. Topics covered here include PCs and Macs, notebook computers, printers, scanners, personal digital assistants, networks, viruses, upgrades of memory or processor chips, and more.

15
PC Shoppers May Find It's Wise to Develop a Taste for Apples

Many people and businesses shopping for computers give little consideration to Apple Computer's Macintosh models. They are making a mistake.

People are leery of the Mac for several reasons. First, it doesn't use the same MS-DOS "operating system"—a computer's basic underlying software—or run exactly the same programs as most PCs, built to be compatible with IBM's design. Second, it is pricier than most comparable IBM clones. Third, it isn't the "standard" in big business. Finally, in its early days the Macintosh was slow and underpowered.

But these arguments, often intoned by salespeople and other advisers who have barely used the Mac, are usually greatly overblown, and in many cases irrelevant. Buying decisions often get mixed up with what I call "computer theology." There are strong Mac and IBM cults among computer users. But religious doctrine isn't a good substitute for informed judgment.

The fact is that for many people and small firms that want to get maximum work done on computers with minimum hassle, the Mac is an excellent choice, with a superior combination of hardware and software.

Apple made popular, and still does best, the easy-to-use graphical approach to computing now imitated by Microsoft's Windows software on IBM-compatibles. Apple's hardware design, closely integrated with the software, makes the Mac easier to set up and much easier to expand than the typical IBM clone. And, in contrast with the early days, there are now multiple Mac models with good speed and power.

On a Mac, you never have to remember precise file names or complex commands to type in. Everything is done by moving around little images, or icons, that represent files. Documents can have real names, such as "Midwest Sales Plan for August," rather than the cryptic titles required on IBM clones. Mac software programs all work much the same way, with common commands, even if they're published by different companies.

Some of this is also true of IBM clones with Windows, but most such features are harder to use than on the Apple, and some are impossible.

The incompatibility problem has eased because there are Mac versions of many leading MS-DOS and Windows programs. These include Microsoft's Word, Works, Excel, and Mail; Lotus Development's 1-2-3, Notes, and cc:Mail; WordPerfect's WordPerfect and LetterPerfect; and Novell networking software. Moreover, every Macintosh can accept floppy disks formatted on an IBM PC, though it takes extra software costing around $69 to make this feat truly practical.

Most Macs come with built-in hardware features that are costly, complicated extras on IBM clones, including networking capability, sound and 256-color video. And you can expand Macs without opening the cover or adding circuit boards: just plug add-on devices into a special socket on the back.

Finally, if you're worried that the Mac is a risky choice consider this: at many big companies where IBM is the nominal standard, Macs have invaded. Even the Software Publishers Association, the trade group whose members' products mainly work on IBM-compatibles, runs its headquarters mostly with Macs.

That isn't to say everyone should run out and buy a Macintosh. It isn't right for all situations, and it has a few significant downsides. The biggest obstacle to buying a Macintosh is its higher price. The Mac's host of built-in features justifies some of the pricing premium Mac commands over IBM clones. But that premium, in my view, is just too high: 50 percent or more on some comparable models. And whether a Mac is right for you depends a lot on how you work and what software you prefer.

If you're using just one or two MS-DOS–based software programs you know and love, and don't plan to explore much new software or to change to a graphical system like Windows, stick with IBM-compatibles. If you're looking for the lowest initial hardware cost, and don't foresee expanding your computers much, bypass the Macintosh. If your company or clients are rigidly locked into a single MS-DOS program that only runs on IBM-compatibles—especially one that has been custom-written or heavily customized—the Mac may be a bad choice. And don't bother if you hate using a mouse.

Furthermore, while there's plenty of Mac-compatible software equal to or better than DOS or Windows programs in word processing, spreadsheets, desktop publishing and graphics, there's relatively little in some other areas. These include sophisticated databases, business accounting, and programs for creating custom applications peculiar to a given business.

But for most small businesses, professionals and families, it isn't smart to overlook the Macintosh.

8/6/92

Mac prices have gotten lower, and Apple has enhanced their compatibility with DOS and Windows software.

16 Do You Really Need the Speed Offered by the New Power Macs?

Over the past decade, Apple's Macintosh computers have generated high customer satisfaction and near-fanatical owner loyalty, yet failed to dominate the computer market. Last year, Apple sold about 15 percent of all PCs in the U.S., while sales of dozens of other brands built to the competing IBM-compatible standard totaled nearly 85 percent.

Critics have long attributed this paradox to three flaws in the Macintosh: a high price, a relatively slow computing speed, and an inability to run programs designed for IBM-compatibles equipped with Microsoft's DOS and Windows software.

Now Apple has introduced a line of aggressively priced, impressively speedy Macs that tries to correct all these deficiencies. It's called the Power Macintosh and is based on a very fast new central processor chip—the brain of a computer—called the PowerPC. It's so powerful it can run three kinds of software: older Macintosh programs written for prior Mac models, new Macintosh programs written for the PowerPC, and even IBM-compatible software (if you buy a special Macintosh program that emulates an IBM-compatible PC and runs DOS and Windows).

After several weeks of testing a mid-range Power Macintosh, I believe it is a beautifully designed PC that squarely addresses the Mac's longstanding weaknesses. But I don't think everybody should rush out and buy one right away.

The Power Macintosh gives Apple, for the first time in memory, clear price/performance leadership over IBM-compatible machines—

the most bang for the buck. Independent lab tests show the PowerPC chip to be at least as fast as the fastest chip used in IBM-compatibles, Intel's Pentium, and much faster at some tasks. In my unscientific tests, the Power Mac ripped through traditionally ponderous jobs like altering complex graphics. It was positively amazing at much more mundane feats—like changing a hundred instances of a word in a twenty-page text document almost instantaneously. The machines are at least twice as fast as the fastest previous Macs and retain all the built-in features and elegant design that have long made Macs easier to use, configure, and expand than other PCs.

The base Power Mac model, called the 6100/60, is officially priced at just $1,819 with eight megabytes of memory and a 160-megabyte hard disk, and was selling this week at one New York discount store for $1,599. With monitor and keyboard, it could be had for around $2,000—way below the typical IBM-compatible with a Pentium chip. Even after adding a larger hard disk and a CD-ROM drive, or more memory and the program that lets the machine run IBM-compatible software, the price of this base model is still below $3,000—hundreds less than a Pentium system. The brawniest of the three models, the 8100/80, with vast memory and a huge hard disk, can run to nearly $6,000 at discount.

But just buying a computer with a fast processor chip doesn't get you anything unless it actually runs the software you use much faster or permits added features in software that are of practical benefit. And that's the catch in the Power Macintosh. The machine's high speeds and increased power can only be achieved when running software that has been revised or created to take advantage of the PowerPC chip. And there are only a handful of such "native" programs available now.

The Power Macs do a great job of running older Macintosh programs that weren't designed for the PowerPC—a tough technical feat—but these programs only run about as fast on Power Macs as they do on standard Macs. And the Power Macs run many DOS and Windows programs acceptably, but more slowly than the fastest IBM-compatibles.

Apple says sixty native Power Macintosh versions of popular programs will be available soon, but many of these are high-end graphics, desktop publishing or design programs, which benefit immensely from the machines' great speed. So if you use a computer for this kind of work, buying a Power Mac soon makes good sense. A few more general business programs, notably the WordPerfect word processor and the ClarisWorks integrated program, will also be available. But bear in mind that if you mainly just write on your computer, the higher speeds of PowerPC and Pentium chips may not make a dramatic difference. You can only type and read so fast.

Many of the thousands of other Mac programs, including very popular packages like Intuit's Quicken personal-finance package, aren't scheduled to be revised for PowerPC. They'll run on a Power Mac, but no faster than they do now.

If you're in the market for a new mid-range computer anyway, the Power Macintosh is an impressive value that's well worth considering. But if you're tempted to replace or upgrade your machine early because you lust after the PowerPC's speed, make sure the new Macs can drastically improve the specific tasks for which you really use your computer. That's the acid test for both PowerPC and Pentium computers, not speed ratings on a lab report.

3/17/94

Even faster Power Macs have since been introduced, and there are now hundreds of native Power Mac programs. But faster Pentiums have also hit the market, and prices of Pentium PCs have plunged faster than expected, erasing much or all of the price advantage of the Power Macs.

17

Apple Tries to Make the Macintosh IBM-Friendly

These words are being written on a computer running Microsoft's DOS and Windows software, the underlying programs that control nearly all IBM-compatible PCs.

Big deal, you say, that's a pretty common setup. But the computer in front of me isn't an IBM-compatible model. It's an Apple Macintosh, which everyone knows can't run DOS, Windows, or application programs that require them. Macs are naturally incompatible with that software, which is one reason many folks hesitate to buy them.

I'm composing this column, however, on a new kind of Mac—one of Apple Computer's groundbreaking line of ultrafast Power Macintosh models that's equipped with a software program called SoftWindows. That package, from Insignia Solutions of Mountain View, California, ingeniously mimics an IBM-compatible, running DOS and Windows, on the Power Mac—without any special hardware. Applications meant for Windows computers then run on the Mac, because it appears to them to be an IBM-compatible. Apple is installing SoftWindows on certain Power Mac models.

Why is Apple doing this? To some extent, it's a matter of survival. While the Mac's system software and user interface are superior to the DOS-Windows combination, most new programs are issued first in Windows versions and sometimes never appear in a Mac version. And many people buying a computer for home or small business use feel uncomfortable with machines incapable of running the DOS and Windows software used by their employers, suppliers, or customers—even though Mac software usually can handle the files created by many of these programs.

So Apple is hoping that SoftWindows will sell Macs to "fence-sitters"—people who generally would prefer a Mac, but want the security of buying a machine that can run DOS and Windows.

After using SoftWindows for a few weeks, I found that it does work largely as advertised. But it has significant limitations, and cannot replace an IBM-compatible computer. It is strictly for people who mainly intend to use Mac software and want only occasionally to run a couple of DOS and Windows programs. Like all attempts to emulate one computer or another, it is not ideal.

SoftWindows adds at least $500 to the cost of a Power Mac. The software is costly, with a list price of $499 if bought separately, and it requires your Mac to have a whopping 16 megabytes of memory and extra hard-disk space in order to simulate a four-megabyte PC. As a result, the cheapest model Apple offers with SoftWindows included is about $3,000 with a monitor and keyboard.

In addition, SoftWindows runs only about as fast as a 386 chip, now obsolete, or a slow version of the 486, depending on which programs you use. Worse, SoftWindows looks to your software like an old PC with an ancient 286 chip, so some newer programs won't run on it. For instance, I couldn't install Visio, the business graphics package, which is a classic example of a Windows program that is unavailable in a Mac version.

Insignia promises a version that will appear to be a true 486, but SoftWindows can't handle PC multimedia software because it doesn't emulate sound cards.

Macintosh owners can upgrade an older machine. Apple offers a variety of upgrades, from $700 to $1,900, that turn many Quadra models and a few other recent Macs into Power Macs. Check your dealer to see if your model is eligible. Add at least $700 on top of that (for software and extra memory) if you want to run SoftWindows on your newly upgraded machine.

Current and prospective Mac owners likely will welcome this IBM-compatibility feature. But it holds a danger for Apple itself. If

Mac users start discovering and relying upon more and more Windows programs that aren't available in Mac versions, they may decide that their next computer should be a real IBM-compatible.

3/24/94

Apple now offers a Power Mac with IBM-compatible hardware built in, and a $699 enhanced IBM-compatible hardware card for other machines.

18
A Multitude of Functions in a Single Component

You know that guy at work who thinks he knows everything about computers—the one who's always talking in technobabble? Well, he's going to hate this column, because it's about a new style of PC that just might begin to move the computer into the realm of appliance, a realm where techno-elitists like him will be far less important. You, on the other hand, as a smart but nontechnical person, may just find out about a computer that makes sense for your home or small business.

This new category is called the all-in-one multimedia PC, and the three top-selling computer makers—Compaq, Apple, and Packard Bell—have each built very nice versions of the design that sell for between $1,800 and $2,200 in configurations I consider acceptable for running the widest variety of software.

Apple pioneered the concept, as it so often does, and its latest version, called the Macintosh Performa 578, has been on sale since spring of 1994. Compaq introduced its new Presario CDS 520 in September 1994, and Packard Bell's new Spectria models are due to hit store shelves soon. I've been testing production models of the three, and I like them all.

These machines look a little like TVs with disk drives. They're one-piece forty-pound units, standing less than eighteen inches high, with full-sized fourteen-inch high-resolution color screens and stereo speakers built in. Unlike traditional computer designs, they have appliance-like controls up front—volume, brightness, headphone jacks, and so forth. All three machines boast a small "footprint"—the amount of space they claim on a desktop or table top—making them perfect for family rooms, bedrooms, or dormitory rooms.

But these aren't stripped-down or crippled computers, like the first all-in-one models in the earlier days of home computers. These 1990s versions have roomy hard disks, relatively fast processor chips, capable CD-ROM drives, strong video and sound systems and, in most cases, ample memory.

They can run all the software a typical business person might use at work, plus do a great job running multimedia encyclopedias, basic desktop publishing, games, educational programs, and all the other things families do on computers. They are also equipped to get you onto the information highway. And the Presario and Spectria can even be used as telephone answering machines and televisions—to tune in to *Oprah* while you work.

Mr. Know-It-All back at the office will try to talk you out of such a machine. He'll contend that the all-in-one design is too limiting. What if you want to add a $1,000 big-screen monitor? Well, few people do. What if the built-in screen goes on the fritz and your whole computer must go in for repairs? Well, few people have spare monitors at home, so if a monitor on a traditional PC breaks down, you're still without the use of your PC. What about expansion—the ability to upgrade to faster processors, add memory, and so forth? Well, unlike the old all-in-one stereos and other dreaded combo appliances, these machines can be upgraded and expanded like any other computer.

So which of these computers did I like best? I consider them basically comparable, with assorted individual strengths and weaknesses. I'd like to give the clear edge to the Compaq, but I can't. I prefer its overall design, and it has some great special features—including a very cool program called Mini-Pilot that controls the multimedia functions and a built-in automated speakerphone. It's also the only one of the three that comes with a modern, fast modem.

But the new Presario is flawed, because Compaq chose to offer it with an inadequate amount of memory—only four megabytes, which isn't enough to handle today's software smoothly. You can only get two configurations—the basic CDS 520 at $1,699 or the CDTV 520, which includes a TV receiver, for $1,899. Both boast a generous 420-megabyte hard drive.

But those prices are somewhat deceptive, because it'll cost you about $200 more to bring the memory up to adequate levels. My strong advice to anyone buying a Presario 520 is to immediately pop in an extra four megabytes of memory. Better yet, Compaq should just offer an eight-megabyte configuration, as Apple and Packard Bell do. Why wait to fix a bad flaw in an otherwise great machine, especially when no redesign is required?

Packard Bell's Spectria comes in three configurations, from an underequipped four-megabyte model at $1,400 to a very well-equipped $1,800 model that has eight megabytes of memory, a 520-megabyte hard disk, and a TV receiver. It's also the only machine whose screen can be plugged into another computer, such as a laptop. It's a worthy contender, and you won't go wrong with it. But it has a slow, old-style modem and lacks the Compaq's best software features.

Which brings us to Apple, for around $2,200. Like all Macs, the Performa 578 has a better, tighter integration of software and hardware than either of the PCs. It has eight megabytes of memory and a 320-megabyte hard disk, and is easily expandable. It can read disks from IBM-compatible machines and is a very solid computer. But its modem is slow, and its basic design, which is a few years old, is showing its age.

None of this will be very persuasive to the office PC snob—the very idea of a powerful PC that looks like a TV is beyond his ken. But it doesn't have to be beyond yours.

9/15/94

For some reason, Packard Bell decided to delay the release of Spectria till 1995. Compaq, as expected, brought out an eight-megabyte version of its machine in January, 1995. Apple and Compaq both cut prices around that time as well. For the fall of 1995, new and more powerful all-in-one computers are due from Apple, Compaq, AST, and others.

19
Adding RAM Power Lets PC Users Bag Higher Performance

You can never be too thin or too rich, according to the old saying. In the case of personal computers, it might be said that you can never have too much memory.

Computer software keeps getting more powerful, putting ever greater demands on PC hardware. To get the most out of the latest programs—especially those designed to work with Microsoft's Windows software on IBM-compatibles—computer owners may have to consider adding more memory.

That's the bad news. The good news is that beefing up your computer's memory is often a relatively quick and inexpensive matter, at least compared with other kinds of computer upgrades. It isn't as easy as computer magazines make it sound; few things are. But you may be able to do it yourself.

Even new PCs can be candidates for such an upgrade, though it may be simpler, if you're just buying a computer, to order it with extra memory. Lots of the bargain computers being sold in droves come with just four megabytes of memory. That sounds like plenty; each megabyte is enough to store a million characters of text. But it isn't enough for efficient performance with Windows programs or the newest software for Apple Computer's Macintosh models, though Microsoft and Apple claim otherwise. In these cases, you need at least eight megabytes, in my view. So, here's a brief primer on adding memory to your PC.

The kind of computer memory we're talking about here is RAM, for random access memory, the temporary storage capacity used by a computer to handle programs and documents being actively used. It's temporary because it resides in special chips that are erased when you turn off the power. That distinguishes RAM from disk storage, such as hard disks and floppy disks, which retain information after the computer is turned off.

Computer users can think of a PC's memory as the equivalent of the desktop or other work surface on which people spread out tools and papers to work on the immediate task or tasks at hand. That pile of stuff is usually temporary; it will be used only until the job is done. In contrast, think of disk storage as a file cabinet. It is used to store the materials for many such tasks over longer periods of time, but the material stored there must first be moved to a work surface before it can be used.

The bigger the work surface, the more different tools and documents you can use handily, without having to dig through file cabinets for each one. Similarly, when you increase the memory, the RAM, of your computer, you are enlarging its electronic work surface and giving it the capacity to work with more and larger programs and documents. More memory also means your PC will run faster, even if it is an older design, because the computer can tap into programs and data from RAM far faster than it can get them from disk storage.

Adding memory is cheap. An extra megabyte of standard RAM for modern desktop computers today costs around $50, depending on where you buy it. You can order memory from the mail-order houses that advertise in the back of computer magazines, or get it from a local retail store.

The most common form of extra memory is a single in-line memory module, or SIMM, a small circuit board shaped like a bookmark with either eight memory chips (for Macs) or nine (for IBM-compatibles) stuck on it. You just pop these things into rows of special little slots inside the computer, usually one or two "banks" of four slots each.

SIMMs come in different capacities; one-megabyte and four-megabyte versions are the most common. They are rated by the speed at which the computer can talk to them, as measured in nanoseconds, or billionths of a second; a lower figure is faster. An ad for a "1 × 9 = 70" SIMM refers to a one-megabyte SIMM with nine chips on it (for IBM-compatibles) that runs at seventy nanoseconds.

Before buying SIMMs, consult your PC manual to determine the speeds and capacities your PC can handle. Check whether your PC requires memory to be added in specific increments, or whether the SIMMs must be arranged in the slots in any special pattern. Also, check inside your PC to see whether the SIMM slots are easily accessible. On some models, you may have to remove some other system components temporarily to get to the memory slots. And never poke inside your PC without first turning it off and unplugging it and then touching a piece of metal to discharge any static electricity in your body (which can damage chips). Inserting SIMMs usually requires no tools, but a small screwdriver may help you align little flexible clamps that hold the SIMMs in place.

Older PCs usually don't use SIMMs, so adding memory to them is harder and costlier. You either have to buy lots of individual little chips and insert them in tiny sockets, or buy a special circuit board for one hundred dollars or more and then fill it with individual chips or SIMMs.

Finally, on some older IBM-compatibles, you may need to add special "memory manager" software to get the ancient MS-DOS operating system to recognize the added RAM. On Macs, the computer automatically uses any extra memory you add.

If any of this confuses or worries you, hire somebody to do the job, or get the store to do it. Despite the obstacles, adding memory to your computer is well worth it. You'll be pleasantly surprised at how much this one upgrade will do to increase the power and speed of your PC.

12/31/92

20 Changing "Engines" Is an Easy Way to Soup Up PCs

Last week I performed a brain transplant on my computer. I tore out the machine's central processing unit, or CPU—the chip that makes everything else work—and replaced it with a new model called an OverDrive chip that is supposed to speed up the computer.

This was probably a foolhardy thing to attempt. For one thing, I'm not exactly handy; I can't even change a vacuum-cleaner bag. For another, the only machine I could experiment on was my own IBM-compatible at home, not the office computer bought from the deep pockets of *The Wall Street Journal.* Finally, I turned down an offer of technical help from the OverDrive chip's maker, Intel. In a few paragraphs, I'll tell you how this effort came out. But first, a little explanation of chips.

There are lots of chips inside every computer—they're the square or rectangular things, usually black, with little metal pins on the bottom. The most important is the aforementioned CPU, which does most of the actual computing, or "processing." It's often the biggest chip in the PC, and in IBM-compatibles it's usually made by Intel.

Over the years, Intel has made a series of ever faster and more powerful CPUs. Early IBM-compatibles used the Intel 8088. The second major generation used a beefed-up CPU called the 80286. In the past few years, the most common chip has been the 80386—this is the minimum chip necessary to run Microsoft's Windows program well. The latest model is the 80486, which has about four times as many tiny transistors baked into it as an 80286.

In computer ads, these chip model numbers are abbreviated, so you see references to "386" or "486" computers. In addition, the ads usually note the speed at which the chip runs, measured in megahertz. A "486/33" is an 80486 chip that runs at a brisk 33 megahertz.

Another variant is called the "SX" chip. These are cut-rate versions of the 386 and 486 in which Intel has crippled special number-crunching circuitry mainly needed for highly complex programs, such as engineering software. A "486SX/20" may be slower at math-intensive tasks than a full-fledged "486/20," but it's still usually a bit faster than a full-fledged "386/33."

The unlucky PC I chose as my guinea pig is an IBM clone made by Packard Bell, with a 486SX/20 inside. Following Intel's very clear instructions, I turned off and unplugged the machine, opened the case, touched my hand to a metal part to discharge any static electricity (which can fry chips), and began the brain transplant.

On my machine, this took all of ten minutes—even for me, working like molasses. I found the CPU chip and lifted a little lever on the special socket that housed it. This had the effect of loosening the socket's grip on the pins beneath the chip. I then effortlessly lifted the old chip out, dropped in the OverDrive chip, and pushed the lever back down.

On many other 486SX computers, the operation is even simpler. These machines have a vacant socket ready to hold the OverDrive chip, so you don't even have to remove your old chip.

Holding my breath, I then plugged the PC in again and turned it on. Everything worked perfectly—only faster. In fact, using a common performance test included in the popular Norton Utilities program, I found that the OverDrive chip had boosted my computer's processing speed by 66 percent. My 486SX was now more than twice as fast as a 386/33.

The OverDrive chip pulls off this speed increase in two ways. First, it adds back the special math circuitry disabled in a 486SX chip. Second, it doubles the speed at which the CPU does some computations—the test software reported that my machine now contained a 486/40, not a 486SX/20. But it doesn't double the speed of all tasks, because the OverDrive chip still talks to the other circuits in the computer at the original, slower speed.

So, should you buy an OverDrive chip, which initially is likely to cost $450 or so in discount stores? Not necessarily, at least right away. Anyone with a 486SX already has a fast computer. Even before I souped up my machine, it was faster than a 386/33. And the OverDrive chip doesn't work in 286 and 386 machines.

Moreover, there are cheaper ways to speed up a computer. More memory can be added, at about $50 a megabyte. And OverDrive chips give off much more heat than earlier models, which could be a problem in some PC designs.

Many people will justifiably want to avoid messing around inside their PCs. Even Intel recommends getting an expert to do it if it "seems risky." I don't believe average computer users should feel impelled to become technicians.

There are other pitfalls. On some PCs, you may have to reset switches inside the machine if you change CPUs. And you can't count on PC companies to help. When I called Packard Bell, the representative had never heard of the OverDrive chip. When I became irritated by this, he hung up on me.

But I am rather enjoying the new speed in my souped-up PC. The only real problem is that my OverDrive chip is just a loaner. I'll have to return it soon—and that means doing another brain transplant.

6/4/92

Intel has since topped the 486 series with the Pentium series of chips, and has launched a family of new OverDrive chips that upgrade the 486s to Pentiums.

21
Smaller Gets Better with the Newest Versions of Portable PCs

Two trends are shaping the future of portable computers: the gradual replacement of monochrome screens with color displays, and the continuing effort to shrink the size and weight of the machines to turn notebook-sized computers into so-called subnotebooks. So far, both innovations have tended to yield higher prices and to require tradeoffs, either in battery life or features. And they have rarely been found in the same product.

Now, however, two of the leading portable PC makers, Compaq and Toshiba, have introduced subnotebooks with a rich set of features and decent battery life. Color screens are available in top-of-the-line configurations of each, but they are machines with very different personalities.

Toshiba's entry, the Portege T3400 series, is a no-compromise product, with a brilliant display and nearly every bell and whistle imaginable. It's the best all-around subnotebook I've ever seen, but it's expensive, ranging from $2,200 to $3,400 (for the color model) at current discount prices.

Compaq's Contura Aero series has some feature compromises and a less imaginative design. But Compaq has also set a new standard, at the cash register. It has priced the Aero so low as to be irresistible to many buyers. You can get a stripped-down, monochrome Aero for $1,400. And for roughly comparable configurations, an Aero is anywhere from $300 to $1,000 cheaper than a Portege at current discount prices.

The handsome gray Toshiba weighs 4.4 pounds (4.1 pounds for

the monochrome version)—about a third less than the typical 6.5 pounds of a full-sized notebook. It's less than two inches thick and takes up less surface area than a sheet of letter-size paper.

The $3,400 Portege T3400CT model I tested is dominated by a dazzling active-matrix color screen that measures about 7.8 inches diagonally. To my eye, it looks as good as the league-leading color display on the IBM ThinkPad. Like all subnotebooks, the Portege has a somewhat shrunken keyboard, but the keys seemed to have nearly full "travel" (up-and-down motion). Also, Toshiba has resisted the subnotebook practice of doubling up important functions on the same key. It has a full set of twelve dedicated function keys, as well as dedicated keys for "home," "end," "page up," and "page down."

To replace a mouse, Toshiba has built in an IBM-style pointing stick, a soft-tipped lever protruding from the middle of the keyboard. It's a good design, but a bit stiffer and less responsive than IBM's. The mouse buttons are large, curved, and placed in a palm-rest area below the keyboard. There are other nice touches, including informative indicator lights and little legs to tilt the machine for comfortable typing.

Another common subnotebook compromise is that the machines lack internal floppy disk drives. But Toshiba has designed an extraordinarily small and light external drive and included it in the Portege's price. Like most other subnotebooks—including the Aero—the Portege features a "PCMCIA" slot that accepts credit-card-size add-in cards. Most subnotebooks use this slot for adding a modem, which in Toshiba's case costs from $300 to $500.

The Portege uses an innovative new lithium-ion battery that claims four to eight hours of life, but costs around $300 to replace. I got between three and four hours on my test Portege. The Portege uses a low-power version of Intel's 486/33 processor chip, which is adequate, and a 120-megabyte hard disk, which might be a bit small for some users.

The color Compaq Aero that I tested sells for around $2,200, plus $200 for the external floppy drive that Toshiba makes standard, for a price of about $2,400—$1,000 less than the Portege. Its processor has about the same power and speed as the one on the Toshiba, but it had a somewhat larger 170-megabyte hard disk (cheaper Aero models have slower processors and smaller hard disks, down to an inadequate 84 megabytes). It's a bit smaller and lighter than the Toshiba—3.5 pounds for the monochrome model, 4.2 pounds for the color version.

In most other respects, however, the $1,000 price difference shows in a more conventional and compromised design. For instance, the color screen is about the same size as the Portege's, but it's a more pallid passive-matrix model that's harder to view from an angle.

The Aero's keyboard seemed cramped, with keys that felt stiffer; it has only ten, instead of twelve, dedicated function keys, and lacks separate keys for "home," "end," "page up" and "page down." The substitute mouse is a small trackball in the lower-right corner, with mouse buttons on the side of the computer. I found the combination to be a bit clumsy, but that's a matter of taste.

Like the Portege, the Aero features an unusual new type of battery. It's a nickel-metal hydride type, in two new standard sizes made by Duracell that will supposedly be much more widely available—and cheaper—than earlier custom-designed computer batteries. Compaq and Duracell say the batteries can yield up to six hours of power (for the larger size battery) and cost $99 and $169 to replace, respectively. I got about three hours of battery life from my color Aero.

Despite its compromises, the color Compaq Aero is a terrific value at $2,400—a powerful color computer that's small enough to almost forget about when traveling. It's not the near-perfect machine Toshiba built, but for $1,000 less, it may be close enough in the eyes of many buyers.

4/14/94

22
Dell's Notebook Keeps Going and Going . . .

Notebook computers these days come with all sorts of bells and whistles—brilliant color screens, exotic communications devices, huge hard disks, and memory capacity. They truly rival desktop computers in most respects.

But any serious traveler who uses these portable PCs knows what he or she really wants: a battery that gets decent life, one that lets you use your computer continuously on a six-hour transcontinental flight. All the fancy features in the world aren't worth a damn when the battery dies out over Kansas City and your report won't be done till Philadelphia.

Well, listen up, you beleaguered notebook nomads: I have found the Holy Grail. It's a full-featured, high-powered, name-brand notebook PC that really gets six hours of battery life and maybe more, depending on your usage pattern. It isn't cheap, but it isn't the most expensive notebook either. It's the new Dell Latitude XP, available only directly through Dell, and it costs from $3,199 to $5,099, depending on the combination of processor, screen, and other variables you select.

In fact, I'm writing these words on a Latitude XP that's been left on for about ten hours and used now and again during that period to run various programs. The rest of the time, it's been idle, mainly in a low-power state imposed by its automated battery-saving program. It's got about half its charge left, according to the little battery gauge on the screen. I'm no engineer, I haven't performed rigorous benchmark tests, and I know the capacity figure will fall fast as I continue to write. Your mileage will vary, especially if you work it harder than I have in this informal test. But the fact I can use it at all after ten hours is pretty amazing.

In addition to the Dell Latitude, I've also been trying out another promising notebook: AST's new Ascentia 900N. Of the two, the Dell Latitude XP stands out, in my view, and not only because of its awesome battery life, made possible by a new lithium-ion battery technology and especially clever hardware and software that micromanages the machine's use of power.

In many other respects, the new Dell shows the kind of careful and elegant design touches that make for a great small PC. This is particularly notable, because in the past Dell has done a lousy job with notebooks. These new Latitudes, however, are the first efforts of a new Dell team headed by some of the Apple executives who designed the path-breaking PowerBook portables before they were lured away by Dell.

Like the PowerBooks, the Latitude I'm using has a very nice keyboard with a trackball at the bottom flanked by broad wrist-rest areas, and little legs at the rear to provide a comfortable typing angle. Unlike the original Apple PowerBook, the Dell sports a full set of function keys and indicator lights. The hard disk is removable, the AC adapter is small and light, the utility programs included are excellent, and the whole thing has a sturdy, polished feel.

About my only complaint with the Latitude XP involves the active-matrix color screen, a high-end, vivid technology. It's not that the screen is bad, exactly. It's bright, sharp, pretty large, and eminently usable. But there's an odd quality to the colors, which appear sort of washed-out when compared with the same shades on other active-matrix notebooks or desktops.

The Latitude model I'm using, called the 450CX, isn't the top of the line. It has a 486 processor running at 50 megahertz, not the faster DX4 chip running at 100 MHz. But it's plenty fast. It has a 340-megabyte hard disk, not the optional 524-megabyte model. But that's more than adequate in a notebook. It costs $4,299—roughly in the middle of the Latitude XP price range—and weighs 6.05 pounds, with battery.

The same machine with a less vivid "passive matrix" color screen, but the same battery life and design details, can be had for $3,199. (Dell also sells a low-priced Latitude line, without the "XP" in the name. These are totally different machines, without the special batteries, though they do let you use two batteries at a time to extend battery life.)

The AST Ascentia has a bigger, more vivid screen than the Latitude, and ships with my favorite electronic mail software, E-Mail Connection. But in all other respects, I found it inferior to the Dell. The keyboard seemed more cramped, with some crucial keys—such as those for home, end, page up, and page down—reduced to shrunken remnants stuck in the top right corner. Worse, the buttons for the built-in substitute mouse—an IBM-style "trackpoint" stick in the middle of the keyboard—are comical, puny things hanging on the edge of the machine that I found hard to operate without making errors.

What's more, the AST model is costlier and heavier than the Dell. I tested the top-of-the-line version, with the fastest processor and biggest screen and hard disk. It costs $5,949, according to AST. A similarly equipped Latitude XP, with its better battery life and keyboard, is $5,099. The Ascentia tips the scales at 6.8 pounds, so it's more of a pain to lug than the Dell. (Like Dell, AST also sells a less expensive, less fancy line, also under the Ascentia brand name.)

And then there's the topic we began with: battery life. The AST doesn't do badly; I got about five hours from it on my low-stress, unscientific test. But that pales compared with the Dell Latitude XP, which still has 19 percent of its power left as I wrap up this column, fifteen hours since the battery was charged. Is that Philadelphia I see down below?

9/8/94

23
Sony's New PDA Is the Pick of a Weak Litter

Sony last week introduced a little computer called Magic Link, and I can report that it's the best personal digital assistant I've ever used. Unfortunately, that's like saying a brewery is making the best nonalcoholic beer I've ever tasted: the competition is so weak it doesn't take much to edge it out, and the winner still leaves you unsatisfied.

Like its unsuccessful predecessors, Sony's product is still too costly and too flawed to be ready for mainstream business users, in my view. It is likelier to be embraced by "early adopters," people willing to pay for new technology, despite its high price and rough edges. But after ten days of toting a Magic Link everywhere, including a cross-country business trip, I'd say it comes closer than anything else to meeting the definition of a really winning PDA: a small, inexpensive, light computer that's controlled by a pen, organizes your contacts and calendar, and lets you communicate easily via voice, fax, and e-mail.

Magic Link's success is partly based on the kind of elegant industrial design for which Sony is famous. But it is mainly due to Sony's decision to incorporate into the device some very impressive software and services from two other companies, a start-up called General Magic and that behemoth called AT&T.

General Magic has contributed a new user interface, called Magic Cap, which I think is the first really successful way of controlling a computer since Apple's Macintosh system, introduced in 1984 and later aped by Microsoft's Windows. It uses pictures of objects in an office—and of buildings in a neighborhood—to represent programs and functions in the computer.

AT&T has contributed PersonaLink, a new on-line service for e-mail and, eventually, shopping and other services. This is a powerful system based on 1990s technology that can easily handle handwritten messages, graphics, sounds, and more. And it permits the user to send out special programs called "intelligent agents" that can route messages in any way he or she wants, or perform other customized tasks using another piece of General Magic software called Telescript. AT&T charges $9.95 a month now, and the base price is expected to drop.

Eventually, you won't need a Sony Magic Link to use Magic Cap, Telescript, and PersonaLink. These products will soon show up on other pieces of hardware, including a PDA from Motorola. And, sometime in 1995, they'll be available for use on standard desktop and notebook computers, both Macintoshes and IBM-compatibles using Windows. For now, though, they're tied into the Magic Link, which is a gray, 1.2-pound machine that sells at discount for a base price of about $850 but is around $1,400 when equipped with enough accessories to make it fully usable. It's about the length and width of a large paperback but only an inch thick.

When you turn it on, you see the main Magic Cap screen—a close-up drawing of a desk with familiar office objects depicted on or near it: a phone, Rolodex, postcard, notepad, calendar, in box, out box and file cabinet. These are all working features that you can access by tapping on them with a plastic stylus or a fingertip.

To send an electronic-mail message or fax, for instance, you just tap on the postcard, which opens a blank message form. Pick a recipient from the Rolodex and enter your text, either by handwriting with the little stylus or by hunting and pecking on a virtual keyboard that pops up on the screen. (If you use handwriting, the machine won't try and translate it to typed text; it just sends or faxes your scrawl as is.) Then you just tap on "send" and the message is deposited in the out box. Another tap or two and Magic Link dials the AT&T service, a fax machine or the America Online service via a built-in modem (which previous PDAs lacked). It not only sends the message you just created, but collects any mail waiting for you and places it in your box.

It sounds great, and it does work. But there are significant problems with Magic Link.

First, the screen isn't backlit, so it's terribly dim in many lighting conditions—so poor that it's barely acceptable. The machine lacks wireless e-mail or faxing capability. That means it still must be tethered to a phone line to communicate. And the modem is as slow as Congress—only 2,400 baud. What's more, the Magic Link quickly runs out of memory in which to store information, so you're forced to buy a $200 add-on memory card. The on-screen keyboard is the best I've ever seen, but it still stinks, so you have to buy a $130 add-on keyboard, which can't be comfortably used except on a desk or table.

Battery life using standard AAA batteries is only a few hours. To get the maximum ten hours or so, you need a $70 lithium-ion battery—not included. The Magic Cap interface works very well in general, but it's hard to customize to your preferences and needs more shortcuts so you can quickly jump from function to function. AT&T's fledgling PersonaLink doesn't yet accept many of the "intelligent agent" commands that AT&T boasts about.

These are some of the reasons I can't recommend Magic Link to most business people. But I'm basically optimistic about the future for all three companies' products. Sony plans a new, improved model next year. And I can't wait to try Magic Cap and PersonaLink on my real computers. I only wish I was as hopeful about nonalcoholic beers.

10/6/94

24 One Task That PCs Fail to Simplify: Adding Gadgets to Your PC

The computer industry likes to boast that personal computers are easy to expand. Just pop a circuit board into a slot inside the box, or plug a cable into a socket on the back, the computer ads say, and your machine can be enhanced with a modem, a scanner, better sound or video, an extra hard disk, networking, or a CD-ROM drive.

These claims are about as reliable as the old adage that "the check is in the mail." In fact, adding extra hardware to an IBM-compatible PC—the dominant PC design—can be a most frustrating experience. Too often, getting new components to mesh with the old takes an aggravating and lengthy process of trial and error.

This conclusion came to me in a blinding flash of insight recently as I was sitting on the floor in my office next to my partly disassembled IBM clone, made by Zeos. I was trying for the fourth or fifth time to fiddle with "jumpers," tiny plastic pieces on several of the computer's add-on circuit boards, or "cards," to get a new sound card to work without disabling the modem or other functions. I finally did it, but it took hours.

If this happens to you, it isn't because you're dumb, and you're not alone. The problem is widely acknowledged in private among computer company officials, even if it never makes it into the ad copy. "The IBM PC architecture is very old," says John Wiersema, an engineer at U.S. Robotics, a top modem maker. "It wasn't designed to handle today's variety of devices."

David Cole, program manager for Microsoft's Windows 3.1 software, admits to similar frustration himself in adding new hardware, saying, "In today's world it's pretty difficult to do."

The problem is that on typical IBM-compatibles, most devices you add must be assigned a special designation called a "COM port," whether or not they actually plug into one of the ports on the machine. But there are usually only four such port designations, and often all four can't be used at once because they try to claim the use of the same two locations in the computer circuitry. This wasn't a problem in 1981, when few add-on devices were around, but today the result is chaos and malfunction. A modern PC with mouse and modem may occupy two such ports before anything else is added.

There are ways around the problem, but most force users to fool with jumpers and tiny switches inside the machine, and to configure software by specifying such arcane information as "base hex address" and "interrupt setting." A regular person who just wants to get work out of a computer shouldn't have to put up with this.

One way to minimize the problem is to make sure your PC has a good, clear manual written for nontechnical people. Neither my Zeos machine nor the Creative Labs' Sound Blaster Pro card with which I was working had a very good manual. Or you can buy a PC equipped at the factory with lots of extras (such as a "multimedia PC"), for extra money.

But there's a more radical option: if you think you'll want to seriously expand your computer, buy one designed from the ground up to make expansion easy.

International Business Machines itself long ago acknowledged the expansion problems of the common IBM-compatible design. In 1987, it introduced a high-end line, Micro Channel PCs, that the company says can be expanded with little or no manual configuration and conflict. But the Micro Channel models, which account for less than 20 percent of IBM-compatible sales, are pricier than standard IBM-compatibles, and require nonstandard internal components, which also cost somewhat more.

Or you could buy one of Apple Computer's Macintosh models. My Macintosh IIci has roughly the same power and speed as my Zeos, and similar features and extras, but the Mac's case hasn't been opened since I set it up (which took just twenty minutes).

The same sound capability I struggled to add to the Zeos came built into the Mac, as did a color video hookup and networking capability. The CD-ROM drive that required an internal adapter card on the Zeos merely plugged into a built-in socket, the "SCSI" port, on the back of the Mac. As many as six devices can be linked to this port by a daisy chain of cables.

A fax modem and a printer simply plugged into sockets marked by pictures of a telephone and a printer. Neither involved any switches or jumpers. The Mac's mouse plugs into the keyboard. In short, the Mac is about as close as you can come today to a mass-market "plug-and-play" computer.

But simplicity has its price. Macintoshes and Mac add-on devices still aren't standard issue in the business world, and they cost more than comparable IBM-compatible equipment, despite recent Apple price cuts that have narrowed the gap.

Moreover, the Mac isn't wholly free of hardware-connection problems. For instance, it can be frustrating to get the chained devices connected to the SCSI port working together just right. Each needs a distinct ID number, and little plugs called "terminators" must be stuck on one or more of them.

Whatever computer you buy, do me a favor. If I ever write that adding a peripheral device to an IBM-compatible is "easy," drop me a sarcastic note.

3/26/92

More IBM-compatibles are now shipping with sound and other features built in, Macintosh-style. But it's still a pain in the neck to expand them.

25 Computer Viruses Are Nothing to Sneeze At, but They're Curable

Companies that make anti-virus software warn that there are over one thousand computer viruses affecting IBM-compatibles, including a strain timed to wipe out certain programs every Friday the thirteenth. And some have trumpeted the discovery of a new virus that may cause crashes on Apple Computer's Macintosh machines.

Just how serious is the virus threat? Must every computer owner buy anti-virus software? The answer is that there is a real threat, but it is easily exaggerated by the anti-virus software firms. Your need for anti-virus software depends a lot on how you use your computers. And though many of the programs are effective, they have downsides.

The independent National Computer Security Association in Washington says that of the thousand-plus viruses known to attack IBM-compatibles, fewer than fifty are common and only about a hundred others have also been found "in the wild"; the rest are known only to researchers. In 1991, the NCSA says, just two viruses, JerusalemB and Stoned, accounted for 74 percent of virus incidents in the U.S.; neither wipes out whole disks, as the much-publicized Michelangelo does. As for the dreaded Maltese Amoeba, the NCSA and others say it hasn't yet been reported in the U.S. In fact, some of the worst viruses mainly flourish abroad. Mac owners face few viruses.

So there's no need to panic, but prudence is in order. Many computers, especially in big organizations, can become infected, and most infections screw up the computer. The worst cases wipe out data or program files.

Lone home users who do little disk-swapping or program-sharing probably don't need anti-virus software. But in most other cases—especially large organizations with many computer users—anti-virus software is advisable. At the very least, hard disks should be scanned for viruses every month or so, and any floppy disk from an outside source should be scanned before use.

Anti-virus programs usually include a scanner, which operates on demand or when the machine starts up, and looks for computer code that matches a set of "signatures" characteristic of known viruses. There's often a separate module that eradicates any viruses found. And there's normally a form of the program that remains in memory at all times to check for viruses. In addition, many programs try to seek unknown viruses by looking for changes in the size and composition of program files on your hard disk, or by monitoring suspicious behavior believed common to viruses.

None of these methods are foolproof. The programs' databases of virus signatures must be updated often to be effective. Their memory-resident modules can goof up other software by hogging memory. And various techniques of finding unknown viruses might be rendered ineffective if the digital vandals think up new methods of infection.

Two programs, "Novi" by Certus of Cleveland, Ohio, and "Untouchable" by Fifth Generation of Baton Rouge, Louisiana, claim such good generic virus detection that you don't need to update for new virus signatures.

Novi seems to offer the more sophisticated approach, monitoring processes inside programs. The company says its generic technology has caught every new virus for four years. But if you buy these products, I'd suggest continuing to scan for known viruses and get updates, which both products allow.

You probably wouldn't go wrong with any of four packages: Central Point Anti-Virus by Central Point, Beaverton, Oregon; Viruscan by McAfee Associates, Santa Clara, California; Certus's Novi; and ViruSafe by XTree, San Luis Obispo, California. I'd place another leading package, Norton Anti-Virus, by Symantec, Santa Monica, California, a whisker behind.

But the NCSA gives higher marks to two lesser-known programs: Dr. Solomon's Anti-Virus Toolkit, sold by Ontrack Computer Systems,

Eden Prairie, Minnesota; and Leprechaun Virus Buster, sold by Leprechaun Software, Marietta, Georgia.

Some top virus busters swear by an Icelandic program that's free to home users and costs businesses just one dollar a computer. Called F-Prot, it's found on database services and bulletin boards, including NCSA's (202-364-1304).

For Macintosh users, two commercial programs stand out: Virex by Microcom, Norwood, Massachusetts, and Symantec's AntiVirus. But there's also a very good free anti-virus program for Macs, called Disinfectant, by John Norstad of Northwestern University, available on many bulletin boards.

3/5/92

26
Putting Your Macs and IBM-Compatibles on Speaking Terms

The conventional wisdom is that you shouldn't mix IBM-compatible personal computers and Apple's Macintosh personal computers in the same office, at least without a costly networking system. Computer salespeople and technicians routinely tell users that, regrettably, the machines aren't "compatible."

But such statements are, at best, gross exaggerations—a classic case of experts focusing on technical barriers rather than practical solutions. In many home and small-office situations, it's easy to share data among IBM-compatibles and Macs without a network.

The Wall Street Journal office in which this column is written features an IBM-compatible and a Macintosh that routinely share files on floppy disks which are swapped between them. This column was begun on a Mac using Claris's MacWrite II word processing program and finished on an IBM-compatible using XyQuest's XyWrite III Plus word processing software.

No technical wizardry is needed to create such a setup—just modestly priced off-the-shelf software. Experts deride this approach as "sneaker net," because it can require carrying disks between computers—but it works.

It is true that IBM-compatibles and Macintoshes use different "operating systems"—the special underlying software needed to run the machines—that prevent them from running the same software programs. An IBM PC's operating system software doesn't recognize a data disk formatted on a Mac, and vice versa. Techies and salespeople focus on this fact. But there are clever and inexpensive ways around that barrier.

This is a problem with three parts. First, can the computers' disk drives physically accommodate each other's disks? Second, can the two computers' operating systems be tricked into recognizing disks produced on the other? Third, can your application programs—word processing, spreadsheets and so on—for one type of computer use files created on the other type of computer?

The hardware issue is the easiest one. Today, every Macintosh comes out of the box with a 3½-inch floppy disk drive that can physically read disks from IBM-compatibles. Newer IBMs sport the same-sized drives, and adding such drives to older IBMs that lack them is inexpensive. Or, you can buy a special disk drive that permits a Mac to read the older style 5¼-inch IBM-type floppies.

But the computer's operating-system software must still be deceived into recognizing each other's disks. Luckily, there are at least three inexpensive (under $100 by mail order) Macintosh software programs that permanently fool the Mac's operating system into recognizing IBM-formatted data disks. They are: Access PC, by Insignia Solutions; DOS Mounter, by Dayna Communications; and Software Bridge/Mac, by Argosy Software. These programs need to be installed just once, and then you can forget about them.

And there's a new utility program for IBM-compatibles that permits them to recognize disks from Macs. It's called Mac-to-DOS, from PLI. It isn't as automatic as the three Mac utilities, but it does the job with minimal fuss.

So, you've got your computer to "see" the disks and files from its alien cousin. How can your programs use the files?

For word processing documents, programs on both computers can usually save files as plain text, a universal format that includes all the words but excludes special formatting such as underlining and italics. Just save a file on one computer as "text" or "ASCII" (its technical name), pop the disk into the other machine, and most word processors will be able to call it up.

Spreadsheet files can also be saved in universal formats. A common one is the Lotus 1-2-3 format, which most spreadsheet programs on both types of computers recognize. Graphics files can also be translated into a common format usable by many programs.

An even better approach is to equip your IBM-compatible and Mac with compatible versions of the same software. That usually allows you to swap files between the machines while preserving all of your special formatting and formulas.

Many major business programs are now available in such "twin" versions for IBMs and Macs. They include the Microsoft Word writing program and Microsoft Excel spreadsheet, the WordPerfect word processor, the Lotus 1-2-3 spreadsheet and Aldus PageMaker desktop publishing program.

There are also special utility programs designed solely to translate files from one computer to the other. Apple supplies such a program, Apple File Exchange, free with all Macs, and there are commercial offerings, such as MacLink Plus by DataViz and Argosy's Software Bridge/Mac, which translates files automatically as soon as they're opened.

There are costlier ways to integrate Macs and IBM-compatibles. These include networks, transferring files over phone lines, and special software and hardware that permit the machines to run programs written for each other. These solutions may make the best sense for large offices constantly sharing lots of files. But for smaller shops, remember this: no matter what the experts say, you can share work between dissimilar computers without a lot of hassle or expense.

11/7/91

Apple has since built its own version of Access PC into every Mac, and has even begun shipping some models with hardware or software that permits the Mac to run IBM programs.

27 Networks Made Easy, or Getting by Without Decoding Token Rings

No computer is an island. That's the slogan the personal-computer industry hopes to get PC users chanting from every office in the land. A raft of software and hardware companies are pushing the idea that, to be truly effective, computers must be "networked"—lashed together with cables so they can exchange data in a flash over a "LAN," or local-area network.

Now Microsoft, the leader in computer software, has begun a multimillion-dollar marketing drive to persuade even the smallest organizations to network their computers. The company has introduced a version of its Windows software called Windows for Workgroups (a "workgroup" being one of those made-up industry terms for a relatively small bunch of office employees working on related projects).

But networking is one of the most confusing subjects in all of computerdom, and it can be expensive. It usually requires extra hardware and software, it often forces PC users to rely even more on high-priced technical experts, and it can force people to change the way they work to fit the design of the system. Moreover, contrary to the industry hype, it isn't necessary to make computers productive in all situations, and it may not even be desirable in some settings.

The basic idea behind computer networking is to allow coworkers to share programs, electronic data, in-house electronic mail, and connections to peripheral equipment such as printers through their individual PCs. It is supposed to enhance teamwork and collaboration and eliminate the need to circulate paper memos and printed drafts of reports and other business documents.

If you pick up a computer magazine or book, you'll see networks described in arcane terms such as "token ring" and "10base-T." This lexicon constitutes a sort of full-employment policy for computer consultants and in-house experts who are paid to oversee complicated networks—like priests who alone can decipher ancient texts.

But there are just two basic models for PC networks, and they aren't hard to grasp. The most common type of network is called "client/server." In this design, one brawny PC is the network's hub, or "server." It is connected to many desktop PCs, called "clients," throughout an organization. The clients typically run programs that are stored on the server. They also call up data stored there, such as changing drafts of a report or a common schedule of meetings. And the server usually functions as an electronic-mail post office.

But the clients are essentially slaves. So everything must pass through the server—even files and messages meant for a coworker two feet away. A client/server network is in some ways a throwback to the early days of computing, when desktop machines were just terminals that tapped into huge computers tightly controlled by a central staff.

The leading brand of client/server network is Netware, by Novell of Provo, Utah. It's high-quality, but it isn't easy to set up and run without technical help.

The other basic model is called "peer-to-peer" networking, or simply "file sharing." In this approach, every PC in a small office acts as both client and server. The machines are cabled together, and each can tap into any of the others, though access is restricted to those files and programs a computer's owner chooses to make public. Peer-to-peer networks are usually much cheaper and easier to set up and don't necessarily require full-time staffs or "network administrators" to operate. They also conform better to real-life work flows, in which coworkers exchange documents in natural patterns, rather than routing everything through some central authority.

The downside of peer-to-peer networking is that it is efficient for twenty or twenty-five people at the most. In larger settings, or offices where vast amounts of data are shared, these networks can bog down.

Peer-to-peer networks were popularized by Apple Computer, which builds networking hardware and software into all its Macintosh computers. Macs can be networked using inexpensive connectors and common telephone wire like that used to plug a phone into a wall jack.

On IBM-compatible PCs, special circuit boards and software must be installed in the computer to set up even a peer-to-peer network. The leading provider of these add-ons is Artisoft of Tucson, Arizona, through its LANtastic networking kits. Microsoft's Windows for Workgroups is another peer-to-peer product.

All networks force users to master such arts as file transmission and security procedures. But client/server networks add a layer to work flow because everything gets routed through the server. They also often add to the office bureaucracy, as network administrators promulgate rules on what software can be used on computers.

Of course, the real competition for both kinds of PC networks is "sneakernet"—the system in which documents are transported by people carrying pieces of paper or floppy disks containing the relevant electronic files. If sneakernet works in your office, you can tune out the computer industry's call to lay miles of cables and hire all those experts.

11/5/92

28
To Be Letter Perfect, Select a Laser Printer That's Right for You

Choosing a printer for your personal computer used to be simple. There wasn't much choice of features, typefaces, type sizes, or styles. But like everything else about computers, printers have become much improved and more varied. The best choice today is a laser printer, whether your PC is an IBM-compatible or one of Apple Computer's Macintosh models. But choosing among laser printers today is far more complicated than it was in the old days. So here's a primer on laser printing.

Without getting too technical, laser printers work essentially the same way photocopiers do. The image from your computer is inscribed on paper using a laser beam (or other light-emitting gizmo) and a dry, fine powder, called toner. The toner sticks to some places on the paper, and not to others, following a pattern of electrical charges.

Though laser printers vary, they all produce output that is sharp enough, bold enough, and neat enough to make for excellent business documents. They use standard paper, not the folded type with holes that people long associated with computer printing. There is no ink or ribbons, and the machines are generally quiet, because there are no metal parts striking the paper and the printers create a whole page at once, rather than hammering the document out line by line. For that reason, laser printers are sometimes called "page printers" or "non-impact printers."

When Apple some years back introduced the first popular laser printer, its LaserWriter, it cost more than $5,000. Today a decent laser printer for low-volume, small-office use can be had for $600 to $1,700, depending on features and options. Unless you or your business never produces documents whose appearance matters, or the cost is simply prohibitive, a laser printer is the way to go.

Laser printers have two main parts. There's the "engine," which does the actual printing, and is usually built by Canon, Minolta Camera, or a handful of other Japanese firms. And there's the computer circuitry, which prepares the image for printing. Indeed, most laser printers contain the same sort of central processing chip and memory found in computers. The speed and quality of a laser printer depend on the nature and interaction of these two parts.

When shopping for laser printers, there are several factors to keep in mind.

The first is speed. Printer ads often rate machines in terms of pages per minute, or "ppm." For personal or small business use, four ppm is probably adequate. But these ratings are misleading, because they only describe the raw power of the printing engine. They don't take account of varying speeds with which the printer's chips prepare documents, or of differences among types of documents—plain text in a single font or typeface prints much more quickly than complicated text or graphics documents.

In addition, lasers work faster when printing added copies of a document that has already been processed than when working on a whole series of different documents, each of which requires preparation. If speed matters, find out whether a fast processor chip (such as a "68020" or higher, or a "RISC" chip) is being used, and whether there's a lot of memory (at least two megabytes, preferably more).

Another factor to consider is the laser's "printer description language." This is the computer code that permits the machine to produce type and graphics in varying sizes without distortion. The standard among design and printing pros is a language called PostScript, supplied to printer makers by Adobe Systems. If you can find a PostScript printer within your price range, go for it.

PostScript printers have come down in cost, but they still occupy the upper end of the $600-to-$1,700 price range. The lower end is occupied by printers that either have or emulate a printer language called "PCL," from Hewlett-Packard. The PCL language has improved greatly, and it can compete with PostScript in many types of printing situations.

A third factor is "connectivity." Most laser printers have a "parallel" port for hookups to IBM-compatibles. Some have an "AppleTalk" or "LocalTalk" port for attaching to Macs. Increasingly, printers are shipping with both types of ports.

Fourth, there's the quality of the output. Nearly every laser printer features output of three hundred dots per inch, or dpi, which I think is more than adequate for most business uses. But scanned photos and some other kinds of graphics, as well as very fine text, don't do as well at 300 dpi as they should. So companies such as Lexmark International and QMS are starting to offer 600 dpi laser printers.

Finally, consider operating costs. With a laser printer, you must periodically replace the toner and a few other key parts, which wear out. In some models, these are separate pieces with varying life cycles. In others, all are swapped out via a single replacement module. One company, Kyocera, claims its new printer, the Eco-Sys, never requires replacement of any parts other than the toner cartridge. But insist on knowing the operating costs per page before you buy a laser printer.

8/20/92

Today, all these criteria still apply, but prices for lasers now start at $400 or so, and most companies offer higher-priced models with 600 dpi output.

29
Fine Printers Offer Little to Users Who Stick to Text

The leading makers of desktop laser printers have begun to offer a new level of print quality and speed at mainstream prices. These companies, notably Hewlett-Packard and Apple Computer, see the new standard they are setting as a near-universal one. But whether you should trade in your old printer for these improved machines depends a lot on what kind of documents you produce. To make an informed decision requires a little background knowledge.

For years, standard laser printers have laid text and graphics down on the page at a resolution of three hundred dots per inch, or dpi. This means every inch of printed material is created on an invisible grid measuring 300 dots of toner (the powdered "ink" used by laser printers) horizontally by 300 dots vertically. That degree of sharpness revolutionized computer printing because, especially for text, it produces documents that look crisp, clean, and professional.

Several companies have offered higher-resolution printers, but these were often very expensive, or very slow, because printing at higher resolutions involves manipulating vastly greater numbers of dots, which requires more processing by both the computer and the printer. For a printer with a resolution of 600 dpi, the square-inch grid measures 600 dots by 600. That works out to four times the dots of a 300-dpi machine—or as many as 360,000 a square inch, compared with 90,000—and thus four times as much work.

Now Hewlett-Packard, the dominant American printer maker, has brought out a pair of sleek, powerful 600-dpi printers, the LaserJet 4 and LaserJet 4M. The basic LaserJet 4, for IBM-compatible computers only, sells for as little as $1,400 at discount, less than the 300-dpi LaserJet III model it replaces.

The LaserJet 4M, which I have been testing, is designed to accommodate Apple's Macintosh computers as well as IBM-compatible PCs. It also includes triple the memory of the basic 4 and has Adobe Systems' PostScript printing language built in. The 4M sells for about $2,000 at discount, also a relatively aggressive price for its features.

Apple, the number two printer maker, has introduced the LaserWriter Pro 600 and LaserWriter Pro 630, a pair of machines similar to the higher-end LaserJet 4M and selling in the same $2,000 range. I haven't tested the Apple models, but both companies' new printers use the same "engine," or basic printing mechanism, made by Canon of Japan. The engine not only prints at 600 dpi, but also uses a finer-grained toner that enhances resolution.

HP's new LaserJets aren't just higher-resolution and affordable, they are also speedy. The company says they can produce as many as eight pages a minute, even while laying down all those extra dots. And the LaserJet 4M I've been testing on both an IBM-compatible PC and a Mac has proved much faster than a mainstream 300-dpi laser printer.

The LaserJets also can send information about their status back to the computer. So, with the right software, the printer could, for instance, post a notice on the screen that the paper tray is empty. Apple printers hooked to Macintoshes have had a similar capability for years.

The HP models are also well-designed. They are fairly compact, at roughly sixteen inches square and about a foot high. They come standard with a 250-sheet automatic paper feeder that slides out of sight into the printer's base, and a second fold-out paper tray that holds as many as one hundred sheets or ten envelopes.

The HP machines have many built-in fonts, including the TrueType varieties used by Microsoft's Windows program and on Macs, and a well-arranged control panel with a bright display. The toner cartridge, which must be replaced periodically, is rated to last a relatively high six thousand pages.

I found that the LaserJet 4M does a much better job with graphics, especially photographs, than my 300-dpi laser printer. Gray areas are much finer and more even, graphic images sharper and richer. But on text, the improvement is only noticeable if you look hard. In my judgment, for standard business documents that are wholly or mainly text, 600-dpi resolution isn't a big leap forward from 300-dpi.

My only gripe is that the 4M occasionally spits out pages with a slight curl at the leading edge. This isn't very noticeable, but it makes the pages tough to feed into a fax machine. HP says it has had only scattered reports about the curling and doesn't regard it as a major problem, though the company is tracking it.

If you print a lot of graphics, or want more speed, the LaserJet 4 is a good buy. Anyone wanting to share a high-quality printer between an IBM-compatible PC and a Macintosh would do well to consider the LaserJet 4M, which—unlike Apple's new machines—can automatically switch between PostScript, predominantly used on Macs, and HP's own PCL 5 printer language, usually used on IBM-compatibles.

If you need to add new printers anyway, you might want to turn to the LaserJet 4; that way, even if you don't think you need 600 dpi, you will get more advanced capabilities, at a reasonable price, that might prove useful in the future. But I wouldn't advise the mainstream IBM-compatible user who for the most part prints text and is happy with current-generation 300-dpi laser printers to rush out and replace them with 600-dpi machines. For standard text documents, 300-dpi printers still seem good enough to me.

2/25/93

30
A Cheaper Route to More Colorful Computer Documents

In the 1980s, as the laser printer gained popularity, the business world was hit by a phenomenon called "ransom notes." Computer users were thrilled that their new printers could produce professional-looking output, with multiple typefaces, in multiple sizes and styles. So they started sending out letters, memos and reports composed of a discordant melange of fonts that resembled the ransom notes that kidnappers—at least in the movies—construct from mismatched characters clipped from a newspaper.

The ransom-note effect has subsided greatly, as people have gotten used to laser printing. But I fear we soon may see a similar esthetic debacle that might be called the "coloring book effect." That's because business-quality color printers have finally dropped to a widely affordable price—about the same as a low-end monochrome laser. And it may be impossible for the artistically impaired to resist churning out boring reports full of red text and green tables that would make *USA Today* look like a tax form by comparison.

Despite this chilling prospect, the coming of quality color printing as a mainstream technology for offices and homes is probably a good thing. After all, the world's in color (even *The Wall Street Journal* occasionally bursts into brighter hues within certain ads). Charts, graphics, and key text passages can be made more understandable in color. It once cost thousands of dollars for a printer that could do a decent job in color, and you often had to use special paper. Now you can get one for around $600, and it can use plain old office paper, just like a copying machine.

With that in mind, I recently tested two first-rate $600 color printers: Canon's BJC600 and Hewlett-Packard's DeskJet 560C. Each uses a printing technology called inkjet, in which a fine mist of ink droplets is sprayed on the page by tiny nozzles. And each comes in versions for both IBM-compatible and Apple Macintosh computers (the Mac version of the DeskJet is called the DeskWriter, and the Mac version of the Canon machine is sold under Apple's label as the Color StyleWriter Pro).

I tested each with straight text documents, in black and several colors; with a chart created in a spreadsheet program; and with some elaborate pictures and stories created in several popular children's programs. I found that, while each machine has its strengths and weaknesses, both are very good. I preferred the overall design of the Canon and liked its color output a bit better. But I give the edge to the Hewlett-Packard in printing monochrome text and in overall speed.

Inkjet printers, to my eye, fall short of laser-printer quality. But there are no modestly priced color lasers. Both the printers I tested are very close to laser quality on monochrome text documents, and their color output was quite pleasing, if less than perfect. In a business, they could produce documents suitable for most common uses. In a home or home office, they would do that and also churn out enough great-looking kids' art to paper every refrigerator door in the land. Neither one is good enough for serious, professional color art or graphics work.

The Canon is newly designed to challenge Hewlett-Packard's dominance of the inkjet market. It features a sleek, compact form with a weight of just under ten pounds, a width of just fourteen inches and a depth of about eight inches (although extending a sliding tray to catch paper as it comes out roughly doubles the depth). There's a separate ink cartridge for black and for each of the three primary colors the printer uses to create its palette of hues. That means you don't have to replace all the colors each time just one shade of ink runs out. Replacement cartridges are priced at around $8 each. The ink also is a new fast-drying variety, which helps reduce bleeding, the effect in which one color oozes into another on the page.

The Canon's print resolution is 360 dots per inch, which is better than low-end monochrome lasers. Every test document came out looking very good. My only complaint about the Canon is that it was quite slow, though the speed may improve as the company revises the software, called a "driver," that controls the machine.

The HP 560C is an older design, and it shows. It's 50 percent heavier than the Canon and is nearly eighteen inches wide by fifteen inches deep. Connections for the power cord and computer cable are inconveniently placed, and it uses a bulky transformer. There's a separate cartridge for black ink, but the primary ink colors are housed together in a single cartridge, so you have to replace all of them when one is used up. Replacement cartridges cost about $20 for black and $30 for color.

But Hewlett-Packard, concerned about Canon's challenge, has enhanced this warhorse with new features. In particular, the 560C prints black-and-white documents (but not color ones) at six hundred dots per inch, just like a high-end laser. The result, on the test documents, was better plain-text printing than the Canon achieved. The HP now also uses special software, called ColorSmart, which automatically optimizes color settings. This resulted in very nice color output, but at a resolution of just three hundred dots per inch. To my eye, it didn't quite match that of the Canon. However, the Hewlett-Packard ran faster in my tests.

The two printers are pretty comparable, and you won't go wrong with either. But if you buy one, control yourself. The world doesn't need more purple prose.

3/31/94

31

Scanning System Lets Your PC Read the Paper

Computers are pretty good at producing paper copies of documents created electronically. But reversing the process has been a killer. Getting paper documents into your computer, turning them into electronic files, and then organizing them effectively has been next to impossible for mainstream users.

There are, of course, many scanners designed to convert hard copy to electronic images, and even elaborate document-imaging and management systems. However, most of these things are too expensive, too bulky, or too hard to install and use for nontechnical folks or small companies. That's a major reason the promise of a "paperless office" has been an empty one.

Now a little start-up company, Visioneer Communications of Palo Alto, California (800-787-7007), has cracked the problem. It has created a small, simple, inexpensive, and elegant scanning system called PaperMax that makes it child's play to load images of paper documents into your computer and organize and manage them. PaperMax is one of the most impressive office-technology products I've seen in years.

The Visioneer product, which lists for $499, consists of two parts. First is the hardware. It's a stationary device that packs most of the functionality of a big, heavy flatbed scanner into a stylish unit that's just three inches deep, less than four inches high, about a foot wide and weighs only two and a half pounds. The whole thing is so small that it can be tucked into the space between a keyboard and the computer or monitor, or transported easily for use with a portable computer. Documents are fed into a slot on the front of the PaperMax and returned through an opening at the top. It attaches to the computer by simply plugging into a serial port. There's no need to insert any circuit boards.

The second part of the system is a beautifully designed software program called MaxMate, which controls the scanner and allows users to organize, view, annotate, and transmit the images of documents scanned by PaperMax.

Operating the system couldn't be simpler. You don't even have to push a button, flip a switch, or manually start up the MaxMate program. At any time, no matter what program you're using, you can pop a piece of paper into the scanner. It automatically turns on, grabs the paper, and scans it very, very quickly. A window pops up on the screen to show the image as it's being received; then the MaxMate software launches itself so you can work with the new image.

In my tests, the scanner handled everything from business letters to glossy fliers to clippings ripped from this newspaper and a crinkled magazine page with a tear in the edge. It even straightens out the image if you put the paper in crooked.

The software is versatile. It presents icons for each scanned document and lets you zoom in on any one. You can annotate the documents with an electronic yellow highlighter or by placing electronic comments and notations on it.

You also can compile documents into "stacks" by dragging their icons into a pile on the screen. MaxMate combines the pages into a single file you can flip through page by page. You can search for documents by file name, by date, or by words in annotations you've made.

Even better, you can create stacks that combine scanned-in pages and electronic documents you create in word processors, spreadsheets, and other programs. You merely "print" from these other programs to the MaxMate software, and the electronic files appear in MaxMate.

The software also has plenty of options for reusing or transmitting scanned images. You can reprint the scanned images or fax them electronically if you have a fax modem and software. You can send them to other computers via electronic mail or floppy disk. Visioneer supplies free software that lets users of Macintoshes or IBM-compatibles without Windows view the scanned document images.

So what are the downsides of PaperMax? It's designed as a single-user business tool to handle a relatively low volume of documents that mainly consist of text and limited graphics. It accepts just one sheet at a time and isn't meant for high-volume scanning. While it can scan photographs, it isn't designed to do professional graphical rendering and manipulation. It also lacks any optical character recognition ability, so it can't translate scanned documents into editable text. The documents exist in your computer only as pictures of the paper originals, unless you buy translation software.

What's more, like many other add-on devices, it must compete for a limited number of serial ports on the IBM-compatible PC. So you may need to reconfigure a mouse or modem. And one feature—in which you can combine electronic documents with scanned images—doesn't work well on computers that use a few models of certain video cards, including those from Orchid and Diamond.

Finally, this breakthrough product is new on the market and may be hard to buy in stores unless you ask them to order it. If you want to get rid of piles of paper and store documents electronically, it's worth the trouble to track down a PaperMax.

2/10/94

The Visioneer scanner has been renamed PaperPort and now sells for $379.

32
Better to Let Those Business Cards Keep Collecting Dust

Admit it. Somewhere in your home or office—probably in the same drawer with the warranty from your answering machine—is a big, dusty wad of business cards you've collected at meetings, conferences, and elsewhere. You're pretty sure these contain a wealth of potentially valuable contacts, and so you know you should copy them into your address book, Rolodex, or computer contact-manager program, no matter how boring that task may be. But every time you think about doing it, something more important comes up—like, say, watching the Weather Channel. So the months roll on, and the wad of cards is approaching the thickness of the Pentagon budget.

Never fear. The computer industry is bringing technology to the rescue—or, is at least claiming to do so. Several small computer-gear companies have brought out friendly looking little machines called business-card scanners. You just feed those cards into these $300-plus gizmos, they say, and the information on them is magically extracted and entered into an electronic address book on your screen. You can then search the information, arrange and rearrange it, print it, or export it to another contact-management program.

It sounds great, doesn't it? With a business-card scanner, it seems, you can actually get organized without all that boring typing. Unfortunately, it isn't that simple. Remember, this is the computer industry we're talking about, where inflated promises are a specialty. I tested a couple of these scanners, using a random sampling from my own pile of business cards, and found that they often mangled names, titles, company names, and phone numbers. They made so many mistakes that I still wound up doing a lot of laborious corrective typing—so much, in fact, that it might have been quicker to type in the data from scratch.

The first scanner I tried was the CardGrabber from Pacific Crest Technologies, Newport Beach, California. This is a sleek little black box, about the size of a Walkman-type tape player, that plugs into the printer port on the back of any IBM-compatible computer running Microsoft Windows. The software that makes it work installed quickly and easily, and the actual scanning process is a no-brainer: just click an icon on the screen, slide a card into the right side of the CardGrabber, and it pops out on the left. If you put the card in upside down, CardGrabber can flip the image. The software grinds away briefly, then displays an address-book form filled in with data from the card, as well as a picture of the scanned card. It also puts up a separate window with the raw text extracted from the card, to help you correct any errors.

The trouble is, the CardGrabber made significant mistakes on about half the twenty or so cards I tested. It had lots of trouble with company logos and other frills. But it also got some pretty simple cards wrong. On the card of the company's own public relations counsel, it failed to pick up the street address and reversed the phone and fax numbers. On my own plain black-and-white card, it failed to read the name of my newspaper, which is printed in our unremarkable typeface, and mangled my phone numbers. Addresses in Washington, D.C., were invariably entered as being in Washington State. Company names on some other cards, including Compaq Computer, Ziff-Davis Publications, and Sega of America, were omitted.

The competing scanner I tested, another Windows-compatible product called CardScan from Corex Technologies of Brookline, Massachusetts, did a little better, but still turned in a badly flawed performance. It placed personal names where company names should go in a number of cases, or thought job titles were names. It also blew Compaq's name and either omitted or mistyped Microsoft, Apple, and the BBC. On the austere card of an esteemed colleague of mine, with the easy-to-spell moniker James M. Perry, CardScan goofed up his name, the company name, the street address, the state, and the phone number (and CardGrabber did almost as badly).

To be sure, some people might be willing to swallow these errors just to get the info on all those moldering cards into their computers, where it can finally be used. What seems like egregious mistakes to me might seem minor to you. Both CardGrabber and CardScan store a picture of the card with each address entry, so you can always refer to the source for accuracy. And hand-correcting the errors might still seem like less work than typing from scratch to some folks, though it didn't to me.

But each of the products has other limitations. CardGrabber expects you to correct each entry right away, after you scan each card. It isn't set up for "batch" scanning of multiple cards. While it doesn't require you to install any internal circuitry in the computer, you must disconnect any printer you have hooked up to connect CardGrabber. Corex's CardScan does allow batch processing of cards, but its scanner hardware is larger and requires that a circuit board be installed in the computer (though the CardScan software itself, available separately for $149, will work with some other brands of scanners).

There are additional brands of business card scanners I didn't get to test, but most use hardware identical to the Corex unit and thus may share some of its limitations, though different software may yield different results. In my view, the business-card scanner is yet another case of high-tech companies putting a technology on the market that's not ready for prime time. It has promise, but still needs more work in the lab.

5/12/94

33
Apple's Camera Is a Computer Gizmo a Boss Will Love

If you're in charge of the office newsletter, you know that in most cases, you can't run a picture of the company president too often. There's the shot of him in front of the new warehouse, or examining the first of the new models to roll off the production line. And let's not forget the classic scene in which Mr. Big, who is rolling in stock options after just five years in the job, tenderly presents some twenty-five-year veteran with a cheap gold watch. It's compelling corporate journalism.

But there's a little problem with all those photos. That newsletter is probably written and laid out on a personal computer, so to get those photos into the next issue takes time and money. You have to take the pictures, process the film, scan the print into the PC with an expensive scanner, then hope it made the transition from film to digital form in tolerable shape. And, if your leader doesn't like the pose, it's not easy to redo it.

Now, Apple Computer is offering a quicker, cheaper way to get photos into a computer—whether to boost executive egos or for any other purpose, including brochures, catalogs, and the like. The company has started selling a lightweight, automated $700 filmless color camera, designed in conjunction with Eastman Kodak, that stores high-resolution photos on a chip and transfers them directly into a computer through a cable.

The camera, called the QuickTake 100, is a sleek, dark-gray gizmo that weighs just one pound, is just a tad larger than a paperback book, and is rounded to nestle in the palm of your hand. Like most Apple add-on products these days, it is expected to work not only with the company's own Macintosh computers, but also with IBM-compatibles running Microsoft's Windows software. (However, it doesn't work with Apple's highly touted new Power Macintosh models.)

The QuickTake 100 isn't the first digital camera on the market. Kodak and others make superior professional models that cost thousands of dollars, or even tens of thousands. And Logitech and Dycam make compact, modestly priced models aimed at the same consumer and small-business market Apple is entering. But the Apple product is the first of a new generation offering superior features at a moderate price. It delivers color for only about $100 more than Logitech's monochrome model, costs much less than Dycam's color model, and has better resolution than either. A number of other companies are expected to follow Apple's lead this year.

Using the camera is a snap. You don't need to be hooked to a computer to take pictures. It runs on three AA batteries, which Apple says will last for about 120 shots. It turns on when you slide open the lens cover, and does focusing and exposure settings automatically. You just frame your shot in the viewfinder and push the shutter button on top. The built-in flash can be set to go off automatically.

The camera's memory can hold up to eight high-resolution color pictures, or up to thirty-two color images at a somewhat lower resolution, and you can mix the two types. A button on the back lets you switch resolutions, and a little screen next to the viewfinder tells you how many shots you've taken, how many the camera can still store, the status of the battery, and more. Images can be stored in the QuickTake's memory for up to a year, but once the internal chip is full, you have to transfer its contents into your computer before you can take more pictures.

To get the photos into your computer, you plug a small cable into the side of the camera and attach the other end to a common serial port on the Mac or PC. Then you launch the QuickTake Mac or Windows software. The program lets you examine the photos in the camera and copies them onto the computer's hard-disk drive. The software also lets you do simple editing of the pictures, including cropping them, and can convert them to a number of standard computer formats so they can be touched up or used in sophisticated graphics, page-layout or word-processing programs. You can also print the pictures on a laser or inkjet printer.

But the Apple QuickTake, like all other low-priced digital cameras I've seen, has definite limitations. Its output looks much better on a PC's screen than printed out on paper. In fact, unless you have a color printer, you obviously lose the benefit of color when making printouts. And even color printouts may be disappointing unless you own a very expensive professional color printer. The pictures work best in electronic documents, meant to be viewed on a screen.

The Apple camera produces pretty nice screen images. But what's "high-resolution" on a computer screen is still far less rich and sharp, to most eyes, than the simple color prints produced by old-fashioned chemically processed film. Black-and-white laser printouts of the pictures are fine for things like the company newsletter, though they may need massaging in high-end software programs like Adobe's Photoshop (which costs almost as much as the camera itself). Even then, the results fall well short of the best that conventional—but costlier—print processes yield.

Still, the Apple QuickTake provides a quick and dirty way to get still images into computer-produced documents. And when the CEO finds out how easily it can cram his or her kisser into the newsletter, you are bound to get approval for the purchase of one.

5/19/94

34
True Confessions: I Was Seduced by a Flashy New PC

This is the tale of how I ignored my own advice, bought a costly new computer packed with unseasoned cutting-edge technology, and lived to regret it—at least for a while. I tell my story to reinforce the point I've made before: unless you're an inveterate technology freak, or enjoy being a guinea pig, you should shy away from the early generations of a new chip or other major computer component because it always takes a while for the industry to work out glitches and incompatibilities in these things.

I also tell this little saga to prove that even if they let you write a technology column in a big newspaper, they can't save you from doing some stupid things with technology. I wanted something fast and cool, and I couldn't wait.

My personal technoblunder, a Dell Dimension XPS P90, costing more than $4,000, gave me nothing but headaches for the first couple of months I owned it. There were failures in the machine's communications, video, audio, CD-ROM, and tape backup systems. Dell clearly screwed up in shipping this popular machine without catching and fixing these fundamental flaws.

I can report, however, that Dell's people were prompt and courteous in helping me correct the problems I encountered. Today, the errant computer, on which I'm writing this column, is humming along smoothly. And to its credit, the company takes full responsibility for the problems in the model I bought, even though some of the glitches involved components Dell got from others.

"There's clearly no excuse for bugs of this magnitude having gotten through our validation process," says Doug MacGregor, a Dell vice president. As a result, he says, Dell is beefing up this process, in which it checks out all supplied components to make sure they work individually and mesh properly together.

That's an admirable attitude, but it would have been slim consolation this summer. It was then that I lost my mind and decided to replace my home IBM-compatible, which was powered by an Intel 486 chip, with a machine built around fairly new components, namely Intel's speed-demon 90-megahertz Pentium chip and some surrounding circuitry called PCI, which also adds to speed.

I settled on Dell's Dimension XPS P90, which also meant I was buying into a new kind of faster hard-disk drive, a relatively recent video system, and a new mini-tower case Dell hadn't used before. This was a recipe for trouble, and it was coming out of my pocket, not the coffers of my employer.

I ordered the machine over the phone, through Dell via normal channels. The first problem cropped up when I tried to play a music CD in the CD-ROM drive and no sound came out. I called Dell's toll-free support number and was asked if I'd mind opening up the machine. I said no, and we discovered that they'd failed to plug in one end of a wire at the factory. I plugged it in.

Next, I discovered that, after making a single call through the modem, the machine's communications system locked up and couldn't make any more calls. This was a flaw somewhere on the "motherboard," the large circuit board that is the heart of every PC, which Intel made for Dell. Dell had posted a special software program on the CompuServe on-line service to fix this problem temporarily, and I downloaded it, resolving that problem. Eventually, I demanded and received a new motherboard.

Then, it turned out that the tape backup drive didn't work properly. Again, Dell put up a software fix on CompuServe, and I downloaded it, used it, and it worked.

But the problems kept mounting. The machine's video system,

supplied by a little company called Number Nine, was flawed. The system was incompatible with the popular programs from a well-known company called Knowledge Adventure and at least one multimedia title from Microsoft. Dell seemed helpless to fix this, so I called Number Nine, which apologized, promised reforms, and eventually sent me a slightly slower version of the video system. That fixed the problems, after I installed it myself. (Number Nine says it has since fixed the problems with the original card.)

Finally, the CD-ROM drive on my hot new Dell broke. It refused to play or even recognize a handful of the disks I tried to run on it. I insisted on a new one, and Dell sent someone to replace it.

So it all worked out, but it took me many weeks, many phone calls, and some repair work of my own to get it right—even though, because of my job, Dell was especially anxious to help heal my computer.

What if I hadn't been a technology writer, hadn't known about CompuServe, and hadn't been willing to fiddle with the machine's innards? I'm sure Dell would still have been helpful; the company has a good reputation for customer service, it did supply fixes for many other owners, and it is planning to send all owners of this model a disk with new fix-it software. But I doubt it would have been quite as responsive or that the problems would have been dispatched quite as smoothly. Mr. MacGregor concedes that, in my case, "there was, to some degree, a sensitivity on our part, that I hope would be given to every customer." But he adds, "It's hard to tell."

Meanwhile, you all owe me one. I feel that I, as a brave technology pioneer, have done a public service for the rest of you, wringing the bugs out of this new technology so you don't have to. If you're feeling really grateful for this and can stop laughing, please send money.

11/3/94

Part III
Productivity Software

The key to computing is software, and this part of the book covers most of it—the business and home programs that get serious work done. The best word processors, spreadsheets, calendar programs, graphics, tax, and personal finance programs are fingered here—along with the odd software that lets you build a deck, type in Finnish, or pick out a new car. There are also explanations of DOS, Windows, and the Macintosh operating system.

35
The Aging Mac Interface Could Learn a Few Tricks from Windows

Apple Computer's strongest asset, the fabled friendly user interface of the Macintosh computer, is getting long in the tooth and needs improving.

What's more, Apple's greatest imitator and nemesis, Microsoft's Mac-like Windows software system for IBM-compatible computers, is superior in certain ways to the decade-old Macintosh interface—the basic screen display a computer presents to the user and through which the computer is controlled.

Let me hasten to add (to cut down just a bit on irate letters from Mac fanatics) that overall, the Mac interface still has the edge. It lets users name files with real English words, provides automatic linkage of documents and the programs that created them, unifies the managing of files and the launching of programs, and does other things Windows can't do. And, when the Mac software is combined with its elegantly designed hardware, the result is a computer that is easier to set up, network, and expand than any machine I've seen that runs Windows. That's why I use a Mac daily, in addition to an IBM-compatible.

But that edge has eroded with each new version of Windows and could disappear entirely if Microsoft pulls off its ambitious plan to revamp the Windows interface and PC hardware, while Apple continues to neglect its crown jewel. Already, in a number of small ways—simple things that affect the user's daily relationship with the computer—Windows is better. Here are some things Apple could learn from Microsoft:

Using menus: On a Mac, when you click with the mouse on the title of a menu, the commands listed there remain visible only while you continue holding down the mouse button. You have to act quickly, and with some dexterity, to scroll down the list and select an item. In Windows, the menus stay down until you dismiss them, allowing ample time to scroll through choices.

Keyboard equivalents: The Mac lacks a way to cause menus to drop down by typing commands from the keyboard. In Windows, every menu title has an underlined letter that, when pressed in conjunction with the Alt key, gives you access to the menu without removing your hands from the keyboard. This is a boon for touch typists and people using portable computers in tight spaces.

Managing screen clutter: On a Mac, the screen can quickly become littered with multiple open windows if you have several programs running simultaneously. You can hide the ones that you aren't using, but that makes it hard to tell what's going on and to click on one of them to bring it to the front. Microsoft lets you clean up the screen by "minimizing" running programs so they appear only as little icons, or graphic symbols.

Built-in applications: Apple pioneered the idea of supplying small programs, like a calculator or small scratch pad, that can pop up on top of the work you're doing. But Windows comes with a much better suite of these "applets," including rudimentary versions of an appointment calendar, an address book, a communications program, a word processor, a painting program, and a solitaire game.

Personalizing the computer: The Mac lets you make limited changes in such elements as the color and pattern of the screen background, or the sound the computer makes when it beeps at you. But in Windows there is a much richer array of colorful customization options, including built-in screen savers, to let users put their own stamp on their electronic desktops.

On-line help: The only standard help system on the Mac is an annoying feature that plants cartoon-like balloons all over the screen to tell you what various things do. Each program you buy has its own inconsistent help system. Windows comes with a consistent, robust help system that most programs share.

The mouse: On a standard Mac, the mouse has only one button, and you can modify only a couple of aspects of its performance—speed and sensitivity. Microsoft lets Windows users customize such things as the size and color of the cursor, and the second button is used in many Windows programs as a shortcut device—to summon a special menu of options, for instance.

Printer selection: On a Mac, you have to open a separate little program called the "chooser" to switch the software settings from one printer to another. In Windows, you can get to that function from the standard print command in many programs.

Task switching: On a Mac, you must use the mouse to switch among several running programs. In Windows, you can do this faster by just hitting the Alt and Tab keys together, or you can pop up a menu of the programs by pressing the Control and Escape keys.

Most of these Windows features can be added to a Macintosh by obtaining extra software. And some are deemed by Mac purists as unacceptable deviations from the user interface conventions espoused by Apple since 1984, guidelines that have taken on the rigid religious authority of Talmudic rulings in some quarters. But Apple engineers have begun to rethink the Mac's user interface. If that effort is to succeed, they can't indulge in the kind of not-invented-here mentality that is the luxury of theologians, not business people.

8/26/93

Apple's market share is still small, and the Mac operating system has changed only slightly. It still needs an overhaul.

36
Growing Panes: The House of Microsoft Has Many Windows

Like a fierce dinosaur, Microsoft's Windows software dominates its realm. It has sold twenty-five million copies in the past three years. And sales of programs that run in conjunction with Windows—relying on graphical icons, pull-down menus and a mouse to make IBM-compatible PCs much easier to use—have surpassed those of programs able to run only with the creaky MS-DOS operating system.

But now a confusing variety of Windows offspring are in the works, or already emerging from Microsoft's labs. Like the genetically engineered dinosaurs in the movie *Jurassic Park*, it's hard to keep track of them once they're loose. So here's a brief field guide to the various species of Windows.

Windows 3.1 is the current mainstream version, designed to run on standard desktop and portable PCs. It accounts for the vast majority of Windows sales, and comes installed on most new PCs. It's an organizing environment from which you can run other software, like word processors. But it isn't a true operating system, the underlying software on every computer that directly controls the basic functions of PC hardware. It can't work without DOS.

Windows 95 is the next mainstream version of Windows, due in August 1995. It incorporates the networking features of Windows for Workgroups and is a true operating system that won't require the separate MS-DOS program. Some Microsoft insiders see Windows 95 as the ultimate "Macintosh killer," because it boasts features that match or exceed the remaining advantages Apple's software has over older versions of Windows. These include a combined file-management and program-launching system and the ability to label files with long, real English names.

Windows for Workgroups is a modified version of Windows 3.1, with functions built in for limited networking of computers among a small group of coworkers. It enables a couple of dozen computers to share files, exchange electronic mail, keep a joint on-line calendar of meetings, and more. It needs DOS to run.

Windows for Pen Computing is shipped installed on a few portable computers that work with a special electronic pen writing directly on the screen. This version of Windows permits users to enter text with a pen. Like all other pen programs I've seen, this one features decidedly imperfect handwriting recognition.

Windows NT has been much talked about lately, but it isn't meant to be used by most computer owners. This program is aimed instead at "servers"—the master computers that control "client/server" networks. A second category of users is expected to be engineers and others who need colossal amounts of computing power at their desks. Anyone planning to run Windows NT at peak form should figure on getting a monster PC with the latest processor, a staggering 16 megabytes of memory and 200 megabytes or more of hard-disk space. On the screen, it looks identical to Windows 3.1, but it is a true operating system, interacting directly with the PC hardware and eliminating the need for DOS.

"Cairo" is planned as the heavy-duty successor to Windows NT. Expected to be ready in 1996, it is rumored to incorporate a radically new file system that will let users conduct sophisticated searches for precise information among many thousands of files.

Modular Windows is the general name for a family of stripped-down versions of Windows that are intended to be built into a wide variety of devices other than standard PCs, including entertainment systems and office machines. The Modular Windows interface is graphical, and it shares underlying computer code with mainstream Windows. But in many cases, what people see on the screens of these devices won't look much like the Windows screens on a PC. Instead of using menus and icons, people will control many of these machines by touching graphical "buttons" on a small screen.

One species of modular Windows is aimed at home-entertainment devices and other new machines that will work through or control television sets. So far, it's only available in Tandy's VIS machine, a disappointing product that plays software on compact disks through a TV.

Another modular Windows variant is being incorporated into Microsoft at Work, a product line intended to provide a standard user interface, and standard communications links, for a new generation of fax machines, copiers, and phones that some big companies are expected to introduce soon.

Microsoft hasn't yet announced any versions of Windows for controlling dishwashers or lawn mowers, but at the rate they're going, I wouldn't rule it out. For Microsoft sees Windows as the Tyrannosaurus rex of both office and home.

7/1/93

37
It's Suddenly Possible to Literally Keep Tabs on What's in Windows

If you work with a computer, one of the most important factors in your overall satisfaction with the machine can be the "user interface," the main screen you use to call up different programs and open frequently used documents.

This isn't critical if your company or organization expects you to use only one program all the time. Then your computer really is devoted to just that one function and your interface is whatever screen design that sole application features.

But if you're using Microsoft's Windows software on an IBM-compatible, you're looking at an interface featuring symbols representing many programs and commonly used documents, and it's important how they're arranged on the screen. The interface Microsoft provides with Windows, a feature called "Program Manager," is hard to customize so the contents of your computer are arranged and organized in your personal style.

As a result, there has been an explosion of software intended to replace Program Manager, software such as Symantec's admirable Norton Desktop for Windows. Microsoft itself is planning a drastic overhaul of Program Manager in the next version of Windows.

Now there's a Windows interface I think is a truly inspired design, one that lets nontechnical computer-users easily organize all the programs and documents on their PCs in a fashion that matches the way they actually work, not the way the computer works. The program is called TabWorks and it's on every new Compaq Computer model. Compaq also sells it separately at $49 for use on any brand of computer you own capable of running Windows (I've used it on two other brands with no problem). It was developed for Compaq by XSoft, a division of Xerox—the company that invented many of the elements of today's standard computer interface, such as the little pictures called icons that you click on with a mouse to launch programs.

TabWorks transforms the main screen of Windows into the familiar image of an open notebook divided into sections with a labeled tab protruding at the right-hand side of each section. It looks like a loose-leaf school notebook, or one of those day planners that people carry around, right down to a drawing of metal "rings" to hold the virtual pages near the left edge of the screen.

This tabbed-notebook design is so much like real life that it's showing up in more and more software programs. All the major Windows spreadsheet programs use it, as do parts of IBM's OS/2 operating-system software. But TabWorks is the only software I've seen that organizes your whole computer using the notebook metaphor.

The key to the program is that you can make up your own sections of this TabWorks notebook, label each with a tab of any color and name you select, and then fill the blank pages of that tabbed section with icons representing whatever programs or documents you pick. To view a section of the notebook, you just click on its protruding tab. To begin working with a program or document stored on a notebook page, you just click twice on its icon. There are no commands to remember, no multiple windows or directories to dig through. And you can reorganize the notebook as often as you like, or even maintain several notebooks.

For instance, you might have tabs for each month, or each employee, or each project, if that's a logical way to organize your work. Within each tab you could have icons representing the same few programs you use each month, plus one representing a particular spreadsheet or database document applicable to that month or project only (you can place the same program or document icon all through the TabWorks notebook without actually having multiple copies of the program or document on your hard disk).

Or, your notebook might divide the contents of your computer functionally. I have a tab called "Column" that includes icons of the programs and documents I use to write these articles. I have another called "Communications" with icons that launch programs that check my electronic mail or connect to my newspaper's computer.

As you add tabs (each of which can have multiple easily "turned" pages), TabWorks automatically creates a table of contents and an index, with their own tabs. These can either locate individual items in your notebook or launch them directly. For items you want on the screen permanently, regardless of which notebook page is open, there's a "button strip" at the far left of the screen. It always remains the same, and its items can be launched with one mouse click instead of the usual two.

Adding items to a notebook is simple. TabWorks begins by converting the groups of icons already set up in Program Manager. After that, you can just select new items from a list of what's on your hard disk, or even "drag" icons of items on your hard disk from file lists generated by the Windows File Manager program directly onto TabWorks pages.

There are a few things missing in TabWorks. I'd like in particular to see icons representing your disk drives, so you could quickly get lists of their contents without running the cumbersome File Manager program. And I'd like to see an icon for your printer that would print any document whose icon you dragged onto it with a mouse. Norton Desktop has both, but it lacks TabWorks' organizational clarity.

Still, TabWorks is the easiest, clearest, most logical interface I've seen for Windows. If Windows confuses you, try it.

11/11/93

TabWorks is now available for non-Compaq computers, from XSoft.

38 Microsoft Expands on the Utility of a Workhorse

In April 1993, the world's biggest software company, Microsoft, started selling a new version of the world's most widespread software program, the MS-DOS operating system. The software industry's marketing machine, as usual, kicked into high gear for the event. To cite one example, the Egghead software chain held special late-night hours to introduce MS-DOS 6.0, the new version. At the Egghead store in my residential neighborhood, the place was quickly jammed with customers forming long lines to buy the $50 program.

But the advent of MS-DOS 6.0 wasn't an epochal event. In fact, the revision didn't contain any fundamental changes to the ancient, complicated operating system, the software that controls the basic functions of the tens of millions of IBM-compatible computers. The new version perpetuated the bewildering DOS interface that has frustrated countless users with its cryptic "C:" prompt and finicky, literal commands like "format a: /n:9 /t:40" (which formats a standard floppy disk).

Indeed, if your PC is working fine now with an older version of MS-DOS, you don't need to buy version 6.0. I know of no current or planned computer programs that require the new version to run, including Microsoft's own graphical Windows software.

So how did Microsoft's marketers entice my neighbors to line up at night for MS-DOS 6.0? By including with MS-DOS a bunch of basic utility programs, many licensed from leading utility software companies, including Symantec and Central Point. Among these are programs that create backup versions of your files, root out computer viruses and optimize memory use. Most important, one of the utilities compresses the files on a disk and thus radically expands the disk's storage capacity.

In effect, Microsoft grafted onto MS-DOS a low-cost multiple utility package and lent its imprimatur to each of the utilities included, thus giving users the confidence that they are safe and compatible. Viewed in that light, MS-DOS 6.0 is a good value and a smart buy for people who aren't already regular users of these key utilities. Unlike the basic features of DOS, these utilities don't automatically run when you install the new DOS on your computer; you must choose to use them initially. None of the utilities are new, and in most cases the Microsoft versions lack some bells and whistles of the stand-alone products. But those products cost much more, and the Microsoft versions include all their basic features.

The two most interesting utilities in MS-DOS, to me, are DoubleSpace, the data-compression program, and MemMaker, the memory optimizer.

DoubleSpace attacks one of computer users' most common problems: too little hard-disk capacity. Standard Windows-compatible word-processing and spreadsheet programs now typically take up 15 megabytes or more, as can Windows itself. The result is that even a 100-megabyte hard disk, once considered quite large, may fill up quickly.

To solve the problem, DoubleSpace squeezes all your data into a "virtual" compressed hard drive that's really one huge special file. This file looks to DOS 6.0 like a regular hard disk, only bigger, usually nearly twice as large (thus the program's name), because the files inside it have been individually shrunk. No content is lost in the process. I've been using DoubleSpace for about a month on both my office and home PCs without any problems. On my office computer, it increased my hard-drive capacity from around 124 megabytes to 230 megabytes or so.

Similar products have been on the market for years, notably Stacker, from Stac Electronics. These products have some features DoubleSpace lacks, including the ability to easily undo the compression. But Microsoft claims DoubleSpace is superior because it is tightly integrated with DOS and starts working almost the instant you turn on the computer. All the normal DOS commands treat the compressed drive like a real one.

If you choose to use DoubleSpace, I recommend backing up your hard disk first, and making several floppy disks with DOS 6.0 that are capable of booting up your computer, in case your hard disk ever crashes. Boot-up disks created by older versions of DOS won't recognize the compressed hard drive or allow you to work with the files inside it.

The MemMaker program examines two special files DOS uses to configure your system, which go by the typically convoluted names of autoexec.bat and config.sys. It then rewrites them so that your computer has more memory free to run programs. In my case, it added nearly 100 kilobytes of free memory, which is a lot.

The new version also includes a few other nice touches. There's a special feature that lets you transfer files between two computers over a cable, and a program that preserves battery life on laptops.

MS-DOS is a fading product, but for now it's a necessary evil. The utilities included with MS-DOS 6.0 make it a little more efficient and easier to use.

4/1/93

Microsoft has revised the compression system in DOS and made some minor changes. The latest version is 6.22.

39
Word Isn't Perfect, but the New WordPerfect Is Too Much for Words

For all the exotic ways people are urged to use their computers, the most popular activity remains word processing—or, as it's known in English, writing. Word-processing programs are still the only really ubiquitous type of software.

Recently, the two dominant publishers of word-processing software, WordPerfect and Microsoft, released new versions of their flagship writing programs for people who operate their IBM-compatible computers using Microsoft's Windows graphical user interface. How on earth, you may ask, could these guys improve or enhance something as well-developed and basic as word processing? The two companies chose radically different approaches, and to my mind, Microsoft's design is a much better bet for mainstream users with typical computer configurations whose focus is on writing and formatting documents.

Microsoft concentrated the improvements in the new Word for Windows 6.0 on ways to speed or assist the actual process of writing, by making the software itself "smart" enough to anticipate and automate formerly manual steps. For instance, Word 6.0 can automatically correct words you commonly misspell as you type them, if you choose, without forcing you to run a spellcheck. And it can automatically analyze your document and format it appropriately, with fonts and spacing and text styles that make it look good. So, users of the new Word can spend less time poring through manuals trying to "learn" the software and more time just writing.

By contrast, WordPerfect, the granddaddy of the category, did far less innovative work on the writing process itself; instead, it fell back on the old temptation to load up its new WordPerfect for Windows 6.0 with a host of features that are only tenuously related to the process of writing. The new version has a complete spreadsheet and a full-blown art program inside, rather than Word's more modest features for making tables and simple drawings. It also includes a program that can index all the words in all the documents on your hard disk and then search for them by word. It's a bit of a throwback to the earlier days of computing, before Windows, when people rarely used multiple programs and instead "lived" in a single product that claimed to do it all.

Each of these new WordPerfect modules is well done, but they and other added features have swollen the program so much that it can't run acceptably on the most common computer configuration advertised today, one with a 486 processor and four megabytes of memory (or "4MB RAM" in technotalk). WordPerfect press releases recommend six megabytes for the program to run smoothly, but the manual calls for eight megabytes. Either way, the package requires owners of many typical new machines to buy extra memory. What's more, it requires at least 10 megabytes of space on your hard disk for a bare minimum of features, and a whopping 31 megabytes to install the whole thing.

Microsoft's Word for Windows isn't slender either, but it's svelte by comparison. It runs acceptably in the standard four megabytes of memory on a 486 machine (though a bit slow on a 386) needing extra memory only if you run other major programs simultaneously. A bare-bones version takes up just six megabytes of hard-disk space; even if you install every feature, it uses 24 megabytes—lots less than WordPerfect.

This isn't to say there's nothing to like about the new WordPerfect. It's a true Windows program, with extensive editing and formatting features. Former users of the DOS (non-Windows) versions of WordPerfect can operate the new version using the old commands, and there are instructional sequences called "Coaches" to graphically teach new ones. Nearly everything in the program is customizable, and WordPerfect includes seventy templates that help users write everything from fax cover sheets to reports to job applications. WordPerfect also has a fabulous system for opening and managing files. You can quickly jump to commonly used directories and can copy, rename, and delete files without launching a separate program.

But Microsoft Word is "smarter" software for writers. In addition to automated formatting and spelling correction, Word automatically lists your most commonly used fonts at the top of the font menu, and lets you open two documents in adjoining windows and just "drag" a block of text from one to the other, using the mouse. You can undo your past hundred actions, and then redo them, if you choose.

Word doesn't have as many templates as WordPerfect, but it includes nine step-by-step "Wizards," to create everything from newsletters to resumes, that actually do the task for you rather than training you to do it. And Microsoft plans an identical version for Macintosh users—a boon to offices that mix both flavors of computer.

There are a few dumb features in Word. One I especially hate is a "tip of the day" that appears each time you start the program to give you a new hint on how to use it. Fortunately, it can be disabled.

Overall, though, Word for Windows 6.0 is the best word-processing software I've seen for Windows, because it concentrates on the writing itself and has taken the first steps toward making word-processing software intelligent. Microsoft is promising more such smart features across its product line. If the company delivers, its customers can spend less time adapting to the software and more time doing their work.

12/2/93

WordPerfect has revised its product to run more quickly in less memory, build in a number of features similar to Word's, and add one or two of its own. But I think Word still has the edge.

40
The Excel Spreadsheet Is New and Improved, but Hardly Perfect

One of the seminal events in the history of the personal computer was the invention of the electronic spreadsheet, a type of software program that permits people to link numbers and formulas to each other and then almost instantly calculate how a change in any one figure affects all the others. It was only after the first popular spreadsheet program, Visicalc, appeared on the old Apple II machine that PCs began to penetrate businesses in significant numbers. And it was the next great spreadsheet program, Lotus Development's 1-2-3, that helped propel the first IBM personal computer to success.

Ironically, however, the spreadsheet is one of the least understood—and therefore one of the most underutilized—types of software. Microsoft studies show the vast majority of spreadsheet users do little more than make lists of data and perform only simple calculations on those lists, such as adding them up.

So, in recent years, the top spreadsheet publishers have launched serious efforts to make them easier to use. Microsoft's Excel spreadsheet for Windows and its chief rivals, Lotus Development's 1-2-3 for Windows and Borland International's Quattro Pro for Windows, each have added shortcuts and automation features that the others have quickly copied.

Now it's Microsoft's turn again. It has released the latest edition of Excel, version 5.0, and it is a mix of catch-up features designed to match innovations from its rivals, plus some original ease-of-use improvements they undoubtedly will adopt soon. In particular, the software giant has tried to build into Excel some of the "IntelliSense" technology introduced earlier this year in Microsoft Word, which causes the software to make intelligent guesses about what users want to do. In addition, Excel has been redesigned so that its menus and commands are almost identical to those in Word.

The result is a very good spreadsheet that inches ahead of its rivals. But it isn't a dazzling new benchmark in the field. Most people can't go wrong buying Excel 5.0, but I was disappointed that the company didn't do even more to make things easier.

Excel 5.0 places notebook-style tabs at the bottom of each spreadsheet, a feature created by Borland to identify spreadsheets better and navigate among them. From Lotus 1-2-3, Microsoft has borrowed "in-cell editing," which allows users to enter and edit data right in its location on a spreadsheet, rather than using a separate area at the top of the screen, as has been traditional. Another catch-up feature is the "pivot table," introduced in Lotus's Improv program, which permits users to view data quickly from different perspectives. For instance, you can view sales by product line for each quarter, or by quarter for each product line, with a couple of mouse clicks.

New features in Excel 5.0 include a "tip wizard," which watches how you work and suggests quicker alternatives. It's a potentially good tool that supposedly learns your habits over time and adjusts to them. However, when you start using the program, it tends to offer gratuitous advice a lot.

There's also a "function wizard" that walks you step by step through the process of entering formulas that use financial, statistical and other functions. It even remembers the ones you use most often. Another nice addition is called drag and plot. It allows you to highlight a range of numerical data, then drag those figures on top of a chart, using the mouse. When you release the mouse button, Excel redraws the chart to include the new figures.

But Excel's designers have placed most of their emphasis on managing lists of data, the task Microsoft says spreadsheet users perform most often. There are three new automation features in Excel 5.0 to make handling lists of data much simpler than in prior spreadsheets. First is an "auto filter" that automatically figures out row and column headings in a data table and lets you view categories of information with a few mouse clicks. An automated subtotals feature makes it much easier to get totals on subcategories of data, such as payroll for specific departments. And automated sorting makes it a breeze to arrange data in a wide variety of ways.

Still, I wish Microsoft had included in Excel many more "wizards," automated routines for creating specific kinds of documents. These might have included profit-and-loss statements or payroll or sales reports. Several other Microsoft programs include such document-creation wizards, but not Excel. In addition, I wonder why the company, which introduced the "auto-sum" button for instantly toting up a column of figures, hasn't followed up with one-step methods for performing other common calculations, such as an "auto-average" or "auto-count" button.

My only other caution about Excel is that it is a very large program. It runs barely acceptably on computers with the most common memory configuration, four megabytes. But if you use very complex calculations, very large spreadsheets or lots of charts, the program becomes too slow for comfort on such machines. Heavy-duty users shouldn't buy Excel 5.0 unless they have at least six megabytes of memory, which adds to the cost of hardware. Also, a typical installation takes around 15 megabytes of hard-disk space, and, if you install every feature, it can top 20 megabytes, so you'll need a hefty hard disk.

Excel 5.0 is a very nice spreadsheet. But I think Microsoft could have done better.

2/3/94

41
The Right Software Lets PC Owners Become Fine Printers

One of the clearest benefits of the computerization of America has been the advent of "desktop publishing": the ability to turn out professional-looking publications using off-the-shelf personal computers, software, and printers instead of costly composing and printing services.

First popularized by Apple Computer for its Macintosh computer line, and now catching on with IBM-compatible computer users, desktop publishing has permeated business, education, and other fields. Many newsletters, business forms, and brochures are now produced this way.

But for many average users, top-flight desktop publishing programs like Quark's $499 XPress and Aldus's $479 PageMaker are overkill—packed with professional features that go beyond their needs and make the programs too complex to learn quickly. Regular word-processing software, on the other hand, often isn't up to even simple page-layout projects.

For these people, who represent the vast majority of potential desktop publishers, software giant Microsoft has hit a home run with a program for IBM-compatible PCs called Microsoft Publisher, which sells for around $129 by mail order.

I was skeptical that Microsoft could make a really useful program that didn't require much of a learning curve. The company is justly known for quality products, including its Word and Excel software, but both require plenty of time to master. And Microsoft's famous MS-DOS program, the basic underlying operating software for all IBM-compatible PCs, is so fiendishly arcane that I believe it has single-handedly discouraged millions of people from becoming comfortable with computers.

But Publisher strikes a masterful balance between powerful features and ease of use. It turns out a wide variety of polished documents that any individual or business would be proud to use. Yet it is inviting, even fun, to use—a model of good software design.

Publisher runs only in conjunction with Microsoft's Windows software, and it makes full use of Windows' trademark features: menus with plain-English commands, graphical "buttons" and icons on the screen that perform various tasks when you simply click on them with a mouse.

The most innovative feature of Publisher is something Microsoft calls Page Wizards. These automated routines create newsletters, invoices, calendars, greeting cards, brochures, expense reports—even paper airplanes. The Wizards first interview you on screen about your basic preferences for the publication in question (How many columns in a newsletter? What information do you want on an invoice?) and then whip it up. Once the Wizards have done their thing, you can customize the results.

With Wizards, even a new Publisher user can create a finished product in a short time. One executive I know never opened the program's manual, but needed less than an hour to turn out a handsome three-page brochure for a local school, complete with graphics.

But Publisher's strengths don't stop there. The program also includes a feature called Word Art, which can take any line of text and print it slanted, curved, vertically, or upside down. It can accept word-processing and graphics files created in a wide variety of other programs, and includes an extensive set of canned artwork that you can drop into documents. Basic commands are all available by selecting little icons at the top of the screen.

Even without using a Page Wizard, I turned out a rough facsimile of my weekly column—complete with shaded logo, illustration, large capital letters, even the little diamonds at the tips of the center rule—in under thirty minutes.

So what's wrong with Publisher? It lacks one key feature: the ability to simultaneously change the style of similar kinds of text (say, all the headlines) in a document. This feature, often called "style sheets" in other programs, can be complicated to use, but it saves lots of time.

More important, though it's made for regular folks rather than pros, you need a fairly hefty computer to run Publisher, because it operates only with Windows. Despite what Microsoft says, Windows runs poorly unless you have a PC powered by at least a 386SX processor chip and two megabytes of memory. You also should have a laser printer. Publisher will work with a dot matrix printer, but the results will be disappointing.

For people with older or less powerful rigs, I recommend GeoWorks Pro, from GeoWorks of Berkeley, California. A rival of Windows, GeoWorks runs well on older machines and includes decent desktop publishing capabilities, along with much more, for about $125. Mac owners seeking an easy desktop publishing program might try Publish It! Easy by Timeworks of Northbrook, Illinois. (But I can't recommend the IBM-compatible version of the same program, which I found clumsy to use.)

If you have the right hardware, however, Microsoft Publisher is one of those software products that can help you get much more from your computer.

2/20/92

The Wizard feature of Publisher proved so popular that it has now spread to many other Microsoft products, and (under different names) to those of some other companies.

42
PC Program Lets Machines Help Bosses Manage People

Good managers spend a lot of their time developing and evaluating their employees, but there isn't much commercial computer software to help them do so. Plenty of programs for managing projects involve tracking certain activities of particular employees for limited periods. But many managers need a program centered on people, not projects, that would help them oversee employees' development, spot problems early, prepare for performance reviews, and schedule raises and other rewards.

Avantos Performance Systems of Emeryville, California, has come up with such a product, an unusual and impressive $245 program called ManagePro that runs on IBM-compatible personal computers in conjunction with Microsoft's Windows software. ManagePro is so useful that, by itself, it may provide the justification some managers have needed to start using Windows on their PCs. Owners of Apple's Macintosh machines will soon get their own version of ManagePro.

Dreamed up by a couple of former management consultants, ManagePro is designed to let managers track their employees' progress against goals, both companywide and individual, set by the bosses.

The program has two linked main modules, for goal planning and people planning. In the goal-planning module, a user establishes objectives for the company or department, and then assigns supporting goals to particular employees or groups.

For instance, a staff member may be handed a task like processing customer complaints faster in a certain office, which may be part of an overall company goal to raise customer satisfaction to 90 percent by a given date. Or she may be assigned a personal goal, such as learning a new computer system.

In the people-planning and development side of ManagePro, users view the business from a personal angle, looking at employees and teams to see how they are doing against these goals. Here the program prompts managers periodically to offer feedback and coaching to each employee, and to reward success or flag failure. Supervisors can establish a schedule for interim and formal performance reviews, which ManagePro will remind them to conduct. The program makes the reviews easier by documenting previous feedback and progress against goals.

ManagePro also offers a built-in "adviser," a collection of people-management tips and strategies written by personnel consultants, which bosses can tap for help in particular situations. The "adviser" suggests providing plenty of recognition for employee successes; for between pay raises, it proposes rewards like sports tickets or dinner for two. The program also comes with a book on managing people.

The software's design is elegant. It has no complicated commands to memorize. Instead, every screen and function is available by clicking with a mouse on bright, clear icons or by selecting plain-English commands from menus. The various screens for viewing data are color-coded and otherwise marked so you always know where you are in the program. The software comes with a clear manual, and a thirty-minute on-screen tutorial gets users up and running.

The goals module of the program lets you define and review goals in three ways: by an outline of the hierarchy of goals; by a timeline that shows the schedules of goals; and by a "status board." This last resembles an organizational chart, with boxes and lines, but it automatically colors each goal green for "on track," yellow for "behind," or red for "critical."

The people-tracking portion of the program has an outline view and a status board, with similar color-coding. But this module is even richer, permitting entry and checking of employees' progress, feedback, pending reviews, recognition, and more.

The linkages among the various screens and modules are particularly impressive. If you establish a new goal in the goals module, it shows up automatically in the people module as being associated with the staffer to whom it was assigned. And you can "drill down" from any screen to see underlying details of goals and employees' records.

The program contains a calendar and an "action list" for scheduling things. It also can print out beautiful reports on all aspects of your staff and goals.

ManagePro can be easily configured to suit the needs and tastes of its users. You can set it to display only the goals or just the people module, or to operate in a simplified fashion within each module, offering fewer screens and features. You can change the terminology for measuring employees' progress, customize various forms for entering data, and more.

The program has only one serious drawback: it's slow. Even on a PC with a speedy 486 chip, I found ManagePro sluggish in bringing up new screens and windows. The problem isn't fatal, but Avantos acknowledges it needs fixing, and says it aims to speed things up in version 2.0.

There are a couple of lesser problems. ManagePro lacks a function for entering an employee work schedule; the company says it is considering adding one. Finally, the program may be hard to find. It is sold by a few mail-order houses, but isn't on many store shelves yet.

It's worth investing some time to locate a copy of ManagePro, because it does what good software should do: it helps people use their computers to do their jobs better without forcing them to become computer experts.

12/24/92

43 Organizer Program Takes a Leaf from Date Books

One hot type of computer software is the "personal information manager," or PIM. These programs keep track of appointments, addresses, phone numbers and more. They are a digital alternative to paper date books, address books, and the venerable Rolodex. And they compete with pocket-size electronic organizers, such as Sharp's Wizard series.

There are two problems with evaluating PIMs. First, software companies use the term loosely. It can cover a simple calendar with limited ability to handle appointments, intended to be called up only once in a while. Or it can refer to a vast, multifunction software octopus that includes such features as serious word processing and data communications and is meant to be on your screen nearly all the time.

The other difficulty is that purchase decisions in this category of software, more than most others, depend heavily on personal work styles and habits. So, while millions of different people can happily use the same spreadsheet with minor modifications, no single PIM works for everyone.

Still, I think one new personal information manager deserves special attention because it is carefully designed to balance a good selection of features, ease of use, and the flexibility to customize the way it works to suit individual tastes. It is a good solution for the large group of computer users who need more than a rudimentary on-screen date book but less than a complex, heavy-duty package.

That program is Lotus Organizer, from Lotus Development, the software company most famous for the 1-2-3 spreadsheet. Organizer, which sells for $99 at discount, is available for IBM-compatible PCs using Microsoft Windows; a version for Apple's Macintosh computers is in the works.

Anyone familiar with a paper date book or address book can be up and running quickly on Organizer. That's because it looks on the screen much like such paper competitors as the Filofax or Day-Timer diaries—down to simulated metal rings holding simulated paper pages.

The pages are divided into sections, identified by tabs labeled "Calendar," "Addresses," "To Do," "Notepad," "Planner" and "Anniversary." Within each section, tabs further identify pages by letters of the alphabet, or year, as appropriate. Click on a tab with your mouse, and the "book" opens instantly to that section.

But Organizer is a lot smarter than a paper date book. The simulated book is surrounded by little icons, pictures representing different functions. Clicking on a picture of a magnet with your mouse lets you grab an appointment on one date in your calendar and move it to another date, with all details intact.

Clicking on a picture of an anchor lets you link one entry to another so that they are connected for easy access. For instance, you might link a meeting listed in the calendar section to an address entry for the chairman of the meeting. To dial a phone number through your modem, you just point to an address entry with your mouse and "drag" the entry onto an icon bearing a picture of a telephone. To print an entry, drag it to a picture of a printer. Records can be sorted, or viewed in different ways on the screen, by clicking on other icons. There aren't any complicated commands to memorize.

Adding entries is also a breeze. You just click on any blank area in the appropriate section and a form pops up that you can fill in. The anniversary section can be used to enter birthdays, holidays and the like into the date book permanently.

The notepad section lets users enter long documents, including text and graphics, that can be summoned anytime. You can even insert material written in other programs. For instance, you might place in the notebook a product price list or an organization chart drawn in other software. Organizer automatically adds each new entry in the notepad to a table of contents.

The planner section provides a grid display on which you can plot the duration of projects using colored bars. Pages in this section, and in the notebook, can "unfold" on the screen so they are wider than usual to show more information.

Organizer can print out its contents in a variety of layouts, including those matching many standard paper date books and mailing label formats. It can incorporate addresses and other records already on your computer, as long as the data are in certain specified formats.

You can rearrange and rename the tabbed sections, eliminate some of them, and combine sections from multiple Organizer notebooks. I added to my own Organizer file some nifty notepad material Lotus ships with the product that contains maps and information on countries, states, and units of measure.

To keep the program easy to use, Organizer's designers left out some features hard-core PIM users may miss. For instance, there's no way to view appointments for more than two weeks at one time. Address entries can contain only a couple of customized fields, and you can sort addresses in only four preset ways. The phone-dialing function doesn't allow for credit-card numbers or other complicated dialing options. Tasks in the to-do section must be tied to dates and can't appear in a separate list that carries over until completion.

Nevertheless, Organizer will fit the bill for lots of people. It is practical, capable software that puts an emphasis on clarity and ease of use.

1/21/93

44
Handy Program Provides Framework for Deck Projects

My weekly column is not called "The Home Handyman." I can pop chips in and out of computers, but anything I try to build around the house comes out looking like a surrealist painting. Once, in a seventh-grade shop class, I submitted a design for a new kind of tool that the teacher drily informed me "couldn't exist on this planet."

But even I could devise a practical backyard deck using a clever software program called "Design and Build Your Deck," the first effort from an intriguing start-up company called Books That Work, in Palo Alto, California.

This $60 program lets you lay out a simple deck just by manipulating an image on the screen, using a mouse. As you change the deck's size and shape, and stairs and rails, the program automatically creates the necessary structural underpinnings and updates a list of materials and a cost estimate.

At any point, you can summon a vast multimedia step-by-step deck-building guide. It's filled with plain-English definitions of construction terms, tips on various elements of the project, and color animations with sound that show how to perform important tasks.

The most impressive feature of Your Deck, however, is its ease of use. It accomplishes all of these feats without requiring the user to memorize any complicated commands or master a palette of drawing tools. There are just seven on-screen icons to use, and their labels make them self-evident: "3D View," "Zoom In," and so forth. Even the pull-down menus of commands bear such simple titles as "Deck,"

"Stairs," and "How-To." The manual for Your Deck is just thirteen pages long.

In fact, Your Deck, which runs on IBM-compatible computers using Microsoft Windows, represents a notable step forward in the software industry's hit-and-miss effort to produce a workable electronic book. Most software programs, including several fine existing packages for designing things around the home, are tools with a broad range of possible uses: they permit you to use your computer to create many different things with many options. But there's a price to this: to master the tool, you often must learn a lot of commands and symbols.

But Your Deck is a great example of an emerging kind of computer program, called content software. These are narrowly focused on single topics, freeing their designers from having to build in a complicated set of controls. The user can get to work quickly, plunging right into the task at hand, just as if she were reading a how-to book on that topic.

That's no coincidence. The chief executive of Books That Work, Stuart Gannes, formerly worked for Time-Life Books on its home-improvement series. His company plans to follow up Your Deck with added volumes in a "Backyard Builder" series, on such topics as landscaping. The program carries the endorsement of *Sunset*, the home-improvement book publisher, and will be sold not only in computer stores, but also in hardware and home stores.

Your Deck surpasses a printed book in many ways. It lets you view your design from the top, the side, or in a realistic 3-D view, at varying sizes. These views can be printed out. You can strip away the top layer at any time to look at the support structure. You can notch or angle corners, and put stairs in various places. The software will even draw in the outer walls and doors of your home in the proper relationship to the deck, and let you wrap the deck around a corner of the house.

The program incorporates national building code practices, so it won't let you make the deck too narrow, or specify beam or joist sizes too small for the structure you design. It doesn't know local codes, but warns users to pay attention to them.

The program also lets you select the types of wood you use, and even includes average national prices so it can keep a running cost estimate (you can edit these for local prices). An inventory of material, tailored to your particular design, can be printed out to form both a cost estimate and a shopping list you can take right to the lumber or hardware store or hand to a contractor. You can even print out a sample contract and a budget sheet.

The reference section includes both obvious tips (don't put nails in your mouth) and obscure ones (how to affix a "lag screw"). Some of the animations are pretty clever. The one on termite attacks is accompanied by the sound of an army drill sergeant calling out a march cadence, followed by chewing noises.

Your Deck does have some limitations. It can't lay out really fancy decks, the kind with scalloped edges or multiple levels. I couldn't see any way to design an opening in a deck for a hot tub or a tree. The program knows only four styles of railing, and the deck and stairs must share the same one.

The designers have also made a mistake, in my view, by including advertisements for tools and lumber in a few places in the program. Supposedly, the ads offer special deals, but these consist mainly of paltry booklets and the like. Ads are expected in a seventy-five-cent newspaper, but in a $60 computer program they're an annoying surprise.

Still, I like this program a lot, and I would love to see more electronic how-to books like it. I'd also like to mail my old shop teacher the lovely deck design I just finished. Maybe I can get him to change my grade.

4/15/93

45
Software for Handling Finances Is Improved, but a Good Competitor Has Arrived

If you use, or want to use, your personal computer to manage your finances, you're in luck. The best software package for doing so—Intuit's Quicken—is getting better, with improved versions that still cost only around $30 or $40 in discount stores. And another publisher, Computer Associates of Islandia, New York, is bidding for instant market share by practically giving away a pretty good competitor to Quicken with the ungainly name of "Kiplinger's CA–Simply Money" for just a $6.95 shipping and handling fee.

For years now, Intuit of Menlo Park, California, has led the way in making it easy to manage your finances on a computer. Quicken has been so useful and so low priced, in fact, that for some folks it justified owning a PC in the first place. After testing the new version for IBM-compatibles running Microsoft Windows, I believe Quicken remains the best program in this category.

But now there is a real competitor to Quicken, at least for Windows users. Simply Money isn't quite as powerful or slick, but it features its own distinctive easy-to-use approach and is a terrific value at $6.95. It has a few glitches, and satisfied Quicken users won't gain from switching to Simply Money. For people just starting to put their finances on the computer, however, it is a worthy alternative.

Quicken has long relied on two on-screen methods for entering transactions: a screen that looks like a check and another that resembles a checkbook register. The new version now adds a third way of entering such things as payments, deposits, and transfers: a calendar onto which you simply drag transaction entries using a mouse.

This calendar feature saves a lot of typing and allows really organized people to plan transactions such as bill payments well into the future. Disorganized people like me, who pay bills whenever the pile of unopened bill envelopes begins to annoy their spouses, can still use the calendar by simply dragging a whole bunch of payment entries onto the day when the pile got too high.

The new Quicken also has a bunch of smaller enhancements. In the check register, you now can pop up a little calendar that lets you pick out a date for a check, or a little calculator to help figure an amount. You can instantly call up a "Quick Report" on your payment history to any payee, right from the register.

Investment tracking has been beefed up substantially, with a multitude of new reports and graphs for viewing portfolio performance in different ways. Setting up loans such as mortgages has been made much easier.

Quicken continues to sport two existing features I like for saving time. Any payment can be sent electronically, for a small fee, through the Checkfree bill-paying service, without using any other piece of software. That spares you the printing and mailing of checks. And if you use a special Quicken Visa card, Intuit will send your monthly statement via modem or disk, and Quicken simply sucks all the details into your electronic file automatically. It costs $3 or $4.50 a month for this service, but it saves a tremendous amount of typing time.

Simply Money introduces its own new user interface: drag and drop icons. Its main screen is separated into three sections: income, accounts, and payees. Each section contains icons, or small graphics, representing income sources, the various accounts into which that income flows, and the various people and companies to which money is paid regularly from those accounts. To enter a transaction, you use the mouse to "drag" one of the icons onto another. For instance, a paycheck would be deposited by dragging a salary icon onto a checking account icon. This method likely will work well for visually oriented users, and masters of the mouse. But for others, it could be confusing.

The program's other unusual feature is pop-up financial advice that appears as you work. These tips are supplied by Kiplinger, the personal-finance publisher, and they will help many people. But I found some of them irritating and obvious. For instance, when I deliberately recorded a huge grocery check, the program noted that it exceeded my grocery budget and suggested I defer it—a useless "tip" since I presumably had already spent it.

Simply Money makes it a bit easier than Quicken to set up accounts, and it has a nice feature that constantly updates the value of your house as an asset as you enter home improvements. But I preferred Quicken's latest graphing, reporting, and investment tracking sections. And Simply Money lacks direct links to an electronic bill-paying service or credit card. The program also failed to print reports properly on my setup and couldn't import Quicken data correctly, making it tough to switch from Quicken.

What's more, the $6.95 price is a little deceptive. Computer Associates hopes to collect much more, over time, from Simply Money users, by selling them special checks that can be printed by their computers, upgrades to the program, and a planned family of other programs. Intuit also makes money on such things, of course, but it isn't claiming to be handing out its software for "free," as Simply Money's marketers do.

Nevertheless, Computer Associates has produced a decent competitor and plans an improved version. That kind of competition is good for all computer users.

9/9/93

46
Graphics Software That's Friendly, Even to Non-Artists

Several trends have recently taken hold in the development of software that promise to make it easier and quicker to get work done on personal computers. First, more programs are emerging that are narrowly focused on specific tasks, rather than on being everything to everybody. Second, software companies are building into their products a degree of automation that lets users perform the most common steps rapidly, without mastering all the commands and tools normally needed to do them.

These approaches make it possible for business people without artistic skills to turn out professional-looking organization charts, office layouts, maps, flow charts, and other business documents. The result is a category of software that might be called modular business graphics, in which you build graphic documents by snapping together their components like kids do with Legos.

For a decade, computers have offered the artistically challenged the promise of real drawing ability. But the machines haven't really delivered, because most drawing programs have been wickedly hard to use for those without good spatial reasoning. Sure, a straight line stayed straight—but making it the right length and thickness, and connecting it to other things using a mouse, was too often a time-consuming struggle for those who, like me, can't draw to save their lives. And art software, like other categories, has suffered from the addition of so many features and controls, demanded by real computer artists, that figuring out how to use them has gotten harder and harder.

So it's good news that this new type of drawing program has

emerged, over about a year. There are around a half-dozen entries in the field, but the leader is Visio 2.0, by Shapeware Corporation of Seattle, Washington, and a key competitor is SnapGrafx by Micrografx Inc. of Richardson, Texas. Visio costs around $125 at discount, and SnapGrafx around $96. Both require computers running Microsoft's Windows software.

Visio presents the user with side-by-side windows on the screen. At the right is a large blank sheet of electronic graph paper on which you create a drawing. To its left is a slimmer "stencil" window containing Visio's key element: an array of pre-drawn objects, called "shapes," you use to put together a drawing. The program comes with twenty stencils arranged around common themes.

For instance, there are stencils with all the shapes you need to create a flow chart, or an organization chart or a space and furniture plan. Others have shapes designed to fit into road maps, bar and pie charts, engineering diagrams, and maps of the world, the U.S., and Europe. The company sells extra sets of stencils and shapes, including collections for home design, kids, landscaping, and marketing, for $79.

The program works on the "drag and drop" principle. To construct a drawing in the right-hand window, you merely click on one of the stock shapes in the stencil window, and, holding the mouse button down, drag its image onto the electronic paper. When you release the mouse button, the program "drops" the shape into the drawing. There's never a need to sketch anything.

Even cooler is the fact that Visio's shapes are "intelligent." If you stretch or rotate them, they change size and orientation without becoming distorted. If you connect them with arrows or lines and then move one of the connected elements, the others remain linked; the lines and arrows behave like rubber bands. And you can type all sorts of text inside them without worrying about running over the borders.

About the only real downside to Visio is that, while the program is based on these simple principles, it is packed with a lot of tools and features for modifying and arranging the shapes and thus can be confusing to novices. In my view, Visio needs a collection of "wizards"—Microsoft's term for automated routines that create basic documents of various types with a single mouse click. These could later be modified by the user. Perhaps a version with fewer complicated tools and a bunch of wizards might be developed for novices at below Visio's $125 street price, which is a bit stiff in a market where software price tags are plunging.

If Visio is too much for you, you might try SnapGrafx. This program also works on the principle of pre-drawn, resizable shapes, but it doesn't rely heavily on drag-and-drop, which can require considerable dexterity with the mouse. And it has many fewer tools and options, making for a simpler, cleaner screen. In SnapGrafx, you mainly add shapes to your documents by clicking on the shape you want, then clicking on an area of the page called a placeholder. The program then puts the shape where the placeholder was. Much of the resizing of the drawings is done by moving little tab symbols—like tabs in a word-processing document—along the screen borders.

But be warned: SnapGrafx is far less versatile than Visio. It offers mainly precooked shapes for creating a variety of charts, and the shapes are less "intelligent." If you want to do office layouts or engineering diagrams or maps, it's tough in SnapGrafx.

Speaking for the artistically impaired people of the world, I'm glad these programs exist. But even so, real artists won't be losing any sleep.

1/27/94

47

Software Aimed at Making Filing a 1040 Less Taxing

There are several places in *The Wall Street Journal* where readers can find informed, intelligent reporting and analysis about the tax laws and strategies for paying lower taxes. My column isn't one of them. I think about taxes as little as possible.

But I've spent many hours trying out the four most popular computer tax programs. So if you want an opinion about which of them makes it easiest to do your tax return, read on.

Here are the contenders: TurboTax by ChipSoft, at $40, and TaxCut by MECA Software, at $35, are the longtime leaders. Personal Tax Edge by Parsons Technology, at $24, is a perennially solid, if unimaginative, performer. And CA–Simply Tax by Computer Associates is a revised and repackaged revision of an older minor product, being offered supposedly for free (if you consider a $9.95 handling charge to be free).

Each of these programs comes in versions for plain IBM-compatible computers running just the DOS operating system and for those running Microsoft's Windows software. TaxCut and TurboTax also have versions for the Apple Macintosh computer. I focused on the Windows versions, which tend to have the most complete set of features.

It's important to remember that these tax software packages are meant to help with completing relatively uncomplicated tax filings, making a trying chore easier. They fill out and print standard Internal Revenue Service and state tax forms, based on information you provide, by taking advantage of the computer's mathematical prowess. Each offers a choice of filling out forms and related worksheets on the screen, or of answering questions in an interview format and letting the software enter the answers on the forms.

However, software isn't a substitute for a tax accountant or adviser. The programs offer some general tax tips, but they can't help you make tricky judgments on how to treat various types of income and spending. Indeed, they typically guarantee only that the tax returns they prepare will be mathematically accurate, not legally sound or financially clever.

That said, here's a quick rundown on the four contenders.

My vote goes to TaxCut for Windows, which in my view does more than any other package to make paying taxes easy. In the past, I thought TaxCut and TurboTax were fairly evenly matched, but MECA has put TaxCut ahead with a host of enhancements and design changes.

Users are greeted with a colorful series of large graphics collectively called the "Navigator." Instead of being labeled with arcane tax terms, they are labeled in plain English, e.g., "personal info" and "for self-employed." Clicking on any of them brings up a choice of answering an interview or filling out a form. Even if you pick the interview, you can see a live form at the bottom of the screen at all times and switch to it instantly to add numbers.

TaxCut excels at this visual presentation of data. When you import figures from last year's return or from a personal-finance program, it lets you see them right next to the corresponding current-year entry. The program runs crisply and prints paper forms quickly. It even has a feature to delete itself from your computer.

My only gripes about TaxCut are that it still lacks a little summary window that constantly updates the tax you owe as you work on your return, and its state tax printouts, unlike the federal ones, aren't accepted for filing, so you have to copy them by hand onto blank state forms.

TurboTax for Windows is a perfectly fine package, but it hasn't changed much lately. It now has fallen behind TaxCut in ease of use, and it is slower. ChipSoft has simplified some processes and terminology, and worked to make its state printouts acceptable for filing. Unlike

TaxCut, it provides a constantly updated summary of taxes owed. But the only significant new feature is a deduction finder, which goes over a completed return before you file it and suggests deductions you might have missed.

Parsons' Personal Tax Edge for Windows is a solid no-frills package that gets the job done for those needing less help. It costs a bit less than TaxCut and TurboTax, and throws in special calculators for computing depreciation and projecting loan costs and savings growth.

CA–Simply Tax is the cheapest at $9.95, and the price is about right. It's the weakest of the four, in my view, with confusing screen displays. I also found it wasn't able to accept numbers longer than eight characters, counting periods and commas. Thus, you can't enter an income of, say, 112,345.98. You have to round it yourself before typing it in.

The two top programs also offer CD-ROM-based versions with multimedia content. Again, I favor TaxCut's approach. ChipSoft seemed to throw a bunch of programs onto its TurboTax platter, including a lot of IRS manuals, the J.K. Lasser tax guide and tax tips. But they aren't well integrated, and reading the long text portions requires a lot of annoying scrolling and zooming. In contrast, TaxCut's multimedia edition adds things directly to the main program, including spoken directions and forty-five down-to-earth tax-tip video clips from Dan Caine, who wrote the program.

Now that you know what tax software to use, read the *Journal* to learn how you might actually save some money on your tax bill. Lord knows, I have no idea.

2/24/94

In 1995, both TurboTax and TaxCut were marred by serious defects, which their publishers scrambled to fix and explain.

48
Four Programs to Ease PC Users into a Job Search

Whether you're a graduating college senior or a business professional between jobs, the search for work can be an overwhelming challenge. It's crucial to think through your qualifications, decide just what kind of job to seek, write an effective resume, organize and track phone calls and appointments with potential employers, and prepare well for job interviews.

Job seekers with PCs can get help in doing all this from a special kind of software devoted to those tasks. There are many programs that turn out resumes and job search–related letters—a big help in and of itself. But some do much more, including maintaining databases of job contacts and calendars of appointments. Still other programs provide expert advice and tutorials on targeting a job search and practicing for interviews.

These programs are representative of an increasingly important category of software: targeted, customized tools designed to automate specific chores like preparing your taxes or drawing organization charts. General software programs, such as word processors and spreadsheets, can perform many of these tasks, but it takes lots of time to learn how to get sophisticated results.

Here's a brief rundown of four job-search programs I consider attractive choices. Bear in mind that you can do most of this stuff by hand, if you lack a computer. It's probably not a great idea to go out and spend $2,000 on a PC while you're out of work just to run these programs.

PFS: Resume & Job Search Pro for Windows: This $39 program, originally published by Spinnaker Software and now by SoftKey International of Cambridge, Massachusetts, is a powerful and well-designed package that turns out handsome resumes in a wide variety of styles. It also has a surprisingly sophisticated contact manager and calendar for keeping track of calls and appointments during a job search.

The program prompts you step by step through the process of filling out a resume and is generally easy to use. It offers ten basic templates for chronological- and functional-style resumes, including special forms for people in technical, military and academic fields. Once a template is selected, you can—with a single mouse click—rearrange your resume in numerous formats and layouts, all well designed. There's also a module for printing envelopes.

The Perfect Resume: This Windows-compatible resume writer, from Davidson & Associates of Torrance, California, isn't as versatile or powerful at constructing resumes as the SoftKey product, and its job-search contact manager is much more limited. The $40 program also lacks a built-in calendar, making use of the lame calendar that Microsoft supplies with Windows. And there's no envelope-addressing feature.

However, The Perfect Resume has three interesting features that PFS: Resume doesn't. The first is an extensive guide to resume-writing and other job-search tips composed by an expert in the field, Tom Jackson. Second is a letter-writing module with templates and canned text. Third is a module called "Resume Express," which interviews you and then constructs a draft resume.

Career Design: This is a very different product from those described above. While it has a modest resume-writing capability, the $70 program from Career Design Software of Atlanta, Georgia, is really a fundamental self-help course in identifying your personal talents and interests and defining a job that fits well with them. It's a series of interactive exercises arranged in three modules titled "Who Am I," "What Do I Want," and "How Do I Get There."

Based on a system used by career consultants, Career Design is intelligent and thorough, guiding the user through a process of discovering his or her real interests, creating a job-search plan and preparing resumes and interview answers. Each of the three modules takes roughly two hours to complete.

However, there's a big drawback to Career Design. It's an old-fashioned DOS program that uses a nonstandard interface, or method of navigating around. It will be unfamiliar and confusing to many PC owners, especially the millions who've bought machines preloaded with Windows-style programs and may never have used older software. I found Career Design confusing to operate, but consider its content valuable.

WinWay Job Interview for Windows: This $45 package, by WinWay of Sacramento, California, is focused on preparing job seekers for employment interviews. It poses two hundred common questions and will even speak them on a PC with a sound card. It then invites you to type in an answer, after studying a hint and suggested answer provided by the program.

The hints range from the basic (even if you have a headache, don't whine about it when the interviewer asks how you are) to the subtle (if asked to describe a failed project, pick one "from a long time ago"). There's even a feature that identifies questions that may be illegal under federal law, and suggests how to handle them.

I was impressed with the program's content and ease of use, but disappointed in the system for rating the answers. The software expects you to rate your own answers, based on four criteria, but there is scant guidance for rating yourself, and the process is of limited value.

So, if you're looking for work and have a PC, you might consider one or more of these programs. And don't forget to shine your shoes before the interview.

5/5/94

49 An Earthling's Guide to Tackling Everyday Tasks

Sometimes I think the big computer hardware and software companies live on a different planet. On their planet—maybe Mars—computers and computer programs are judged by their lists of "features." On mine—and, I suspect, yours—the only real test of these high-tech products is how well and how easily they perform practical, specific tasks that matter to average users.

Yet for years, the king of computer software has been the generalized tool—the all-encompassing, multi-featured word-processing or spreadsheet program. To perform such specific, tailored tasks with these general tools, you have to get pretty deeply immersed in the intricacies of the programs.

There have always been exceptions to the trend—specialized programs such as tax software that focus on tailored tasks. But only a few have been done well.

Now, however, a new class of tailored, task-oriented software is emerging, mainly from smaller companies. These programs won't let you analyze the GDP of India, but they will solve real-world problems without requiring users to get a computer science degree.

One example is a package that guides you step by step through electrical repairs around the house. It's called Get Wired! and is by Books That Work of Palo Alto, California, which has done several similar do-it-yourself projects. Get Wired!, which sells for about $20, explains the mysteries of electricity and wiring with text, pictures, and animation. My favorite feature is a wiring simulator that lets you lay out very quickly a proposed fixture or outlet and graphically warns if your plan will short out the neighborhood.

Two of the most attractive programs are published by Parsons Technology of Hiawatha, Iowa, a company that gets little attention because it isn't on either coast and mainly sells its dozens of programs by mail order (800-223-6925).

One Parsons program is The Home Buyers' Companion and the other is The Car Buyers' Companion. Designed for computers running Microsoft's Windows software, the packages have some flaws and limitations, but they get the job done with a minimum of hassle. And their cost is unbeatable—$19, plus $5 for shipping, gets you both programs and a slim combined manual.

The Home Buyers' Companion starts by interviewing you to determine your basic financial circumstances—gross income, savings, monthly debt, and so forth, as well as local interest rates and taxes.

Then, using the data collected in the interview, it rapidly creates a series of easy-to-read analyses that help you study your home-buying options. One of these, called Dream Solver, tells you the maximum home price and monthly payment you can afford, based on common guidelines (that you can alter if you choose). It suggests ways to afford more and shows the ratio of housing costs and total debt to your income. A second analysis figures your closing costs, and a third estimates your tax savings from a proposed mortgage, complete with pie charts.

There are specialized calculators that create detailed loan payback tables and figure how long it takes to pay off a credit-card debt. There's a module that compares your mortgage with a proposed new one, to help decide on refinancing. And there's a module that indexes home prices and salaries in different states and major cities, based on government data.

The program has some drawbacks. It ignores a major issue in many home-buying decisions—the impact of selling an existing house on the affordability of a new one. And it doesn't cover adjusted-rate mortgages.

So it's a very basic buyers' tool, but it costs less than a termite inspection and doesn't require crawling around the basement.

The Car Buyers' Companion works similarly. It first ascertains your preferences in a car, including a price range, using a module called a Car Finder. You can specify a general style, such as a minivan; a preference for front-wheel, rear-wheel, or four-wheel drive and a preference for domestic makes, imports, or all makes.

Then, based on your choices, the program generates a list of current models you should consider. If you select one, the program displays two analysis screens. One, called Showroom, contains a brief description of the car; the other, called Payment Estimator, figures total and monthly costs for a base model, a loaded model or an average-priced model. There's also a module that helps you figure fuel costs, and another that lets you compare the costs of buying or leasing a car.

This program is fine as a starting point in car-shopping, but its usefulness is limited by two glaring lapses. First, the car descriptions are just dry statistics. They lack any rating, review, or opinion from the many magazines and other sources that evaluate cars. Second, the program doesn't let you add or subtract optional features from the cars, to see the effect on the price. Still, like the home-buying program, The Car Buyers' Companion is a helpful basic tool, and much less annoying than browsing through shark-infested showrooms.

Parsons is on the right track with these two programs, and I hope the company will consider beefing them up while retaining their simple design, even if that adds a few dollars to the price. Whether or not that happens, it's clear that Hiawatha, Iowa, is located on the planet Earth, not Mars.

6/9/94

50
An Energetic Sidekick to Help You Organize Your Life on PC

One of the most famous computer programs of all time was an inexpensive little piece of software called Sidekick, a sleek electronic address book, appointment calendar and notebook by Borland International. For many early users of IBM-compatible computers, Sidekick was the first program that could pop up on the screen and be used without requiring them to first quit any other program they might be running. At the time, this capability was largely limited to Apple's rival Macintosh machines. It wouldn't become common on IBM-compatibles until the advent of Microsoft's Windows in 1990. But Sidekick was ahead of its time.

Alas, as Borland became a very large software company, specializing in $500 databases and spreadsheets, it let Sidekick languish and die. Now, however, after getting bruised by bigger competitors, Borland is working to redefine itself as a leaner, nimbler company. So it has revived Sidekick, releasing a new Windows version appearing in stores for $29 under the Simplify brand name.

This time around, Sidekick must contend with a crowded field of so-called personal information managers, or PIMs, all of which claim to do the best job of managing your appointments, your lists of contacts and your notes. But after testing the new Sidekick for a couple of weeks, I found it to be a fast, capable, satisfying piece of software that stands out from the others, despite a few rough edges typical of a new product.

Picking the right PIM is more a matter of personal style than is the choice of any other type of software. For me, however, a PIM must be simple enough to use without much study and fast enough to speed through searches and data entry. Lotus's Organizer is a good one by these tests, but Sidekick is just as convenient and, I think, more flexible and powerful.

Some much-touted new PIMs, such as Ecco by Arabesque and InfoCentral by WordPerfect, are too large and comlex, I find. These boast many features but also have a daunting computerish feel and focus more on the relationships among bits of information and less on simplicity and speed.

By contrast, Sidekick is built for rapid entry and quick retrieval of information in familiar forms. There are three main modules—a calendar, a card file, and a notebook. Each looks like the paper version it emulates, and each uses a tabbed notebook metaphor for navigation. For instance, in the card file, you can skip to different parts of your address list by clicking with a mouse on tabs labeled alphabetically. In the calendar, clicking on the tabs switches among daily, weekly, monthly, or yearly views. In the notebook, tabs let you switch among categories like personal and business.

The card-file section, where you store addresses, uses an index card metaphor. All the cards are displayed on the left, with just their first lines visible. You can select a card with the alphabetic tabs, by manually scrolling through the list or by typing a name in a search box that progresses through the list as you type letters. Once you select a card, it becomes fully visible on the top right. You can enter or change information by typing on the cards. At the bottom right, you can choose to display a variety of information, including an appointment or to-do list from the calendar module.

Address cards can be dragged across the screen using the mouse to perform certain actions. Drag one to an appointment list and it automatically enters the name for an appointment. Drag a name to a picture of a phone and Sidekick dials that person's number through your modem. Drag one to a wastebasket icon and the card is deleted.

The daily calendar section is dominated by an appointment schedule, flanked by lists of to-do items and phone calls. Entries made on this daily form automatically appear on the weekly and monthly views, and multi-day entries are displayed using colorful banners. You can set recurring events, reminders and so forth. The notebook module looks a bit like the card-file function, but it allows free-form entry grouped by subject. You can also produce short form letters here.

Sidekick can import and export data from a variety of common file formats, though not to and from a Sharp Wizard pocket organizer. It prints reports, labels and address book pages in Day-Timer, DayRunner, Filofax, or Franklin format.

Lots of things are customizable, from the arrangement of lists on a screen to the module Sidekick automatically displays when run to colors used on various screens. You can create a row of icons to directly launch other programs you use often, and can install a special menu in other programs that will instantly summon Sidekick.

What about those rough edges I mentioned? I found that the program could use more and better keyboard controls when a mouse is inconvenient to use. It also could use built-in lists of states and other common data to save manual entry time. I'd also like to see one-click appointment entry in the week and month views, and the ability to start and end appointments at odd times, instead of on the quarter hour, half hour and hour.

But Sidekick for Windows represents a strong first effort, and it won't hog your computer. It comes on a single floppy disk and requires just three megabytes of hard-disk space. The manual is a slender seventy pages, and is clearly written. Sidekick for Windows deserves a look.

6/16/94

Sidekick, currently in its second revision, is now published by Starfish Software, a start-up founded by Borland's longtime chairman, Philippe Kahn.

51
Dov'è l'Autobus? Software Lets You Type the Query Properly

Comment allez-vous? Je vais bien, merci, et vous?

That's the kind of sophisticated foreign language expertise the American education system gave me after only eight years of French classes. (As I recall, it means: "Where's my tour bus? I can't find it anywhere, can you?") It's no wonder we run rings around all our trading partners, posting huge trade surpluses month after month. Or maybe not.

Of course, "foreign" languages aren't just a headache for Americans. It's been my experience that the average taxi driver in Moscow, his brain dulled by the discredited communist education system, has managed to learn just one English phrase: "Five dollars, please." And over in Brussels, Belgium, I'm told, the European Union is forced to pay thousands of bureaucrats just to type out vital documents—like the regulations governing sausages—in languages ranging from Greek to Portuguese.

So maybe the world needs a little foreign-language help from its personal computers. At least that's what Accent Software International, a little Israeli company, is hoping. It has released Accent, a multilingual word processor for computers running Microsoft's Windows software. It lets you write using the alphabets of thirty mostly European languages, including those that use the Roman alphabet, like French and Spanish, and a couple that use their own, like Greek and Russian. An add-on module for Arabic and Hebrew will be released soon, and a Japanese module is promised. Modules covering Cantonese, Mandarin, and Hindi are also under development.

This slick, powerful $299 product is really designed to let people who already know a foreign language easily create documents in that tongue—or in several of them at once. Accent doesn't claim to do comprehensive translation, a feat I have yet to see done well by any off-the-shelf PC program. There is a limited translator built in, but that's not Accent's main function.

Accent features a language menu with little flags and country names. When you choose a language from this list, Accent automatically reconfigures your PC keyboard with the standard keystrokes and layout of the keyboards of whichever country you select. Then, using a keyboard guide that pops up on screen, Accent lets you produce all the characters, diacritical marks, and punctuation marks each language requires, but are either missing from standard English word processors or take a lot of work to enter.

In addition, Accent features spellchecking in any of seventeen languages and built-in thesauruses in nine languages. The standard find-and-replace function works in any language. You can even change all of Accent's menus, dialog boxes, and help screens so they appear in any of eight languages: French, Spanish, Italian, English, German, Russian, Portuguese, and Finnish.

And you can mix and match many of these features. For instance, I'm writing this in Accent using the English-language keyboard, but I just clicked a couple of times and changed all my menus into Finnish, including one titled "Ohje," which for all I know could refer to orange juice. (Unfortunately, now I can't remember which menu I need to use to change everything back to English, and the Help screens are full of words with double-dots over the letters.)

As noted above, Accent doesn't claim to be a full-blown translation tool, but it does include a little translation utility from Berlitz that handles twelve thousand common words in each of the Big Five Western European languages: English, French, German, Spanish, and Italian. Type in a word in the source language of your choice, and the program instantly displays its equivalent in the other four languages.

If you type in "software," for example, you find that the word is the same in four of the five major tongues, except French, which uses the handy term "logiciel." The French also insist on calling a computer an "ordinateur," which lacks a certain catchiness (I like the Spanish term "computador," which conjures up the image of a Macintosh fighting a bull).

Accent also sports most of the core features of standard Windows word processors, including mail merge for producing form letters and a tool bar full of icons. Accent also allows the creation of tables and the insertion of graphics into text files, and can import files created in other popular programs and export files in other programs' formats. All in all, it's a very well-designed product.

But Accent is hardly perfect. The program sucks up over 20 megabytes of space on your hard disk if you install every feature, and runs a bit slowly in the minimum four megabytes of memory it requires. It ran fine on a Compaq 486, but crashed on a speedy new Dell model powered by a Pentium chip whenever I tried to use the word-counting feature and sometimes when I tried to export a file. In addition, some normally reliable features, such as the spellchecker, seemed to crash annoyingly often when multiple large programs were running on the Pentium while Accent was in use. The company is checking into these glitches.

Accent is also hard to find in America. As far as I know, it isn't carried in stores or the major mail-order software catalogs. The sole vendor appears to be an outfit called Softmart in Pennsylvania (800-535-5256), which also provides technical support for Accent users.

But if you do a lot of writing in a language foreign to your own, Accent may be your answer, despite these problems. As they say in Paris, "Quelle heure est-il?"

7/28/94

52
Two New Programs Do Single Tasks Cheaply and Well

The computer software business seems to be increasingly dominated by a few big companies—especially giant Microsoft. But I'm happy to report that little companies continue to do innovative work, turning out clever programs that break ground Microsoft has yet to traverse.

In this column, I'll review two such new programs for Windows users. One, called QuickXpense, provides an easy way to prepare your expense accounts and then spits out the data on a near-exact replica of your company's own proprietary expense-account form. The other, Gift Maker, lets you sit at your PC and design T-shirts, baseball caps, coffee mugs, and many other gift items, then order a factory to produce your creations at the click of a mouse. Both programs are inexpensive, focus on doing a single practical task well, and put great emphasis on customizing your work.

I hate doing expense accounts. I'd rather watch Congress debate textile quotas than fill out those tedious forms. As a consequence, I'm always really late turning them in. In fact, the hard-working folks in my newspaper's accounting department are no doubt cracking up right now at the mere thought that I'm writing about the topic. But I'm the perfect guy to check out the new QuickXpense software because it's supposed to make the process so much easier that even offenders like me will shape up.

After a month of working with QuickXpense, I think it might just do that. I have used QuickXpense over the past few weeks to churn out numerous accountings, and it performed very well, speeding up the process immensely.

Here's the way it works: when you first run the $69 program, from Portable Software of Redmond, Washington, it asks which form you want to use—either one of the fifteen generic forms the program provides or an electronic version of your own company's form (more on this later). Then, depending on that choice, it asks for the boilerplate details required by that form—e.g., your department, location, etc. It takes account of company cars, credit cards, cash advances, foreign currencies, and the like.

Then you enter your data in an electronic checkbook register like the ones in personal finance programs. This register is smart. It sorts your receipts by date and type, so you can enter them in any order. It memorizes entries, such as the names of people, restaurants, and hotels, and fills them in automatically the next time you type the first few letters of their names.

Once your receipts are entered, the software automatically calculates all the totals, enters the information in exactly the right spots on the expense form—even your own company's form—and prints it out or dispatches it via electronic mail.

Portable Software will create a digital version of your company's form, as it did for mine. This is free for the first division of any Fortune 1,000 company that sends in its form, or for any smaller company that buys at least two copies of the program. It's $50 for all others. QuickXpense is so far available only directly from Portable Software (800-626-8620).

With my expense accounts out of the way, I was able to become the proud owner of the world's first official "Personal Technology" baseball cap. I designed it myself, on my PC, using the second of these two innovative software packages, Gift Maker. This $40 program is published by Maxis Corporation of Orinda, California, the maker of SimCity.

The idea behind Gift Maker is that you dream up a design—including graphics, photos and/or text—and then order, via modem or by sending a disk through the mail, any of forty gift items bearing your masterpiece. The items, made by a third company, Artistic Greetings of Elmira, New York, range from a $9.95 pennant to a $68.95 jacket, and they include ceramic tiles, clocks, polo shirts, teddy bears, and more.

The program makes this all pretty easy, even for the nonartist. It comes with hundreds of design templates, canned graphics, and special fonts. You can also import graphics and digitized photos created in other software or send in regular photos. You simply pick out an image of the gift item you want, then select graphics and type in text in that image. You can pick colors for various elements of your design, add shadows and special effects, and change the size and placement of the elements.

When you're done, you just enter the addresses where you want the things sent, enter a credit-card number, and click to either put the design on a floppy disk for mailing or blast it to Elmira via modem.

The system basically worked fine on my hat and on a T-shirt designed by my twelve-year-old son. But a few glitches arose. We were surprised to find that you can't select the exact point size of your typeface and that the program won't automatically center your design when you're done, forcing you to do it by hand.

Also, prices on some of the items can be steep. A $13.95 T-shirt, for instance, becomes $19.95 if you want designs on both sides and $23.45 if you include a single photo. Add $4.01 for shipping, which can take up to two weeks, for a total of $27.46. If you want overnight delivery, it would be $39.95—a lot for a T-shirt.

More importantly, Gift Maker crashed—freezing my whole computer—a couple of times while I was trying to transmit my orders.

Gift Maker is otherwise a clever, well-designed piece of software that a lot of folks will find useful. If only I could use it to make a personalized green eye-shade I could wear while doing my expense accounts.

10/27/94

53
Some Powerful Data for Computer Users on the Move

If only life were simple as *Star Trek*, at least when it comes to computers. In the wildly popular science-fiction TV series and movies, the poor, emotional humans of the future are helped to coolly and logically analyze their worst problems by the ultimate portable PC—a friendly walking android computer aptly named Commander Data.

Today's personal computers are supposed to perform a similar role. But despite the computer industry's typically overheated claims, the machines still aren't all that useful in helping to solve life's problems. At least in this primitive century, most computer software is still too general and too hard to use to offer the kind of personalized, detailed help you can get from a human expert, or even a book, when faced with a big decision or dilemma in your life, like a household move.

But gradually, with the introduction of faster machines, smarter software and CD-ROM disks that can hold tons of detailed information, a few companies are building inexpensive programs that offer people the kind of pinpointed information that just might be uttered by a brainy android. One example that recently crossed my desk is a program called Smart Moves, which is an amazing repository of data about every major metropolitan area in the U.S., designed to help people who are moving to a strange city decide which neighborhoods they want to live in.

For thirty bucks, anyone with a robust PC running Windows can call up detailed tables, maps, and community profiles packed with a vast array of statistics that rank central cities, suburbs, and rural towns in such categories as housing, crime, taxes, schools, and the detailed demographics of what kinds of families live where. In each category there are numerous statistics available for viewing, such as the concentrations of families with kids under six or of entry-level houses, or areas with the lowest property taxes or the fewest burglaries. The categories can even cover such arcane areas as which communities use oil heat or well water the most, or which attract the most transients or professionals or people with college degrees.

Smart Moves isn't the product of a mainstream software company but of a huge relocation firm called PHH in Overland Park, Kansas.

That's good and bad for computer users who buy it. The good news is that PHH understands the kinds of issues on the minds of people moving or being transferred. It has incorporated lots of its own proprietary data on housing prices and housing markets into the software, along with a ton of government census and crime data, as well as some data from other firms.

The bad news is that the design of the software isn't up to the best software industry standards—it's pretty clumsy and frustrating in a variety of ways. It isn't exactly hard to use; it just doesn't follow standard conventions, doesn't display its data as well as it should and gives too few clues as to how to use its features.

For instance, if you call up a table of data that has more than a half-dozen columns, the ones to the right are cut off and can't be viewed—yet the program never warns you. There's only a slim manual, and the help screens are only fair, in my view. I judge the program barely acceptable in the ease-of-use category; be prepared for a measure of confusion and aggravation.

Nevertheless, such hassles may be worth it for anybody preparing to move to a new metro area, because there's a gold mine of information in Smart Moves. Color-coded maps show where each part of an area ranks on whatever factor you've selected. The same data can be displayed in table form, and the program ranks the communities on whichever factor you like.

There's a good searching feature, which allows you to assign weights to various categories. You can also modify the way the program computes some measures. There are also detailed reports on particular communities, which can be printed out. These will rate the communities, on a hundred-point scale, for various factors and provide text and charts.

The program crashed occasionally and was incredibly slow in some phases of its operation, especially during the early stages of a research session, when it's loading in the basic data for a given metro area. I recommend using it only on machines with eight megabytes of memory and at least 10 megabytes of free space on the hard disk. It comes on a CD-ROM, but PHH will send you floppy disks if you need them. The company made a recent change in Smart Moves to fix a screen display problem on high-resolution monitors; if you need this, PHH says it'll supply it.

PHH says Smart Moves is available in stores, but it will also sell the program directly at 800-210-8852. The data are from the second quarter of 1994. Updates will be offered to registered users for $20.

It's a shame that Smart Moves isn't better designed; the company plans a second version that I hope works better. But PHH is on to something important: putting powerful information into the hands of average people.

12/8/94

54
An Introductory Tour of Windows 95 (née "Chicago")

If you still think Chicago only refers to a city on Lake Michigan, then you haven't been reading the big computer magazines lately. I can't blame you—they're not exactly beach material for most of us. Not to worry, though. Read on, and I'll fill you in on what has the computer press so fired up, but I'll be using much smaller words.

"Chicago" is the code name Microsoft uses to describe Windows 95, an all-new software program designed to totally replace both Windows and DOS, the nearly ubiquitous pair of programs that control tens of millions of IBM-compatible personal computers. It is a special type of program called an operating system, which means it governs the way other software and hardware products interact with the computer. It also defines the user interface, which is computer jargon for the basic design of the menus, icons, and other features that people use to run their computers.

Because so many people and businesses depend on DOS and Windows, Microsoft's candidate to replace them will have a huge impact on the way people use computers and on the computer industry itself.

Microsoft is aiming to finish Windows 95 and start selling it by August 1995, an ambitious timetable. It's too early for me to critique its strengths and weaknesses and recommend which computer users need it. But the company has released hundreds of thousands of test, or "beta," copies of Windows 95, offering the first clear look at the details of the huge project.

So here's a basic description of Windows 95, which will arm you for that backyard barbecue at which the neighborhood computer expert insists on disclosing what he read about it in the magazines. Bear in mind that the features and improvements discussed below are still in the test stage, and Microsoft must still eliminate numerous bugs. That's a gargantuan challenge, especially since the company has had trouble in the past with the first versions, or major revisions, of its products.

Windows 95 is technically an improved version of Windows, but it sports a radically different look and feel and includes so many other fundamental changes that it's best thought of as an entirely new program. It's the final leg in Microsoft's long march to give IBM-compatible computers the relative simplicity and ease of use of Apple's Macintosh machines, still the gold standard in user-friendly computing.

In Windows 95, Microsoft has junked most of the clumsiest elements of DOS and Windows and appropriated a long list of features from the Mac's operating system, as well as some elements from IBM's rival OS/2 operating system. Microsoft has also introduced a few original major elements that these competing platforms lack. Nevertheless, Windows 95 will be instantly more familiar to veteran Macintosh users than to users of DOS and Windows. Judging from the test version, Windows 95 stands a chance of finally closing the gap with the Mac.

Gone are the awkward limitations on the naming of files that produced documents with unhelpful names like "APRILSEX.RPT." Windows 95 users, like Mac owners, can use long, real-English file names, like "April's export report." There's no longer any need to use the separate File Manager program to copy and move files among different directories on your hard disk, or among different disks. As on the Mac, you can do so by merely dragging little icons representing files between folder icons or disk icons. You can see the contents of your computer by clicking with a mouse on a little picture of a PC labeled "My Computer."

One major innovation in Windows 95 is a task bar, a strip at the bottom of the screen with buttons for every program and document you've opened, that allows you to switch among them with ease. In addition, the task bar contains a start button that you can click any time to launch your most-used programs, or open any of the last fifteen documents you created.

Like the Mac, Windows 95 aims to automatically detect such devices as printers and modems and properly configure itself to use them. It has built-in networking, making it easier for users to lash together multiple computers.

Like OS/2, Windows 95 aims to have full-fledged multitasking, the ability to run several programs at once without one slowing the others down or stopping them cold if it crashes. In other words, you should be able to write a report in one part of your screen, while downloading data in another through your modem and printing in yet a third program. The Mac and the current version of Windows use a feeble system to try to simulate true multitasking, with sometimes disastrous results.

Windows 95 is to have simple built-in programs for sending and receiving electronic mail and faxes, as well as much speedier printing than current systems. It is being designed with powerful built-in multimedia features for playing video and sound.

On top of all this, Microsoft is promising that Windows 95 will seamlessly run existing DOS and Windows programs. And the company claims it will run at least as well as Windows does in any PC with at least a 386 microprocessor and four megabytes of memory. These may be the acid tests for Microsoft.

So now you'll know what your computer-crazed friends are talking about when they invoke the name of the Windy City. And brace yourself—Microsoft is already working on the *next* version of Windows, code-named "Cairo."

7/7/94

Part IV
Going On-Line

Nothing is hotter these days than using a computer to go on-line, and here we'll tell you how, from buying a modem to linking up from hotel rooms, to sending and receiving electronic mail. There are also reviews and explanations of the Internet, America Online, Prodigy, and CompuServe, and tips on how to contact the White House and protect your kids on-line.

55
E-Mail Delivers a First-Class Package of Useful Simplicity

Electronic mail is an increasingly important form of business and even personal communication. But it's way too complex and costly for average computer users, right?

Wrong. Just about anybody with a personal computer and a modem—the device that hooks computers up to the phone system—can subscribe to a commercial e-mail network for reasonable prices. Then you can use a variety of software, including some simple programs, to exchange messages from your screen with millions of people in the U.S. and abroad.

Both American Telephone & Telegraph and MCI Communications, the titans of long-distance phone service, also offer commercial e-mail services, called AT&T Mail and MCI Mail. Another popular service is run by CompuServe, the big on-line database service owned by H&R Block.

In most cases, you simply bang out messages to send, and read messages you have received, while "off-line"—that is, when you're not connected to the system. Then, at the touch of a key or the click of a mouse, the software will automatically dial up your service, rapidly send all the messages you've composed since your last call, and just as quickly pull into your own computer any messages others have left for you.

Each user has an "electronic mailbox," a small part of the disk storage space on their systems' mainframe computers. Each mailbox has a distinct address, plus a separate password for security. Users can find addresses in on-line listings.

These commercial e-mail systems even allow you to send messages to people who lack computers: for an extra fee, you can direct that any message be delivered as a fax or letter. For another additional fee, some services will print faxes and letters on copies of your own letterhead with copies of your signature.

Most of the big services also permit members to send and receive messages to and from account holders on competing networks, and to people who belong to in-house e-mail systems at large companies that have configured their networks to connect to the outside world. In most cases, you can also link up with people who use the Internet, a vast interlocking system of computer networks mostly at universities and government agencies.

This adds up to a tremendous tool for individuals and small businesses, a way to help even the playing field with the big boys. Sitting in a home or storefront office, with any mainstream brand of computer, an e-mail subscriber can compose a single message and, with a single keystroke, fire it off to dozens of suppliers or customers. One minute she can get the same instant price updates long available to big companies, and the next minute she can send an e-mail note to her daughter at college.

Because the systems hold mail for members until they call in, they avoid the problem of "telephone tag." And since the computers transmit messages quickly, you can cram much more information into a brief e-mail call than into a regular voice message. Commercial e-mail rarely swamps users with floods of messages, unlike in-house corporate e-mail systems, where messages are free and don't require placing a phone call.

So how much does it cost? In most cases, you can reach the commercial e-mail systems by placing a local call or dialing a toll-free number. Users are typically charged only for messages they send, not those they receive. The cost is based on the length of the messages, not the time spent on-line. For long documents, e-mail can get costly. For small letters, it can be quicker and cheaper than overnight delivery services.

Pricing plans vary. They can be complex. The basic charge for my favorite service, MCI Mail, is $35 a year. Each message costs 50 cents for the first 500 characters, or roughly 75 words. The second 500 characters, and each of the next several 1,000 characters, cost a dime. The rate drops to a nickel per 1,000 characters beyond 10,000 characters. A message as long as this column would cost about $1 to send through MCI Mail to anybody in the U.S. or abroad.

Software is a crucial issue. It's best to use special programs called "front ends," which streamline and automate the process of writing messages, dialing into your service, and reading and storing your e-mail. MCI and AT&T both offer their own front-end software, but several other programs are better, in my view.

One is the Wire, from Swfte International, a $90 front end for MCI Mail customers with IBM-compatible PCs running Microsoft Windows. CompuServe's $30 membership kit includes a good program, Information Manager, in versions for DOS, Windows, and Apple Computer's Macintosh. Software Ventures' $140 Microphone program for the Mac and Windows also includes good front ends for MCI and CompuServe.

It would be ideal to have one piece of dedicated, simple software that can automatically manage your mail on multiple services. One Button Mail, from Sigea Systems of Weston, Massachusetts, an IBM-compatible program that handles both MCI and CompuServe, is great but costly at $250. Hewlett-Packard plans to introduce this spring a $99 Windows front end that can handle four major e-mail services.

One final advantage of e-mail is worth mentioning. I have yet to receive an electronic junk message declaring, "YOU MAY HAVE WON A MILLION DOLLARS." But if some sweepstakes company reading this wants to give away a lot of money via e-mail, I can be found on the Internet at the address "Mossberg@wsj.com".

2/4/93

56
New Software Helps E-Mail Users Avoid That Boxed-In Feeling

What if every telephone company used a different system of phone numbers, some with more or fewer digits, others mixing letters and numbers and odd symbols? And what if you had to dial a different access number to call users of each company's system?

The telephone system would be even more unwieldy than most of us think it has become in recent years. Every business and individual would have to consider either joining multiple phone systems and mastering several arcane numbering schemes, or calling only subscribers that also use their base company.

Yet this clumsy scenario approximates the commercial electronic-mail system today, the only e-mail alternative for millions of small businesses and individuals who lack the kind of in-house electronic mail common in large organizations.

These people must open accounts with one or more separate e-mail providers, such as AT&T Mail, MCI Mail, and CompuServe. Each has its own incompatible addressing scheme, and different commands for sending and retrieving messages. Each has its own access number, and a separate subscriber listing. Each has its own proprietary software for automating e-mail operations.

It's possible to call most of them using a single, generic communications program, if you're a skilled computer user—but these don't work for every service, and they offer less automation than the various services' own custom software. And there is a way to send messages from one service to users on another one (if you know their address), by the loose alliance of computer networks known as the Internet, to which most of the systems are linked. But the commands to do this can be tricky and rigid.

So most users of commercial e-mail either restrict their messaging to a single system, or join several of them and struggle with multiple software programs.

Recently, however, ConnectSoft, a small company in Redmond, Washington (800-234-9497), introduced an inexpensive, easy-to-use software package that consolidates and automates access to two of the biggest systems, MCI Mail and CompuServe, and makes it easy to use the Internet to reach people on many other systems—even the internal e-mail systems of private companies and other organizations with links to the Internet.

The $49 program, called E-Mail Connection, works on IBM-compatible PCs running Microsoft's Windows system, and has a clean graphical interface. It bills itself as the "universal e-mail interface" because it replaces the proprietary software from MCI and CompuServe and maintains a single address book and filing system for messages received and sent on the two systems. The program also can be used to receive and send internal e-mail over corporate networks based on either Novell or Microsoft networking systems.

I've been using E-Mail Connection every day for several months, starting with prerelease versions, and have found it to be reliable, easy to use, and efficient. It has a few flaws, but gets the job done better than any other commercial e-mail package I've seen.

Installing E-Mail Connection is fairly painless. You click on an on-screen button marked by a colorful MCI or CompuServe logo, and enter—one time only—your account and password information for the services, and the phone numbers you use to reach them. A separate screen lets you configure the software for your PC and modem. After that, a single click orders the program to dial one or both services, automatically retrieve any messsages waiting for you there, and transmit any messages you've composed off-line in the program's very nice built-in editor. You can also order E-Mail Connection to dial in automatically and check your mail hourly, daily, or on nearly any other schedule you choose.

The built-in address book is very well done. Addresses can be entered manually, or the program can be instructed to add the sender's address automatically from any message you get. MCI and CompuServe addresses are treated in an identical manner, and you can add addresses for people on other systems—such as America Online, AppleLink, or private corporate networks—so long as they are linked to MCI or CompuServe via the Internet. The program automatically fills in the Internet codes for popular systems.

E-Mail Connection is excellent at archiving and organizing your messages. You can set up your own custom "folders" to sort messages for later reference. The program will even let you set up "rules" by which it will automatically do the sorting for you, based on the identity of the sender or a word or phrase in the message's heading.

The program has a few weaknesses. It lacks a connection to the large AT&T e-mail service, even by an indirect Internet link. It can be slow to launch and to switch screen displays (though it is speedy at message retrieval). It can't send and receive messages while you simultaneously perform other functions, and there's no way to merge or synchronize address books stored on two different computers.

But ConnectSoft says it plans to remedy these problems in a future revision, and it's already working on adding more e-mail systems. A Macintosh version of the program is also planned.

Someday, maybe e-mail services will be as interchangeable and compatible as the regular telephone companies. Until then, E-Mail Connection is a good way to bring some order to the chaos.

8/19/93

57
Dialing Up Details on New and Improved On-Line Services

It's been a while since I've reviewed the major commercial on-line services—those huge repositories of news, data, and electronic messages you reach through your modem. Recently, competition among these services has heated up fiercely, with new features and prices. So here's a brief introduction to the three general-interest consumer services—CompuServe, America Online, and Prodigy—as well as news on some new competitors scheduled to show up soon.

CompuServe still has the richest offerings, but it has been the slowest to change and can be much costlier than the other two services, especially if you make heavy use of some of its best features.

The fifteen-year-old service, owned by H&R Block, claims 1.6 million subscribers. It has added relatively few significant features to its traditional core of news and "forums"—bulletin boards that are especially strong on computer advice and support. The most important recent addition has been an on-line edition of the weekly magazine *U.S. News & World Report.* But a number of interesting things are in the works, including access to parts of the Internet network and a Windows program called Navigator that lets you scan the system quickly and so save money.

CompuServe members pay $8.95 a month for unlimited access to news, weather, sports, stock quotes, and basic references. Using anything else—including the valuable forums—costs a stiff $8 an hour at standard modem speeds, and a truly painful $16 an hour for high-speed modems. It also costs extra to send more than sixty electronic mail messages monthly, and to receive electronic mail from people on other services. But the service is adding some lower-cost technology that may allow price cuts.

America Online (AOL) remains the hottest, easiest-to-use, and most interesting of the services. During 1993, the upstart system more than doubled its membership, hitting five hundred thousand, due to aggressive pricing and the introduction of many features.

AOL offers *Time* magazine on-line, as well as the *Atlantic Monthly*, the *Chicago Tribune*, and features provided by National Public Radio and C-SPAN, among others. It even has introduced a user-friendly way to reach parts of the vast but complex Internet on-line system.

When it comes to basic news and reference services, America Online lags behind its competitors, but the company says it has deals in the pipeline to remedy that over the next few months. Also, its explosive growth has caused problems; during the past few months, the service has crawled at times, though it seems to have recovered lately.

America Online charges $9.95 a month for the first five hours you're connected, regardless of modem speed or the features you use (with a few minor exceptions). After that, it's $3.50 an hour. Electronic mail is free, period.

Prodigy, a joint venture of IBM and Sears Roebuck, finally has started to improve its garish, jumbled look and confusing system for navigating among features. The new main screens are cleaner and simpler, with black text on white (instead of the awful colored text on black) and color-coded "buttons" to take you to various features and ads that hide their gaudy graphics unless you ask to see them. There's also a Windows version of the Prodigy software, with menus, and a companion program that lets you compose and read electronic mail off-line.

That's the good news. But the bad news is that the improvements affect only a small minority of Prodigy's screens so far, and the new look was accompanied by stiff price increase. Prodigy's new pricing structure is complex and can get expensive. The service charges a standard flat fee of $14.95 a month for unlimited-use "core" services, such as news and reference. But bulletin boards cost $3.60 an hour after the first two hours, and electronic mail costs extra after thirty messages a month. There also are extra charges for software downloading and certain premium games and financial features, and you can only send e-mail to people on other systems with the off-line mail program.

Prodigy now offers features in which cable TV networks will post viewer information. After losing members due to the price rises, the service claims to have recovered to about a million household subscriptions, with about two million users.

Some new services are due to enter the fray. Apple Computer plans a service called eWorld, which lets users navigate among features using a 3-D map of a fictional town in which the buildings represent the sections of the service. eWorld will be available only on Apple's Macintosh computers at first, but an IBM-compatible version is planned. AT&T also is believed to be about to launch an on-line service, built around e-mail. Microsoft is working on another service, and a major trade-magazine publisher is readying a new service mainly for people interested in computers.

So keep those modems oiled and ready, but have your wallet open. There's a lot to do out there on the commercial lanes of the information highway, if you're willing to pay the tolls.

1/6/94

Since this was written, the competition among the Big Three services has heated up, and each has cut prices. But America Online remains the hottest service, and has more than tripled its membership in just one year, to well over two million, overtaking CompuServe in the United States.

58 The White House Lets You Turn On Your PC and Tune In to Politics

Sometimes it seems that President Clinton is everywhere. You can't turn on the TV or radio, or open the newspaper, without encountering him announcing another new policy or holding a town meeting.

Now the Clinton White House is even in touch by computer. The administration has set up special databases and bulletin boards on a number of popular on-line services available to any computer user. For the first time, there are official White House electronic-mail addresses on public services anyone can use.

The main reason for all this, of course, is a political one. The White House can propagate presidential speeches, statements, and interviews onto millions of disk drives and computer printers by tempting their owners to download the material. There's also an advantage for computer owners: they can talk back to the White House through e-mail.

So here's a guide to establishing electronic links to the Clinton White House, using any IBM-compatible, Macintosh, or other popular PC equipped with a modem, phone line, and communications software.

- If you belong to the CompuServe information service, you can send the White House an e-mail message at the address "75300,3115". You can also tap into a large library of official White House documents, updated daily, by using the command "Go Whitehouse". These documents, which can be downloaded into your own computer, range from weighty speeches and daily press briefings to the official proclamation of Irish-American Heritage Month.

The same "Go Whitehouse" command also lets you participate in bulletin-board discussions: on-line electronic debates about Clinton administration policies. These range far and wide; a recent conversation on CompuServe was about how to stop the Central Intelligence Agency from monitoring the discussions there.

- If you belong to the competing America Online service, you can send the White House an e-mail message at the address "Clintonpz". You can tap into a similar library of White House documents, and a similar bulletin board, by using the command "Whitehouse".

- If you belong to MCI Mail, you can send the White House an e-mail message at the address "White House". You can also reach a repository of White House documents with the command "View White House".

- If you have access to the Internet, you can send the White House e-mail messages via the commercial services even if you aren't a member of them. The Internet isn't user-friendly, so you must use one of two ungainly addresses: "75300.3115@CompuServe.com" or "Clintonpz@AOL.com".

To send the White House e-mail, or download documents from the on-line libraries, you'll have to follow the rules for the particular service you're using and use the commands built into the software through which you're connecting to them. If you're using a commercial service, like CompuServe, America Online, or MCI Mail, you'll also incur their standard usage fees.

Computer jockeys who are comfortable with complex commands and can link into the Internet have another option. They can subscribe—free—to electronic deliveries of White House documents, which are routed automatically to their electronic mailboxes. This experimental service can be requested with a message to the Internet address "Clinton-Info@Campaign92.Org" (you must use the word

"Help" as the subject of your message). This service should be used sparingly; it isn't designed for high-volume traffic.

Another service for computer experts on the Internet is an on-line database of recent presidential documents maintained at the University of North Carolina. Internet users can reach this trove by using the command "telnet sunsite.unc.edu" and logging in with the word "politics".

Before PC junkies get too excited about this digital democracy stuff, however, let me inject a few notes of cold reality. First, the president himself isn't a routine computer user, according to White House aides, and he doesn't personally tap into these on-line messages and comments. Eventually, he or other officials may make guest appearances on-line, but don't hold your breath.

Second, the backward White House computer system doesn't receive the electronic messages directly, and the mail isn't answered electronically. Instead, the e-mail messages are delivered to the White House on disk, where they are printed out and answered by low-level workers through regular paper mail. So, if you want an answer, you must include your postal address in the e-mail message.

Third, the presidential staff doesn't participate in the discussions on the White House bulletin boards, or read them fully.

If the White House doesn't suit your fancy, electronic alternatives abound. There are bulletin boards and databases devoted to the Republican Party and Ross Perot's United We Stand organization, on both CompuServe (type "Go Politics") and America Online (type "Issues").

CompuServe also has a bulletin board where members debate the views of the conservative radio talk-show host Rush Limbaugh ("Go Issues"). An independent on-line service for conservatives, called National Town Hall, is jointly run by the *National Review* and the Heritage Foundation think tank.

So be a good electronic citizen and crank up those computers. If we could only vote this way, we'd never have to leave the house.

3/18/93

Mr. Clinton is a little less visible these days (early 1995), now that Republicans have captured Congress. But these on-line White House sites still do a brisk business, and have proliferated. On the colorful World Wide Web portion of the Internet, there's a graphical "Welcome to the White House" feature, which can be reached by typing: "http://www.whitehouse.gov". Not to be outdone, Congress has established its own World Wide Web site, named "Thomas," after Thomas Jefferson. It's at: "http://thomas.loc.gov".

59 With eWorld, Apple Begins an Onslaught of On-Line Services

Attention cyberspace travelers: if you're confused by the Internet and tired of today's commercial on-line services, some of the biggest names in computers will be happy to take your money for membership in a bunch of new commercial services.

This second wave hit the beach recently as Apple Computer launched eWorld to compete with the Big Three established on-line services: CompuServe, Prodigy, and America Online. In 1995, Ziff-Davis, the preeminent publisher of computer magazines, joins the fray with Interchange. And Microsoft, the Tyrannosaurus rex of the digital kingdom, expects to introduce its own service soon thereafter. In this column, I'll focus on eWorld (no, that's not a typo; it really starts with a cutesy lowercase "e").

In the best Apple tradition, eWorld, which I've been testing for several months, is the most graphically attractive and easiest to use of the current services. It is splashed throughout with colorful watercolor-style pastel graphics and bold logos identifying sections. The effect is to reduce the sense that this is a typical computer environment, and to give users the feeling of a friendly electronic community.

In the same vein, navigation is done intelligently. The opening screen depicts the eWorld service as a town, with cartoon-like buildings representing key offerings within the service. You click with your mouse on a building and immediately jump to the part of the service it represents. Click on a library, for example, and you get to an on-line version of Grolier's *Encyclopedia*. Electronic mail is found by clicking on a post office. In addition, each section of the service is color-coded, and each major screen has a consistent set of symbols down the side that bring up information and directories.

The service has a decent, if mostly unremarkable, selection of content for a start-up: news from Reuters and *USA Today*, stock quotes, e-mail that connects to the Internet, bulletin boards, shareware programs you can download, and reference materials.

But eWorld also starts life with some limitations that could make it less attractive to users than some of its competitors. Unlike Apple's most notable products, the eWorld software isn't groundbreaking or revolutionary, and it could well be outclassed by the Ziff and Microsoft services. To get eWorld up and running quickly, Apple licensed the basic software from America Online. While it has revised the look and feel of that software, it's stuck with the underlying capabilities inherited from America Online, which don't include some key features expected in the next round of competitors. These include multimedia on screen and the ability to browse through or download multiple things simultaneously.

What's more, eWorld suffers from two of Apple's usual mistakes: it works only on the company's Macintosh computers, and it's priced a bit high. The snazzy software will be shipped with every new Mac, and current Mac owners can get it free (call 800-775-4556). But a version for the vastly greater number of people using IBM-compatible machines with Microsoft's Windows software won't be out till 1995.

Apple is charging $8.95 a month for eWorld, but that includes just two free hours of connect time, only during nonbusiness hours. After that, it's $7.90 an hour during business hours and $4.95 an hour on evenings and weekends. All parts of the service are covered by those prices; there aren't any premium surcharges yet. That price structure is probably cheaper than CompuServe's for most people, because CompuServe charges extra for many features and for high-speed modem connections.

But for anyone using it more than two hours a month, eWorld costs more than America Online. AOL charges $9.95 a month with five free hours, and bills just $3.50 an hour after that, night or day.

Ultimately, eWorld and its competitors will be judged mainly on two things: the value and uniqueness of their content and their success in establishing an on-line "community." Apple's offering has few active bulletin boards so far, but it stands a good chance of becoming the major electronic community for Mac fans, especially since Apple's older and costlier on-line service, AppleLink, will soon be folded into eWorld.

Building unique content will be a tougher challenge. So far, eWorld has only a handful of unusual offerings. *Inc.* magazine has an area for small-business people; there's another section called Working Solo, devoted to the concerns of people working out of their homes; and Apple's longtime public relations firm, Regis McKenna, has created a database of marketing and PR tips. There are some syndicated political columns I haven't seen elsewhere on-line, and a strong collection of features about arts and leisure. There's a lot of information about the Macintosh, including an Apple on-line customer service center.

But there's not much in-depth sports or corporate news, no archival news databases and only limited archives of software for downloading. The news feeds aren't updated often enough, in my view. And some promised features have "under construction" notices on them. Apple says all this will improve, but these are merely the sorts of features available elsewhere. For eWorld to be a big hit, beyond its current customers, Apple will need to make it as distinct and exciting as the Mac itself.

6/23/94

Apple has since been forced to lower prices for eWorld.

60
Internet, a Vast Link That Isn't Missing, Can Be Hard to Find

Listen to a dedicated computer hobbyist, a person who spends hours a day using a modem to exchange messages and data with other techies, and pretty soon (if you can penetrate the jargon) you'll hear him or her gush about something called the Internet—a giant "network of networks" that links millions of computers around the world.

Pick up some of the many recent news articles about the trendy idea of building a national information highway to link homes and businesses, and you're likely to find the Internet portrayed as today's prototype of that data thoroughfare. Talk to high-tech political activists, and you'll hear the Internet described as a kind of national town hall, the center of an emerging digital democracy.

So, just what is the Internet? That's not an easy question to answer succinctly, because the thing is technical, designed by techies for techies. What follows is a general, simplified primer on the Internet.

The Internet may be used by millions of people, but it's not a mass medium. It's a formless mostly unregulated system for linking computers. For now, it is useful mainly to technically adept folks at government agencies, colleges and universities, and some large companies. Most other computer users—in other words, most people—can't gain access to it without great effort and some cost. And once they enter the net, they must deal with a system of commands and acronyms that isn't easy to learn.

The whole thing was started by the Pentagon in 1969 as a way to link, over dedicated phone lines, large computer databases that could be shared by military and government officials and academic researchers. Today, a big chunk of the system is run by the National Science Foundation. But there are many thousands of "servers"—big computers all over the world holding data on many subjects—linked through the Internet.

In recent years, the Internet has grown explosively, as businesses have begun to tie their computers into it (despite a little-enforced rule against "commercial" use) and ways have been found to let people outside the government and colleges dial into the Internet over regular phone lines.

Unlike commercial computer services, such as CompuServe or America Online, the Internet isn't really owned by anyone or run by anyone. There isn't even a complete, unified list of all the databases available or of all the people on the Internet. So finding the right data file or person can be a chore.

Perhaps the most common use of the Internet is electronic mail. Students and faculty members at colleges around the world routinely send and receive e-mail over the Internet, and people who use corporate e-mail systems, or commercial services like MCI Mail, can reach people on campuses, and each other, by using Internet addresses—a sort of universal code.

These e-mail addresses generally look like this: "username@location.xxx." In this example, "username" refers to a person's code name or address, and "location.xxx" to the server or e-mail system on which his or her electronic mailbox resides. For instance, my mailbox on America Online can be reached by Internet users (or by members of other commercial services, through Internet) by using the address: "Waltm@aol.com" ("com" means America Online is a commercial server on the Internet; college addreses have ".edu" at the end, and government sites end with ".gov".)

A second major use of the Internet is the posting of public messages in electronic discussion groups called "news groups" on a system called USENET reached through the Internet. These are like bulletin boards or forums on an array of subjects, from TV shows to politics to jokes.

The third primary use of the Internet is to tap into large computer databases and search through them to download data files on various topics that the owners of the databases have chosen to share on the network. (Note: this is not the same as illegally "hacking" one's way into private files.) There are several competing software systems for browsing and searching these remote computers.

In general, the Internet isn't very user-friendly. Most of the software for using it is a throwback to the old days of computing, requiring users to memorize commands and type them in with just the right syntax. There are a few programs, mainly for Apple's Macintosh computers, that put a graphical user interface on portions of the Internet.

If you're not at a college or government agency, you can find many commercial computer services that offer e-mail exchange with the Internet, but going beyond that isn't easy. A few local computer bulletin boards offer connections to the Internet. The Delphi on-line service, run by General Videotex in Cambridge, Massachusetts, lets you search and download data on the Internet for $23 a month for as many as twenty hours of use.

Companies also sell direct dial-up links to the Internet. Performance Systems International, of Reston, Virginia, provides access to the Internet for $29 a month, which includes the necessary software for IBM-compatible computers. A nearby company, InterCon Systems, of Herndon, Virginia, sells the same service for Macintosh computers.

A good book for Internet novices is *The Internet Companion*, by Tracy LaQuey and Jeanne C. Ryer, from Addison-Wesley. You can also find many guides and tip sheets on the Internet itself, if you can figure out how to get on. Good luck.

5/13/93

The Internet has surged forward in recent months, and it is easier to use than it was. A new graphical point-and-click feature has been added, called the World Wide Web. But it still has a way to go before becoming a real mass medium.

61
Services Compete to Escort You Through the Internet

Nearly everyone with a computer by now has heard of the Internet, a sprawling system of connected computer networks packed with information, electronic conversation and news. Politicians, writers, and business leaders regularly hail the thing as a prototype for the much-touted "information highway," which is supposed to wire us all up to each other so we can watch videos, learn trigonometry, and buy fake diamonds anywhere, anytime.

(Note to readers: as this column has just used the magic words "information highway," the current journalistic practice allows me right about here to insert a bad pun or dopey metaphor comparing the Internet to a real interstate roadway. However, as a public service, I am refraining from doing so.)

There are just three teensy problems with the Internet that its boosters overlook. First, unless you're inside a university, government agency, or big company, it can be very difficult—and expensive—to find a company that sells access to many of its features, beyond electronic-mail transfers. Second, the Internet mostly relies on complicated, old-fashioned software that requires memorizing lots of arcane commands. Finally, the Internet can be confusing because it has no organizing structure.

Those barriers are beginning to fall, however, as big national on-line computer services compete to attract customers by creating easy-to-use software systems, or interfaces, for connecting to and cruising the Internet. Most on-line services permit users to send e-mail to people on other commercial services or networks, using the Internet as a transfer mechanism. The competition is aimed at opening up many more Internet functions to members.

First to cross the finish line in this race is America Online (AOL). It has rolled out a feature called Internet Center that uses the familiar AOL system of icons and menus, controlled by clicking a computer mouse, to navigate through the Internet.

So far, America Online's Internet Center has three parts covering three Internet services, beyond e-mail. One allows users to tap into thousands of Internet bulletin boards, called news groups, on topics from politics to music to sex, travel, and art. A second lets members subscribe to mailing lists, in which information and commentary on selected topics published by aficionados worldwide is automatically forwarded to their e-mail box on AOL. Finally, America Online is in the process of adding a third service: point-and-click access to many databases at universities and elsewhere that are based on two popular computer systems called "Gopher" and "WAIS."

AOL also organizes the Internet material, letting you pick what you like from lists or search for topics. Best of all, these Internet services are included in AOL's standard price of $9.95 a month for five hours, and $3.50 an hour for time on-line past five hours. No special phone numbers or software are needed. You just dial into AOL using the usual number and the same software, and type the key words "Internet center".

This good news for Internet novices is tempered a bit by the fact that America Online has grown so fast that it can be difficult to dial into it. While the capacity problem has eased greatly since the company was forced to turn away callers during the winter of 1993–94, I still find it harder to dial into AOL than other services, and run into more delays on-line, especially at night. The service is also down for routine maintenance three mornings a week from 6:00 to 8:30.

The other big services, CompuServe and Prodigy, are promising similar easy-to-use Internet access soon. But at first they are likely to cover only news groups, and might be priced at a premium above the services' monthly flat rate.

Delphi, a smaller national service, already offers complete Internet access. But Delphi's Internet gateway uses a confusing old-style command system and it charges a small monthly surcharge for Internet use. The company promises an easy Internet interface by 1995.

Even smaller outfits are jumping into the race, though most are local firms that lack AOL's reach. One of them, Computer Witchcraft of Louisville, Kentucky, offers an easy-to-use Windows interface called WinNet Mail. But it only covers e-mail and news groups, and users outside Louisville incur long-distance charges in addition to the basic fee of $8-an-hour, or surcharges if they use the company's 800 number.

A little New York City company called Pipeline offers a particularly slick Internet interface that lets users access news groups, search databases, and tap into a wide range of Internet features and functions by just clicking on icons or menu items with the mouse. The Pipeline breaks down Internet choices into subject areas, and even lets users do multiple things at once, like reading e-mail while downloading a file. Non–New Yorkers must call long-distance, but the company says that, in a matter of weeks, people outside the city will be able to dial into the Pipeline through local phone numbers in many big cities. These outlanders will pay a surcharge of up to $5 an hour over the basic rate, which is $20 a month for twenty hours, plus $90 for the proprietary software (which is waived if you subscribe for three months).

Each of these companies hopes to become the home base for tens of millions of computer users, the place from which they communicate electronically with people and databases worldwide, via the Internet. Whoever makes it easy and cheap to do that will come out on top.

4/7/94

In early 1995, Prodigy added access to the newest and coolest feature of the Internet, the World Wide Web. AOL and CompuServe are in the process of doing so. Meanwhile, the Pipeline has launched a nationwide version featuring free local phone numbers in many cities.

62
All the News You Want, When and How You Want It

Some years ago, Columbia University conferred upon me a master of science degree in journalism. This document, I know now, was something of an academic oxymoron. Despite a long career as a newspaper reporter, I have yet to discover the "science" of journalism (though my office resembles the site of a lab experiment gone horribly wrong). Still, I keep trying to figure out what Columbia meant. So I was intrigued to discover a forty-dollar computer program called Journalist.

The software, for computers running Microsoft Windows, isn't one of those programs that purport to replace reporters by automatically composing news articles, thank heavens. Instead, it turns out to be an effort to replace editors, letting the user select and arrange news stories according to preference. In fact, they could have called it Editor, though that name has kind of a cranky ring to it and raises the prospect that your PC might start yelling at you a lot and rewriting your perfectly good prose for no apparent reason. (Note to my editors: just kidding.)

What the Journalist software does is to dial into the Prodigy online service and cull through its database of daily news and statistics, retrieving only the articles on topics the user has said he or she wants. Then, it places these stories, tables, and charts into a mini-newspaper, laid out according to the user's preference, which can be printed out. In effect, Journalist lets you act as the editor, instead of relying on professional newspaper editors.

This kind of thing will become increasingly important as a flood of undifferentiated news and other information becomes more easily available to anyone with a computer. Already, Dow Jones News/

Retrieval, an on-line service run by the company that publishes *The Wall Street Journal*, offers a feature called Clip, which just gathers stories on those companies or topics that users specify. The CompuServe on-line service offers a similar capability in its extra-cost Executive News Service.

But both are fairly expensive. There are also several personalized news services, devoted to producing such "custom" news, but these cost even more.

By contrast, Journalist, from PED Software of San Jose, California, works with the relatively inexpensive Prodigy service. (An earlier version from PED works with CompuServe.) This is a big cost advantage, but the approach has some drawbacks. Most of the news on Prodigy is distilled from wire service stories, which tend to be drier, less analytical, and less often exclusive than stories produced by major papers. In addition, Prodigy doesn't carry local news, editorials, comic strips, and other material offered by your morning paper.

Journalist works like a page-layout program. The screen shows a blank newspaper page, with a row of icons to its left. Each icon represents a type of story that the program can fetch from Prodigy—headline news, weather forecasts, business stories, stock quotes, sports news or articles on entertainment, computers, travel, and health.

You create your newspaper by clicking on an icon and then marking off a section of the blank page, called a frame, in which you want that kind of news to show up. When you're done with the layout, you click on another icon, and Journalist logs onto Prodigy and retrieves all the stories that match your selections, placing them where you specified.

This can be a time-consuming system to master. To make it simpler, there's a function called assistant that automates much of the selection and layout process. In general, the Prodigy version is much easier to use than the CompuServe version, which I found pretty daunting. But Journalist has some significant limitations and drawbacks.

For one thing, it works very slowly. If you have a large or complex paper to fill, it can take ten or fifteen minutes a page. For another, the level of customization is limited. You can specify that you only want news, quotes, scores, or weather for a particular company, team, or city. But you can't get stories containing only a particular phrase or name (unless you use the CompuServe version and subscribe to CompuServe's extra-cost clipping service).

In addition, the resulting newspaper is extremely hard to read on the screen without endless zooming and scrolling. Predicting what the printed version will look like is also next to impossible, because there's no print preview feature. The program also automatically adds pages during printing to contain material that overflows from the frames you include in your layout, but you can't control the number or design of these extra pages. The company says it is working to fix many of these flaws, and to add features, in planned versions of Prodigy and CompuServe.

I'm sure computers will get better at filtering the news, but I'm not all that sanguine about the prospect. If people read only stories about topics they think, in advance, would interest them, they will lose the opportunity to encounter the unexpected article that could enlighten or enrich them. I'm convinced, for instance, that many readers over the years have been helped personally or financially because they read stories in the *Journal* that seemed at first to have nothing to do with their particular business or personal circumstances, but which the editors thought might be of benefit.

If we come to rely exclusively on computerized filters to decide what we need to know, we risk adopting electronic blinders. And that can't be good for the future of either democracy or free markets.

5/26/94

63
Keeping Your Kids Away from Creeps as They Play On-Line

One of the benefits of owning a personal computer is the opportunity to explore such on-line services as CompuServe, Prodigy, and America Online, as well as the loosely organized worldwide network of linked computers called the Internet. Each is a virtual community where people from all over the world, who might never meet in real life, can strike up electronic friendships.

But there's a dark side to this exciting phenomenon, one that's too rarely understood by computer novices. Because they offer instant access to others, and considerable anonymity to participants, the services make it possible for people—especially computer-literate kids—to find themselves in unpleasant, sexually explicit, and even dangerous social situations.

The on-line services all have rules banning bad conduct and, fearing possible government-imposed restrictions, have stepped up the policing of on-line abuse. But parents could do more to protect kids from these disturbing situations. And I've gradually come to adopt the view, which will be controversial among many on-line users, that the use of nicknames and other forms of anonymity must be eliminated or severely curbed to force people on-line into at least as much accountability for their words and actions as exists in real social encounters.

Here are some examples of the problems and a brief practical guide to fighting back.

While you're reading this article, your ten-year-old son or daughter could easily be wandering into a raunchy or perverse sexual conversation with twenty mostly male adults known only by nicknames, whose real identities may be difficult or impossible to determine. Or he or she could be downloading hard-core pornographic photos and video clips. Both situations would be unlikely to occur in nonelectronic, real-world settings.

Even worse, there are more than a few creeps prowling the on-line services right now who use the access and anonymity they afford to reach victims more easily than they could in real life. They tempt kids into meeting for real-world or fantasy sex, peddle pornography and drugs, or pitch investment scams. These same odious operators harass anyone signing on with a female name with a flood of crude come-ons and even pose as women themselves to gain the confidence of women.

I don't believe government censorship, or the banning of some topics on line, is a healthy solution. But parents and other adults can act to lessen the danger. Several of the services, including America Online, Prodigy, and CompuServe, have various types of controls that let parents lock their kids out of portions of the on-line world where trouble is likeliest. Familiarize yourself with these and use them. You may even want to choose one service over another based on the degree of control it offers. The venerable Genie service lacks any such controls, as does Apple's eWorld service (though it plans to install them). The others do much too little to publicize them.

The most important areas to keep kids out of, in my view, are so-called "chat" or "CB" sections, in which people conduct simultaneous, real-time discussions under the cloak of anonymous "handles." Another dangerous feature you should consider disabling is the so-called "instant message"—a real-time one-on-one conversation through which some creep can contact a person he thinks is young or female. Bulletin boards, in which public messages are posted over a longer time period, tend to be safer, unless they're devoted to a sexual or other topic you'd like your kids to avoid. Electronic mail is private. You may also wish to bar your kids from less regulated or unregulated services, including the vast Internet, where there isn't any central authority.

Beyond that, I think it's time now for the services to jettison the long tradition of allowing members to hide behind "handles" or nicknames. In general, people should conduct themselves on-line under their real names, or not at all. In the same vein, I think the services should delay granting new members access for twenty-four or forty-eight hours, as many local bulletin boards do, while they verify that the applicants are really who they say they are—and not merely that their credit cards are good.

I know many women and some public figures like the freedom of taking an assumed name for protection, and that the nicknames can help people gain acceptance on line despite unpopular business, political, or ethnic ties. But I believe that these legitimate interests are far outweighed by the mask such nicknames now provide for abusers. In an electronic world where real names were the norm, for instance, many fewer women would need to seek aliases to feel safe.

The worst offender on this nickname question is America Online, a service I otherwise like. On AOL, "screen names"—not real names—are standard, and members can have multiple nicknames and change them at will. AOL also places a greater emphasis on the most dangerous forms of communication, "chat" sections and instant messaging. Prodigy and CompuServe generally reveal automatically the real names behind account numbers, but even they permit handles in their "chat" areas, saying fans of that format like the anonymity.

Maybe so. But unless parents get vigorous about this, and the services take more drastic steps than they have, I fear this terrific resource could be hobbled just as it's taking off, by a consumer backlash or heavy-handed government regulation.

6/30/94

64

When Shopping for a Modem, Faster Isn't Always Better

They're doing it to us again. Just when you may have thought you had a handle on understanding modems—those devices that let PCs connect to other computers and to on-line services over telephone lines—the computer industry has introduced a new, and particularly confusing, standard for these gizmos.

Let's look into the new standard, and go over the whole process of buying a modem, whether it's an add-on to a computer or built into a new machine.

The easiest way to think of a modem is as a telephone for your computer. Regular phones—the entire telephone system, in fact—are designed to carry voices. Modems are mainly designed to transmit and receive computer data over this voice-based network. The material transmitted by modem can range from simple text-based documents such as electronic mail messages, to the special computer-file types that contain spreadsheets, sounds, pictures, video, and more. Nearly every modem today also has the ability to send documents from a computer's screen to a fax machine and to receive on the PC screen documents faxed from a fax machine.

When you look at a modem in the store, the box is crawling with technoterminology that hardly anybody understands. But there really are only two basic characteristics of a modem that will matter to most people. The first is its physical configuration—is it an internal model or an external model? The second is the speed at which it is capable of sending and receiving data, a crucial issue since many on-line services charge by the hour, or even the minute.

Most modems for IBM-compatible personal computers are internal, including nearly all of the ones that come with new computers. These internal models have several advantages: they save desk space, they are usually a bit cheaper than external models—they don't require an electrical outlet (they draw power through the PC itself), and they don't take up one of the serial port connectors on the back of your computer. But like any other internal circuit board, they can be daunting to install or replace for most people, and they have no visible indicators to tell you what's going on while you're on-line.

I prefer external modems, which are optional on IBM-compatibles and prevalent on Apple Macintoshes, because they're easy to hook up and they have lights that give you positive confirmation that you are still connected and that a download or other transmission is proceeding. (I've criticized these little lights for having cryptic labels, and that's still true. But they're useful anyway.)

Speed is the other key factor. Modem speeds are measured in bits per second or BPS (a bit being the smallest unit of computer data). This is sometimes called "baud," but that's actually a different and more complicated measure so BPS is the one to use.

Modems usually have one speed for computer data and another for faxing. The fastest modem speed that's widely supported today by commercial and corporate networks you might dial into is 14,400 bits per second, usually called 14.4, fourteen-four, or fourteen-dot-four. These 14.4 modems usually have a faxing speed of 9,600 BPS. They now cost around $100 to $150. Older modems with data speeds of 9,600 BPS or 2,400 BPS are cheaper but should be avoided because they are just too slow.

Here's where that new industry standard comes in. Many modem companies have now brought out models that claim to work at a high speed of 28,800 BPS.

These 28.8 BPS modems promise great benefits, but for most people, they aren't a good choice for several reasons. First, none of the leading on-line services can handle data at this new speed, and few other computers can either. Second, even when the on-line services can handle the new speed, probably late in 1995, they're likely to charge a premium for that faster service that will partly or wholly wipe out any cost savings the speed increase brings. Third, the 28.8 BPS modems are roughly twice as expensive as 14.4 BPS models—about $250 to $300.

Finally—and here's the really confusing part—many of the 28.8 modems on store shelves can't be relied on to connect at full speed to other 28.8 BPS modems because they don't meet the international standard for modems of that speed. This standard is set by some international panel of engineers and covers lots of technical matters too dense and boring to enumerate here (even if I could). But all you need to know is that the standard is called V.34. If you insist on buying a 28.8 BPS modem, make sure it says on the box that it complies with the V.34 standard. Don't buy a modem that supports a standard called V.FC or V.Fast or any other V that's not V.34. These are unofficial standards cooked up by impatient modem companies while waiting for the slow-moving international committee to define the official standard.

The only exception is a few nonstandard 28.8 BPS modems that can be cheaply upgraded to the official V.34 standard. One example is the best-selling U.S. Robotics' Sportster, which now comes in an official V.34 version. Older Sportsters that met only the V.Fast standard can be upgraded to V.34 by popping in a chip the company will send you for $29.

Sorry for all the jargon, but you'll need to look for it on the box if you absolutely must have the fastest modem, no matter how impractical it is. For the rest of us, 14.4 BPS will do fine.

9/29/94

65 Things You Really Need to Know About Staying Plugged In on the Road

The computer industry has sold a lot of portable personal computers by promising that they would enable their owners to conduct business with the home office over phone lines from hotels and other remote sites.

But like so much else connected with high technology, that pledge is easier made than redeemed.

It's true that a laptop computer equipped with a modem can transmit and receive documents over almost any phone line, giving it the potential to function as a remote business center. All you have to do is connect the machine, using a standard telephone wire, to a modular phone jack, and then dial up your office computer using your communications software. But getting those connections to work often takes much more experience and technical skill than the computer ads suggest.

I learned this the hard way. For several years I traveled around the world for this newspaper covering the secretary of state. The reporters aboard his plane were supposed to be pondering great world events, but we often had to focus instead on how to get our laptops to work from various hotels. One highlight of our journeys occurred in Moscow when a Cable News Network reporter finally linked his laptop PC to CNN's Atlanta headquarters by yanking the phone wires out of the wall in our hotel and wiring his modem directly into them.

You don't have to go to such extremes to hook up a laptop in your hotel room. But you must overcome two basic obstacles.

First, the telephone hardware in hotels is often hostile to making connections. Spare phone jacks are rare; those already in use for the phones are often hidden behind heavy furniture; and some phones are wired directly into the wall without a plug-in phone jack.

Second, the system for making calls can be complicated, sometimes requiring that all calls go through an operator or use a long string of numbers. That can make it tough to set up your software to dial into the home office.

So, here are a few tips from a seasoned laptop lugger that might help you overcome these hurdles. Most of this advice also applies to portable fax machines.

- Look for a hotel that provides spare phone jacks. These are still rare but are growing in number. One example is the new San Francisco Marriott.

- Failing that, always carry three inexpensive items: a long spare phone wire, a coupler to connect two phone wires and a Y-adapter—a gizmo that lets two phone wires plug into a single jack. With these three things, available for a few dollars each at Radio Shack and similar stores, you can usually avoid using the wall jack at all. For instance, you can plug the Y-adapter into the back of the phone and then plug both the line from the wall and the line to your PC's modem into it.

- For hotels where the phone is permanently "hard-wired" to the wall and you can't plug anything in, consider buying two costlier devices. One is an acoustic coupler, which connects your modem to the phone's handset via rubber cups that fit over the mouth and ear pieces.

The other is a special connector that fits between the handset and phone and provides a phone jack for your modem. One source for these gadgets is Unlimited Systems of San Diego, California, which makes both types of devices in the U.S. and sells them under the Konexx brand name. Each costs eighty to one hundred and fifty dollars.

• Make sure before you leave that you have communications software that can accommodate long phone numbers. Hotels often require that guests use extra digits when calling outside lines. Some programs will let you set up an automatic dialing entry that conforms to the hotel's particular system, so the computer can just dial away. Hint: you can build pauses into these programmed phone numbers using commas between the digits. That way the computer will wait for an outside dial tone before proceeding.

• Also try to learn how your software can be set up to handle situations where you dial on the phone itself or give an operator a credit card number orally. This can be tricky and may require a close reading of the software manual.

• If your company's computers aren't set up to be dialed directly, you can subscribe to a public service such as MCI Mail. The service will assign you an electronic mailbox into which you can deposit documents from your laptop computer. Then, your associates back home can call the same service and retrieve the documents from the mailbox for use at the office.

• Instead of toting a printer along on trips, consider equipping your laptop with a "fax modem"—a modem equipped to send faxes. Then, if you want a printout of something on your laptop's screen, just send it downstairs to the hotel's fax machine.

They don't teach things like that in business school. And, in an ideal world, you shouldn't have to know about them. But for now, keep in mind that using a hotel room as a computer center usually takes some extra effort.

1/30/92

Part V
Multimedia and CD-ROM

No area of personal computing has grown as fast as multimedia software distributed on CD-ROM disks. This part of the book includes reviews of some of the more interesting disks, as well as critical appraisals of the difficulties of getting multimedia to work right, and of finding the right disk on store shelves.

66
Taking the Latest CD-ROM Disks Out for a Spin

Someday, we may all be cruising down the "information highway," driving a vast array of "interactive multimedia" programs on our televisions. These programs will convey knowledge and entertainment through video, audio, and text we will control and customize by using a simple remote control.

But this road trip won't start anytime soon, despite a recent spate of breathless media coverage. One reason is that computer programmers, print publishers, and entertainment producers are still jointly struggling to produce interactive multimedia programming worthy of the billions of dollars in cabling and electronics being installed to carry it.

Their main proving ground today is the exploding number of personal computers equipped to play CD-ROM disks, which can store the large video and audio files that interactive multimedia programs require. A flood of such disks has come out in recent months.

Taken together, the latest crop shows a few things. First, the stuff is getting better, as Hollywood production values creep in. Second, as always, such production values sometimes crowd out editorial quality. Third, many of the most ambitious disks seem to be showing up first in the Macintosh market, not the much larger IBM-compatible market. Finally, the biggest companies don't always do the best work.

Here's a look at some of the most interesting titles to cross my desk recently. Each costs under $100 in discount stores and catalogs.

Clinton: A Portrait of Victory: Time Warner published a conventional book of good black-and-white, behind-the-scenes photos of the president's

1992 campaign by the veteran *Time* magazine photographer P.F. Bentley. But the company's multimedia arm, Warner New Media of Burbank, California, has blurred the photojournalism's impact in this CD-ROM version by mixing it with an adoring melange of Hollywood-style hero worship.

This includes an opening sequence with the president's face superimposed on an American flag while patriotic music accompanied by one of his speeches plays in the background. There are also little movies of several Clinton speeches. The disk works on both Macintoshes and IBMs, but the movies play only on the Mac.

Seven Days in August: Warner New Media did much better with this first-rate multimedia history of the 1961 Berlin Wall crisis, when American and Soviet forces nearly clashed. Users can relive the event day by day, through footage of old newscasts, a panel discussion of experts, and excellent vignettes of the fallout-shelter craze in the U.S. and daily life in Berlin, Germany, and Berlin, Wisconsin. Included are examples of 1961 rock-and-roll songs and TV shows and coverage of the 1989 fall of the Wall. It's for Macintosh only.

Newsweek Interactive: *Time*'s rival has taken a different tack, launching a quarterly interactive magazine that includes long pieces on a special topic (it's the environment in the first issue) as well as articles from *Newsweek* and *The Washington Post*, which owns the magazine. I found the thing generally well done, with an easy-to-use command system that lets users switch back and forth from continuous narration to a mode where topics may be searched. There are ads, but they don't show up unless the user selects them. So far, the product only works on Sony's portable CD-ROM player, but an IBM-compatible version and a Mac version are in the works.

A Hard Day's Night: Tiny Voyager Company of Santa Monica, California, which consistently turns out the most elegant multimedia material, has done it again. This Mac-only disk contains the complete 1964 Beatles movie, with "Can't Buy Me Love" and other great tunes.

Included are the complete text of the script as well as critical essays on the film, the Fab Four and the music.

All of these are linked so that, for instance, you can click on a song title in the middle of text and instantly see and hear the song. The market may be limited for a program that plays a black-and-white movie in a small window on a Mac, but the disk is an artistic triumph.

***Dinosaurs* and *Dinosaur Adventure*:** Software giant Microsoft offers *Dinosaurs*, a CD-ROM packed with beautiful, detailed drawings of the ancient beasts and short articles describing them. Users can search for dinosaur facts through an index, with a time line, or by clicking on icons that resemble Flintstones-style stone tablets. There are audio clips of what dinosaur roars may have sounded like, but the disk lacks animation and video, and I think it pales next to *Dinosaur Adventure*, the latest offering from little Knowledge Adventure of La Crescenta, California. *Dinosaur Adventure* has movies of robot dinosaur models in action, plus two games and a storybook for kids, as well as the sort of still pictures and articles Microsoft's disk has. The two products are for IBMs only, though Microsoft plans a Mac version of *Dinosaur*.

***Mayo Clinic Family Health Book*:** This disk, by Interactive Ventures, of Eagan, Minnesota, contains a rich body of clear medical advice that can be called up interactively by the user. Available in Mac and IBM versions, it's augmented by scores of well-done audio clips, color images, and animations illustrating common maladies and medical procedures.

4/22/93

67
Fix Your Faucets, Visit the Parthenon: That's Multimedia

The hits just keep on coming—would-be hits, that is. Software publishers keep churning out stacks of new "multimedia" titles each month, mainly on CD-ROM disks, the high-capacity platters that look just like audio CDs.

Many try to use photos, video clips, illustrations, and sound to emulate Hollywood "production values." Most fail to approach this smooth look and feel, or have hopelessly weak content. Others are a tremendous pain to get working right, especially on IBM-compatible computers, which often require special video software and hardware or memory configurations that can vary from disk to disk. But a few of the dozens that cross my desk are worthy of note, in my view. So here's a brief rundown on one batch of titles I liked.

Medio Multimedia, a little start-up company in the shadow of giant Microsoft in Redmond, Washington, hit the ground running with its first three CD-ROM titles, each in stores at about $39. One, called *Exploring Ancient Architecture*, lets you visually "walk" through Egyptian temples, the Parthenon in Athens, Greece, and other famous structures, using 3-D animation and realistic illustration, while a narrator explains their architectural features and significance.

Another Medio title, *The JFK Assassination: A Visual Investigation*, explores both the official account and various conspiracy theories of the 1963 murder. The disk includes the famous Zapruder home movie of the assassination, as well as other amateur films and still photos, which can be viewed at various sizes and speeds. There are photo maps, background explanations, and more.

The third Medio CD-ROM is *Midnight Movie Madness*, a compendium of trailers for laughably bad old horror and science-fiction pictures—annotated with smart-aleck comments, trivia quizzes, and an introductory video by comedian Gilbert Gottfried. After careful study, I concluded that Godzilla displayed more screen presence in the 1968 epic *Destroy All Monsters* than Zsa Zsa Gabor did as the boss of an all-female planet in the 1958 classic *Queen of Outer Space*.

The Medio titles run only on IBM-compatibles using Microsoft Windows. The video on them can be choppy or grainy, depending on your system. But they show ambition and creativity.

Another winner is the second title from a clever start-up, Books That Work of Palo Alto, California. It's called Home Survival Toolkit: Home Repairs, and comes on floppy disks, not CD-ROM, for IBM-compatibles running Windows. The $35 program is basically one of those thick fix-it-yourself books transferred to the computer screen with sound, animation, and good graphics. There are databases on paints and adhesives, stain removal, and the toll-free numbers of home-product makers. It also has special calculators for figuring out how much paint, concrete, or attic ventilation you need. While testing the program, I used it to fix a leaky faucet by just printing out the relevant section and keeping it by my side as I worked.

There are two new entries in what I consider to be the single-best multimedia software series, Living Books, a wonderful collection for kids by Broderbund Software of Novato, California. For tykes, there's a richly illustrated and wonderfully narrated version of "The Tortoise and the Hare" fable. For older grade-schoolers, there's an anthology of silly poems by Jack Prelutsky called *The New Kid on the Block*. Like other Living Books, they invite kids to click on words and pictures to make funny stuff happen on the screen. The animation is TV-quality, and every child I've tried these on has loved them. They come on CD-ROM, in versions for Macintosh and IBM-compatibles, for around $35 each.

Innovative Voyager of New York has a new $40 Mac CD-ROM title called *Planetary Taxi*. It teaches kids—or adults—about the solar system by sending the player off in a space taxi to pick up passengers and take them to various planets. The disk is packed with striking photos and videos of the planets.

Microsoft has updated and improved two of its multimedia CD-ROM titles for Windows, the $85 *Encarta Encyclopedia* and the $55 *Cinemania*, a database of movies. In the 1994 versions of each, video clips have finally been included, and the presentations have been cleaned up considerably. New articles and reviews have been added. These products still could be better, but they are following the admirable Microsoft path of constant incremental improvement.

Finally, I want to mention a CD-ROM title that isn't really multimedia. It doesn't have sound or moving pictures, but it does include street maps of every U.S. town and city, and it can quickly home in on streets, blocks, zip codes, and area codes to display maps that can be pasted into other documents or printed out. The product is the new $125 version 2.0 of *Street Atlas USA*, from DeLorme Mapping of Freeport, Maine. It now comes in fully compatible Windows and Mac versions, which makes copying and printing maps much easier.

Even the best multimedia titles can be hard to find in stores, but they help make a good case for ensuring that your next computer has a CD-ROM drive, good sound and video and ample memory. Thus equipped, you can trace Zsa Zsa's career, fix a faucet, or get a map of a neighborhood fifteen states away. It sure beats staring at spreadsheets all day.

11/18/93

68
Behind the Hype Lurks the Darker Side of Multimedia

The computer industry's marketing battalions have been in full cry about the virtues of multimedia software—PC programs featuring combinations of animation, sound, video, text, and graphics. In fact, the advent of multimedia on the computer has been a key reason for the surge in home computer sales, especially of models with sound capability and CD-ROM disk drives, the equipment needed to play the high-capacity platters on which most multimedia software is distributed.

I've recommended some such programs myself, and will continue to do so. But it's time to reveal the dirty little secret of the industry marketers, the dark side of multimedia: in many cases, getting multimedia hardware and, especially, software, to run on a typical IBM-compatible computer can be a frustrating—even impossible—task.

A case in point: when a much-publicized multimedia health-care simulation program, SimHealth, was issued to great publicity in late 1993, at least one computer-savvy White House staffer and others (including yours truly) couldn't get it to work without help from its publisher, Maxis. The software required users to answer detailed technical questions about components of the computer, and some obvious choices didn't seem to work. The program was rushed out before testing was completed, has been improved and Maxis no longer owns it. But the syndrome is widespread.

Neither the basic PC hardware nor the underlying operating system software, which controls IBM-compatibles, was designed to produce singing, dancing video on the screen. Modifying these systems for multimedia can mean altering the computer's configuration in ways that mess up the more mundane components, such as modems and word-processing software. Some products require you to know highly technical terms to even understand their explanations of how they are changing your machine's configuration. Worse, there are some products that reconfigure key aspects of your computer without informing you at all. In all these categories, game software is the worst offender.

So here's a brief rundown of the kinds of problems you face in getting multimedia products to run on your computer. This discussion is limited to IBM-compatibles. In general, users of Apple's Macintosh computers face very few of these problems, because a single company—Apple—makes both the hardware and the operating system and has made sound, graphics, and video a priority.

The first multimedia problem many IBM-compatible users encounter comes when they try to add sound capability and/or CD-ROM drives to older machines. This requires opening the computer and installing at least one, or maybe two, flat cards jammed with chips into special slots. In too many cases, this requires hours of maddening adjustment of tiny switches, or software settings, to prevent the new equipment from disabling things like modems and mice. It's much better, if buying a new computer, to get one with stereo sound and a CD-ROM drive built in.

Even if you clear this hurdle, however, hours of aggravation await you as you try to install and run multimedia software, especially games and other programs that don't take advantage of Microsoft Windows, but rely on the older MS-DOS operating system. I estimate that a third of the multimedia programs I've tested lately have caused problems.

One problem is what the White House and I faced: programs that expect you to know the make and model of your audio and video circuitry, and even complicated configuration information about them. One such program is the game Mad Dog McCree, by American Laser Games.

Worse is software that requires you to make big changes in the basic configuration of your computer. Some of these programs tinker with special configuration files, called "autoexec.bat" and "config.sys," in ways most users don't (and shouldn't have to) understand and that can goof up Windows or other programs.

Still other software refuses to run or even to install unless you somehow find and run a "driver" for something called "VESA" video, a new standard that most software doesn't use. Another group of programs tries to seize all your computer memory, or utilize an older type of memory management that most modern programs don't use.

Among the products I've found guilty of one or more of these traits lately are a game called The 7th Guest, by Virgin Games; a program called Sid & Al's Incredible Toons, by Dynamix, and some games from Sierra On-Line. In some cases, software makers suggest you create a floppy disk, configured only for their products, and start your computer using the floppy instead of your hard disk. That's not only cumbersome, it's a throwback to 1981 computing that wouldn't be necessary if the software worked better with standard machines and with Windows.

Some companies do a great job of this, including Knowledge Adventure and Medio. Infocom's fascinating new game, Return to Zork, gave me no trouble. Nor have any of the Microsoft multimedia titles. So it can be done.

It's time the rest of the computer industry gets the message that computer users shouldn't have to be techies to use multimedia.

1/13/94

69
Journalism and Art Adapted for CD-ROM Use

The world seems awash in multimedia computer software, designed to bring interactive mixtures of video, sound, text, and photos to people with computers equipped to play CD-ROM disks. Publishers are cranking the disks out fast in hopes of reaping big bucks from the millions of people buying those computers. It has become such a big business that *Entertainment Weekly* magazine has added a multimedia section to complement those covering television, cinema, and other more established arts categories.

Alas, however, much of what passes for multimedia isn't worth stuffing into your computer, and it can be hard to tell from the boxes. Here are some of the more interesting titles from the many that have crossed my desk.

The most innovative CD-ROM I've seen in a long time was created by Peter Gabriel, the award-winning British rock-and-roll star who has long used computer graphics to produce terrific music videos. Titled *Xplora 1: Peter Gabriel's Secret World*, the $50 disk lets the user wander digitally among a rich array of features, including numerous Gabriel songs, interviews, a history of Mr. Gabriel's work, and original art based on the music. There are four complete videos, including the delightful "Steam," a commentary on sexism and stereotyping.

But *Xplora*, produced by Mr. Gabriel's Real World Multimedia and Brilliant Media of San Francisco, is much more than a catalog of the singer's work. There's a section about unusual musical instruments from around the world. Another section features personal themes, including family photos and videos about political repression. Still another section takes users behind the scenes of Mr. Gabriel's work, including a tour of his rural English music studio, where you can try revising a Gabriel song.

My only complaints about *Xplora 1*, which is aimed at teenagers and adults, are that it uses several competing and overlapping navigation systems, and that it is available only for the Mac. Interplay Productions, the distributor, promises a version for Microsoft Windows.

How do you teach the dusty texts of Greek mythology to a video child of the 1990s? Answer: turn mythology into a video game, grounded in the myths themselves. That's the approach taken by Luminaria, a start-up software company in San Francisco. And the result, a $40 disk called *Wrath of the Gods*, succeeds with flying colors.

In the game, available for Windows and Mac, the user plays a young man, abandoned at birth by his royal parents, on a quest to find and reclaim his kingdom. He travels through ancient Greece, encountering puzzles, challenges, and obstacles drawn from mythology, such as the Hydra and the Minotaur.

The situations aren't identical to the myths, but the mythological parallels and backgrounds can be read at any time and are helpful to solving the puzzles. More direct hints are available, for a price of five points, from an animated oracle. In fact, all the characters in the game are moving videos, not drawings, though the video motion can be a bit choppy.

Wrath of the Gods is laden with humor, there's little or no violence, and you can't die (you just go somewhere else, like Hades).

It's presumably easier to get folks interested in Michael Jordan, the World Series, and the Super Bowl, than mythology, but a CD-ROM from *Sports Illustrated* doesn't take that for granted. The magazine's *1994 Multimedia Sports Almanac*, produced by StarPress Multimedia of San Francisco, is as visually fresh and interesting as the sports events it covers.

The $40 disk includes 40 minutes of videos covering the events of late 1992 through late 1993, the magazine's complete text from that period, plus 1,200 pages of statistics, 450 color photos, and several trivia games. The interface features bright, responsive animated controls and even comes on a single disk that works on either PCs running

Windows or on Macs. (To save some of you a phone call, I'll tell you it doesn't include the annual swimsuit photos: it's only about sports.)

Finally, there's a CD-ROM from Cable News Network that could have been a contender, but isn't. It's called *CNN Time Capsule 1993* and was produced for the network by Vicarious Entertainment of Redwood City, California. Its strongest feature is its one hundred video clips, each covering a "defining moment" in the news last year. These are edited by CNN news people with a skill and flair rarely seen on multimedia disks. Other nice features are the price—about $29—and the fact that, like the *Sports Illustrated* CD, it comes on a single disk for both Windows and Mac.

What ruins *CNN Time Capsule*, however, is its user interface and some shaky news judgment. The disk contains no menu of all hundred events. To pick one, you must manipulate a scroll bar and stop at the right title as it flashes by. If you manage this feat, you'll find that the top news story of 1993 wasn't the Middle East peace treaty, the new Clinton presidency, the attempted coup in Russia, or the devastating Midwest floods. No, it was the Waco, Texas, shootout between federal agents and religious cultists, a story with plenty of breathless CNN video footage. The Bobbitt genital-mutilation trial outranks the California wildfires and the Nafta treaty.

Which goes to show that multimedia computer programs, like all forms of art and journalism, aren't necessarily good just because they're novel.

4/21/94

Vicarious has improved the CNN program greatly in its second version, with a much better interface and better news selection.

70
Baseball and Computers Team Up to Score with Stats Software

For serious baseball fans with computers, 1994 brought the proliferation of a new type of baseball software. Baseball and computers are a natural match. No other sport is as frequently analyzed in so many different mathematical permutations that have such long histories. The recent spread of "rotisserie," or fantasy, baseball contests has raised interest in all these figures. And where there are numbers and statistics, software is sure to follow.

So the latest baseball programs aren't simulated games you play on screen. They are high-tech reference works that let users pore through mounds of real baseball statistics, review players' careers and famous moments, and use a modem to get daily updates of scores and stats. One of them is even designed to be used at the ballpark. I've been looking at four of these baseball reference programs. Each is quite distinct and requires a different computer configuration, but any of them would make a dedicated baseball fan happy.

For basic computers that run Microsoft Windows, there's the *Major League Baseball SportsGuide* from Momentum Development of Ashland, Oregon. The $34 program is a sort of grab bag of baseball-oriented data and utilities. None of these modules is terrific, and the overall program has a sort of ragged feel that left me unsure how to get from one part to the other at times. But there's a lot going on in there.

The software includes statistics and standings on all current players and teams, schedules and calendars of games, a datebook and address book, ticket information with stadium maps, and simple trivia games for every team. In addition, there are screen savers and "wallpaper" designs to decorate your screen, based on each team's logo.

For $30 a season, you can also use a modem to retrieve scores and player stats, and the software will automatically update its data.

If you're one of the few to own one of Apple's Newton personal digital assistants, you can indulge a love of baseball with a $100 program called Fingertip for Stats. This software includes stats on both current players and teams, and an abridged version of Bill James's baseball encyclopedia, which contains data on Hall of Fame players and career leaders in various categories. There's a trivia game and a feature that lets users download fresh statistics and news for about twenty-five cents a minute, or an average of a dollar a day. And because Fingertip for Stats runs on the pocket-sized Newton, it even includes an elaborate electronic game-scoring module you can use in your seat at the ballpark—if you can make out the Newton's dim screen and keep mustard from dripping on it.

By far the most impressive of the new baseball programs is *Complete Baseball* from software giant Microsoft. It's designed for Windows users whose computers have CD-ROM drives, and it's expected to sell for around $60.

The prerelease version I tried out is a gorgeous product that encompasses the entire history and current status of the game and is richly illustrated with color photos, drawings and audio and video clips. *Complete Baseball* includes the entire text of the excellent reference work *Total Baseball*, including not only statistics on every player and team in baseball history but also well-done articles tracing players' lives, the course of each season and every aspect of the history of the game. There's even an article on women in baseball.

Extra material from other sources, such as *New York Times* articles about the book's hundred greatest players, covers moments like Henry Aaron's record-breaking 1975 home run and Ted Williams' .406 season in 1941. The trivia game is challenging and interesting. For $1.25 a day, Microsoft will offer via modem an electronic baseball newspaper containing fresh scores, stats, news and even a daily photo.

Because *Complete Baseball* is an unreleased product, it has some bugs and flaws that I can't certify will be gone when Microsoft releases it, but the company promises to wring them out. There are also a few design limitations in the program that won't be fixed right away. The daily updates are kept separate from the underlying data, so career statistics don't get updated. Printing is a clumsy process in some parts of the program, and you can't view on a single screen the statistics for multiple years in a player's career.

If you can't wait for Microsoft, or don't use Windows, the text of *Total Baseball* is also available on a CD-ROM for IBM-compatible and Macintosh computers that comes packaged with the $50 book itself. But this is a bare-bones product, with less material, fewer features, and none of the beauty of Microsoft's offering. And it only appears to go through the 1992 season.

Baseball has had trouble lately developing new young fans. I suspect these new software programs will help to snag some of those high-tech kids who spend more time at the computer than the ballpark.

4/28/94

The 1995 edition of Microsoft's Complete Baseball *is even better.*

71
Using CD-ROMs to Bridge the Gap in History Education

The only news articles more common than those hyping the new information age are the ones reporting that schoolchildren don't know a thing about history. If you can believe these reports, most teenagers think the Great Depression was the bad feeling they once got when they couldn't get tickets to a Meat Loaf concert.

Now the information age is offering a possible solution to the history education gap. A number of publishers are releasing multimedia CD-ROMs that aim to bring history to life on computer screens in a way that might appeal to children of the video-game era. These are "interactive" titles, which let users wander among vast amounts of video and text to absorb history in their own fashion.

The trouble is, such programs are so new that nobody knows for sure how to do one just right. All seem captive of the medium from which the material was mainly drawn: there are big differences between CD-ROMs that are based on books or periodicals and those that evolved from film or television productions.

Here's a look at four recent historical CD-ROMs, covering such topics as the D-Day invasion of Normandy, the Nixon White House, and the twentieth century. All are intended for computers running Microsoft's Windows software. They're so new they may be tough to find, but all should sell for between $40 and $60 at discount.

Normandy, the Great Crusade: This CD-ROM is being published by The Discovery Channel, in conjunction with a television documentary of the same name being aired by that cable network. It shows. The disk is a beautiful piece of work, with handsome graphics and audio narration that's professional and compelling. Film clips are well-edited and liberally used.

The story of the invasion is enhanced in a variety of captivating ways—from animated maps, to the texts of letters from soldiers, to segments of radio broadcasts. The disk essentially takes a polished TV documentary and allows the viewer to enter and leave it at any point.

Unfortunately, this television approach means the disk's research features are weak. The text articles included are relatively skimpy. There's no way to search for words, to copy material to a word-processor document or print it out. Still, I can imagine my teenager absorbing much from this program.

The D-Day Encyclopedia: This CD-ROM, from Simon & Schuster and Context Systems of Hatboro, Pennsylvania, is just the opposite. This disk has a wealth of text material, but it seems like a book slapped onto a screen with some movie clips, without much thought to the nature of the new medium.

I found the organization and the integration of text and video to be clumsy. The maps are hard to read on screen, and a picture of a real tapestry used as an organizing device is also tough to make out.

This is mainly a research product, and it permits you to copy and print material. But amazingly, you can't search for words in the text-only article titles. Overall, *The D-Day Encyclopedia* doesn't make it as a CD-ROM, in my view.

The Haldeman Diaries: Much was written about the news value of this digital account of the Nixon White House by the late president's top aide, Bob Haldeman. I tried to look at it from a user's point of view to see if it works well as a piece of software. The answer is a qualified yes, though the program is more for researchers than casual browsers.

The disk, from Sony Electronic Publishing, uses a simple metaphor as a main menu: a drawing of a desk, with a variety of objects on it. Click on the movie camera, and you get a menu of numerous home movies Mr. Haldeman shot in the White House. Click on the diary, and the text of his journals appears. A photo album yields still photos, and so forth. Navigation is clear. You can search for words, or find a date by clicking on a little calendar. Pictures, movies, biographies, and diary entries are linked, and you can print out material.

My only problem with the disk was that it sometimes behaved unexpectedly. Clicking on the newspaper lying on the desk didn't summon up press articles, but merely references to news events in an appointments log. The search feature seemed, on occasion, to miss things or be inconsistent. And the program crashed periodically. But some of these flaws may be attributable to the fact that I was reviewing a prerelease version. All in all, this is a well-done and fascinating CD-ROM.

Time Almanac of the 20th Century: This CD-ROM, by Compact Publishing of Washington, D.C., is the best of the digital historical almanacs I've seen. Particularly impressive is the number and variety of video clips, including silent footage from the early 1900s. There are economic charts, maps, and, of course, the text of many *Time* magazine articles. Research is made easier with a word-search function and the ability to copy or print material.

The disk is organized in two main ways: by decades and by themes. But I found the theme articles confusing, because you enter them from the section of the program covering the time period the authors thought most appropriate, even if the articles span other eras. For instance, the video of the 1989 Tiananmen Square massacre in China is part of a theme article on communism that is accessed from the decade of the 1920s. Still, there's a lot of value on this disk, and it would appeal to young browsers.

The only thing better would be a disk that lets kids study the League of Nations and order rock-concert tickets. Watch this space; I'm sure somebody will do it.

6/2/94

72
Leonardo's Ideas Fly and Woodstock Rocks on Two CD-ROMs

Most of the multimedia CD-ROM titles that cross my desk aren't good enough to recommend. A lot of them are "shovelware," the contents of a book poured onto a disk with some sound and graphics, but with little thought to designing the whole thing as a computer experience. Once in a while, however, a disk shows up that features both interesting content well-suited to the screen and a usable interface for "interactively" viewing and browsing.

Two such disks have caught my eye recently. One is about Leonardo da Vinci. The other is about such people as Janis Joplin, the late rock singer. One is for children who wish to explore the mind of the great Renaissance man. The other is an excuse for aging baby boomers like me to reminisce about the Woodstock rock festival. Both are well-done titles, but the better of the two is *Leonardo the Inventor*, a $40 disk from InterActive Publishing of Spring Valley, New York.

Leonardo the Inventor, which includes on a single disk versions for both Apple's Macintosh computers and PCs running Microsoft Windows, is aimed at older kids. But exploring this handsomely crafted title is such a rich, engaging experience that plenty of adults will enjoy it as well. It focuses not on the great fifteenth century artist's paintings, but on the numerous designs for startling machines found in his notebooks. These designs foreshadowed such modern inventions as the helicopter, the drawbridge, and the deep-sea diving suit.

From the opening seconds, the disk envelops the reader in rich illustrations and period music meant to invoke the Renaissance. A crisp, professional narrator's voice gives the feeling of a high-class television documentary, a feeling reinforced when an ink sketch by Leonardo of a prototype flying machine leaps off the page in animated flight.

Soon, however, the user is given control of the documentary, through an easy-to-use contents screen and a detailed index. The main section of the disk is devoted to Leonardo's inventions, but there also are sections devoted to his biography, a brief review of his artistic work, a time line matching the events of his life with events in the wider world, and a bibliography. Any of these can be viewed, in any order. The whole thing is so well done it's hard to believe it was created for its publisher by a little-known digital design firm in Jerusalem, called SuperStudio.

For each invention, the program offers an explanation, complete with animations and narration, a relevant quote from Leonardo, plus a video clip showing how Leonardo's idea was eventually carried out in the modern world. In addition, some musical inventions include interactive demonstrations of instruments.

The software also has a sense of humor. There are three full-fledged computer games, based on the inventions, including an excellent one involving escape from a Pentagon-like fortress of Leonardo's design. And there are funny animations involving the Mona Lisa I won't reveal.

Not everything the designers tried here works. Many of the videos depict technologies that bear little relation to Leonardo's inventions—for example, a fire truck ladder is compared with a device for scaling castle walls. And a collection of 3-D animations, to be viewed with special cardboard glasses the publisher supplies, is an unimpressive gimmick that detracts from the title's overall class. Despite this, *Leonardo the Inventor* is a very nice piece of work.

So, in its own way, is the Woodstock retrospective CD-ROM from Time Warner Interactive of Burbank, California. This $30 disk for Macs or PCs running Windows, produced for the Time Warner unit by Opcode Interactive, is based on the famous 1970 documentary film about the festival, another Time Warner property. It's also part of a commercially inspired effort to tempt middle-aged baby boomers to spend some of the money they've accumulated since abandoning antimaterialism.

There are videos of performers and attendees, lots of still photos, biographies, and discographies of the artists. A trivia game tests users' knowledge of the 1960s. Correct answers are rewarded with the phrase "Far out!" while wrong guesses draw the comment "Bummer."

The user makes her way through the Woodstock disk with on-screen controls that strain to be funky (the button for returning to a prior screen is labeled "Take Me Higher"), yet still are clear enough to work well.

But the heart of the Woodstock title is the music. It opens with Joni Mitchell's anthem to the festival ("We are stardust, we are golden. . . .") sung by Crosby, Stills, Nash, and Young, and includes eight full performances, complete with lyrics. The spirit of the era is captured by a video clip of Country Joe McDonald singing the "I-Feel-Like-I'm-Fixin'-to-Die-Rag," with a bouncing ball leading the viewer through its antiwar lyrics ("One, two, three, what are we fightin' for?").

There's a little too much uncritical emphasis on the drug culture, for my taste. I could have done without a goofy feature that lets you paint vibrating psychedelic scenes that suggest a marijuana haze.

To its credit, however, the title includes video interviews with a few attendees that hint that everyone wasn't drawn to Woodstock in 1969 by social conscience. In one, a young man en route concedes he's going because "there's a lot of girls here, and they're probably a lot freer than other places."

And that's the way it was.

8/4/94

73
CD-ROM Software That Quietly Goes about Your Business

The Wall Street Journal recently reported that sales of CD-ROM drives were soaring and were expected to continue doing so. But the article also noted that market researchers believe many PC owners aren't using their CD-ROM drives, which allow computers to run software and read data stored on high-capacity platters resembling music CDs.

That may appear paradoxical, but it isn't as surprising as it seems. I suspect most of those who possess, but don't use, a CD-ROM drive didn't go out and buy one to add to their old machine. Instead, they received the drive as part of the standard configuration of a new PC. In fact, the CD-ROM drive is fast becoming part of the basic complement of features on all but the cheapest computers.

My guess is that these owners of idle CD-ROM drives think them useful only for playing the flashy multimedia entertainment and education software with which the term CD-ROM is most closely associated in the press. If you've reached this conclusion, think again. There are lots of CD-ROM disks that don't sing, dance, or slay dragons, but just sit in your PC quietly providing volumes of useful information. Some employ audio or video to augment their contents. But they are mainly textual, not graphical, and use the disk's vast storage capacity to provide business information or to support research.

Here's a random selection of just a few of these dull-but-practical CD-ROMs I've tried; there are many more, in the same and other categories. Most let you copy and/or print selections from their contents. Many lack a pretty interface, and some take more effort to learn to operate than the software I normally recommend. But they just might give you a reason to use that CD-ROM drive you paid for.

There are a variety of phone and address directories available on CD-ROM, all of which use the computer's power to store and rapidly search through mounds of data. These combine local listings into broad national or regional databases, containing millions of names, addresses, and phone numbers. They let you search for people or businesses, even if you only know a part of the name or some other fragment of information.

One I tried is called the *Eleven Million Businesses Phone Book*, from American Business Information of Omaha, Nebraska. This $40 disk claims to include "virtually every business in the U.S. and Canada." Using it, I was able to locate not only big businesses, but my neighborhood pet shop and the submarine-sandwich joint at the beach resort I just visited. The disk permits you to retrieve five thousand detailed listings for up to one year, after which it stops working and must be replaced. The company offers a similar disk covering seventy million households. Both are for PCs running MS-DOS or Windows. These products and their competitors don't generally include unlisted phone numbers.

Allegro New Media of Fairfield, New Jersey, offers the searchable text of twelve business how-to books on a $60 CD-ROM called *Business Library, Volume One*. The disk, for Windows, also contains three business-oriented videos. The books aren't world-famous titles, but they cover advertising, marketing, sales, accounting, careers, real estate, and my personal favorite: "How to Get People to Do Things Your Way."

For $70, you can get a CD-ROM that claims to list the names and contacts for every federal domestic-aid program, including "federal grants, loans, services, scholarships, mortgage loans . . . surplus property, government auctions and much more." The disk, for MS-DOS and Windows, is called *Information USA* and is published by Infobusiness of Orem, Utah. There are limitations to this disk, however. I found I could only print the entries I wanted, not save them as text files or copy them for insertion into a word processor.

You can get the full text of 1,750 great works of literature and other books and documents on a $129 CD-ROM for IBM-compatibles called *Library of the Future*, from World Library of Garden Grove, California. The disk includes all the works of Shakespeare, Aristotle, Twain, Chaucer, and many others; all the Sherlock Holmes mysteries; the Bible, the Koran, and the Book of Mormon; and the U.S. Constitution and Federalist Papers. It's a rotten way to read these works cover to cover, but a great way to search for key phrases and references across a vast range of titles.

An outfit called the Bureau of Electronic Publishing, in Parsippany, New Jersey, offers a competing $40 *Great Literature* CD-ROM for both IBM-compatible and Macintosh computers with over 1,800 famous works of literature and nonfiction. For those who just want the essence of the great books, especially students, the company also offers the famous *Monarch Notes* series of literary summaries. The $50 *Monarch Notes* disk includes nearly every book a teacher might assign and runs on both IBMs and Macs.

Other companies offer low-cost CD-ROMs containing thousands of fonts, illustrations, and photos. I recently picked up for under $20 a CD-ROM crammed with hundreds of inexpensive shareware programs. Several companies now offer CD-ROMs that contain street maps of nearly every locality in America. And the list goes on and on.

So, even if you're not interested in multimedia, you can still get your money's worth from that CD-ROM drive that came with your computer. Some of your hipper friends will call you boring, but can they get the phone number of that place in Rehoboth Beach, Delaware, that makes great Italian subs? I think not.

8/18/94

74

Computer Toys That Don't Require a Child's Supervision

Attention, grown-ups with computers! You don't have to spend all your time in front of that screen typing things into word processors (the way I'm doing now). You don't have to be locked in spreadsheet hell forever! Sure, it seems like all the cool new computer programs are for kids, those ungrateful little urchins who already have more stuff than they deserve. But even if you lack the joystick reflexes of a twelve-year-old, don't despair. An exhaustive investigation by this columnist has turned up at least five really neat computer programs we grownups can use to pursue hobbies, plan purchases and trips, and just to amuse ourselves. They make great gifts and can be played again and again.

Best of all, most are interactive programs that let you control how they unfold and work with your personal data and preferences. All you need is an IBM-compatible PC that runs Microsoft Windows (alas, only one comes in a version for Apple's Macintosh). For several of the programs, you will also need a CD-ROM drive. (I'll indicate which.)

3D Landscape: This terrific multimedia package from Books That Work of Palo Alto, California, will let you create a detailed layout for your yard, right down to the plants, trees, and shrubs you want and the best positions for them. You first select the plantings from a large database, in which you can search for varieties that do well in various parts of the U.S. and in various light and moisture conditions and that meet numerous other criteria you choose—down to what color blossoms they yield. Then you drag images of your selected plants wherever you want on an image of your yard.

The $50 program, which comes in CD and floppy-disk versions, is smart enough to show you where the plants' shadows will fall on any date or time, based on the latitude and orientation of your yard. It will even show how the plants you select will look after five or ten years. You can view the yard from the top or on a slope or in 3-D. There is also an extensive how-to section, with text and animations, and various calculators for figuring things like soil acidity. You can even print out a materials list with estimated prices for your design.

Popular Mechanics New Car Buyers' Guide, 1995: Another program by Books That Work, this $30 CD-ROM is the best automobile software I've seen, allowing you to do extensive comparison shopping before setting foot in the dreaded showroom. You simply tell the program what style, price, safety and other features you're looking for, and it generates a list of choices, complete with illustrated reports on each model. You get all the specs, color pictures of the exterior and interior, and even a limited ability to see each car in different colors. Price estimates are provided and can be printed out.

There's a complex and sophisticated options feature, with prices, for building just the model you want, and loan and lease calculators that use the actual price figures for the cars you're considering. There's also information on car-buying tips, ratings where available on model safety and warranties, and detailed reviews from *Popular Mechanics* for about fifty cars.

Rand McNally TripMaker: This $45 floppy-disk program lets you create detailed itineraries for family or business car trips, reflecting your preferences for daily driving distances and various intermediate stops. You can set up the route manually or use an automated step-by-step process called Trip Guide that will even suggest vacation destinations and sightseeing stopovers from an internal database. The program produces a list of written directions and a map, which can be printed out. My only complaint is that, surprisingly for Rand McNally, the maps do a poor job of labeling small local streets.

Family Tree Maker, Deluxe CD-ROM Edition, Version 2.0: The long-winded name of this $59 program is misleading, because this is a full-fledged genealogy program, not just a way to mock up family trees. It lets you create a detailed database of all your relatives and their relationships and can even incorporate photos if they have first been transferred to a Kodak photo CD disk.

Not only that, but the program's publisher, Banner Blue Software of Fremont, California, has built in a list of one hundred million deceased Americans. The program tells you what sort of historical government records contain information on each person—Social Security records, census data, military records and so forth. You can then go to a library and look up indexes to the relevant records, or Banner Blue will sell you a CD-ROM containing detailed indexes to the records for about $25, in most cases. The indexes alone often contain key dates and other data.

***Dilbert* Screen Saver:** Scott Adams' *Dilbert* comic strip chronicles the frustrating, stupid and petty world of the typical American office worker. This $45 floppy-disk program, from Delrina of Toronto, Ontario, lets that caustic commentary decorate the screen of either a Windows PC or a Mac.

There are numerous scenarios, including one where a character reads a budget in disgust, rolls it up and uses it to smack a manager—whom you can name after a real boss you hate. In another scenario, a group of executives are shown falling asleep, one by one, during a boring presentation. In yet another, called Secretary with a Crossbow, secretaries everywhere can live out their dreams of revenge.

So, grown-ups: enjoy these five programs without any pesky kids around. Unless, of course, like so many of us hapless breadwinners, you need their help to get the blasted computer running.

12/1/94

75
So Many CD-ROMs, So Few Ways to Find the Ones You Want

The CD-ROM revolution is running into a huge roadblock: it's nearly impossible for consumers to buy the software disks with any confidence that they know what they're getting. The shopping experience for interactive and multimedia software on CD-ROMs is frustrating and unsatisfying, and it's getting worse.

Thousands of CD-ROM titles are flooding the market, overwhelming retailers' shelf space. Most of these programs still must be searched out at computer stores, especially superstores like CompUSA and Computer City. But nontechnical folks often dislike venturing into these places, where disk drives, memory chips, and spreadsheets are the standard fare—not titles on the life of Leonardo da Vinci or on financial planning—and clerks are too often scarce and poorly informed.

Worse, there's no way to "browse" through potential CD-ROM purchases, even though many electronic titles contain far more content than a hefty book and typically sell for much more: between $30 and $100. Though computer stores often have enough PCs on the floor to run the space program, customers are rarely permitted to use them freely to try out CD-ROM titles.

There are good reasons for this, from the retailers' point of view. It's easy for unskilled or malicious shoppers to disable a computer temporarily by entering the wrong commands. And every CD-ROM title for IBM-compatible machines seems to require a different complicated software configuration. But it still results in a bad, blind shopping experience for consumers.

I believe these factors conspire against greater variety and quality in the CD-ROM marketplace, favoring games and titles that use established characters from television and films. These kinds of disks can be assessed and selected more quickly, without detailed browsing, and appeal more to the men and teenage boys who enjoy hanging out at computer stores. Indeed, small software developers routinely complain that they can't even get buyers from the big stores to look at titles other than games or character spinoffs. And if other titles somehow make it onto the shelves, they complain, they're expected to become hits within a month or so or they're yanked.

All this sounds like a job guarantee for guys like me who write reviews of CD-ROM titles, because reading such reviews, or hearing about titles from friends, seems to be the only way to know what's out there. Reviews will continue to be important, as they are for books and music CDs. But there are too many titles for reviews and word-of-mouth to do it all, and we reviewers never know if, when, or where a title we recommend will be available to readers. There's just no substitute for browsing through books or hearing selections from CDs on the radio or TV or in-store listening kiosks before buying.

One solution is for other types of stores to handle CD-ROMs, but my experience with these alternatives has been disappointing. The excellent Borders chain of large, upscale bookstores has started adding "new media" sections packed with CD-ROMs. The atmosphere is certainly better than in a computer store. But, like computer stores, Borders isn't providing customer-controlled PCs and unstructured browsing.

Blockbuster, the big video-rental chain, tried renting CD-ROMs in its San Francisco–area stores during 1994. It declared the test a success and plans to expand it. But according to media reports, the chain found customers mostly rented games, mostly for CD-capable game machines, not computers. Blockbuster also complained that customers found it baffling to get many CD-ROM titles to run right on their home IBM-compatible PCs. (Macintosh users had a much easier time.)

I suspect the solution to the browsing problem is a digital one: special machines and special disks designed to give consumers a taste of many titles in one package. In stores, there's a need for sealed, automated computer-driven kiosks in which customers could sit and quietly browse some titles. Microsoft has installed stand-up kiosks for its titles, but somebody should make sit-down ones that feature non-Microsoft titles as well.

The best solution of all may be sampler CD-ROMs that can be played at home, offering consumers the opportunity to try out limited versions of titles on their own machines and then buy the ones they like over the phone.

An excellent product like this already exists for children's software. It's called Club KidSoft and can be ordered (800-354-6150) for $7.95, or through an annual four-disk subscription for $29.95.

Microsoft (800-583-0040) and Voyager (800-446-2001), another major CD-ROM publisher, offer sampler CDs covering their own product lines, for $4.95 and $9.95, respectively. (I like Voyager's new slogan for its generally high-class product line: "Bring your brain.") A magazine called *CD-ROM Today*, which sells for $7.95 a pop, also includes with each issue a sampler CD of titles the magazine wishes to promote.

Several companies have tried and failed to sell CD-ROM–based catalogs containing general software, mostly traditional programs like word processors that sell on floppy disks. However, I don't know of a CD-ROM sampler disk for grownups, covering CD titles only, that covers multiple publishers and has a centralized purchasing mechanism built in. But such a product is certainly needed if innovative titles and curious consumers are ever to have a chance to find one another.

12/29/94

Part VI
Kids & Games

Nothing sells computers like the argument that the kids need one. But it's not easy to figure out what software to buy for them. Here, we offer some suggestions, and cover some adult games as well. In addition, there's a tip on keeping kids away from the grown-ups' files on the computer, and why you should avoid the most advanced of the game machines.

76
Breathing Easy When the Kids Borrow the PC

When school opens every September, the thoughts of U.S. parents are supposed to turn to the question of how to make their offspring smart enough to compete with all those brainy tykes who never seem to take long vacations.

Increasingly, this means letting the kids get their jelly-stained mitts on the family computer. Of course, in many cases, the machine was bought in the first place on the theory it would help make the children computer-literate. But you may also have it loaded up with your finance and tax records, or reports for the office, or private electronic mail.

The last thing you want is to have your fifth-grader or teenager mucking around in those files, reading them, misplacing them in odd places on your hard disk, or even deleting them altogether.

So, what's a parent to do?

There are relatively inexpensive ways to customize and control access to the computer so kids can only call up the programs and files that you want them to use. For years, there have been "menu" programs, especially for IBM-compatible computers, that let computer owners control and restrict a user's choices.

Now there's a $30 program designed expressly to manage young kids' access to your computer, and to do other things to enhance a child's computing experience. This clever and colorful package, for both IBM-compatibles and Apple Computer's Macintosh models, is called KidDesk. It's made by Edmark, an educational publishing firm based in Redmond, Washington.

Apple itself is also offering a simple Macintosh access-control program called At Ease, which it says is aimed at neophytes such as "kids and chief executive officers."

The more general menu programs are often quite plain-looking, and aren't designed specifically for kids. But they're usually inexpensive, and they get the job done. These programs let you set up a menu of available choices that appears when the PC is turned on. The child has access to only those choices you preselect, and you can lock out such items as access to file directories by requiring the entry of a password only you control.

These menu programs are too numerous to list here, but two good examples are "MenuWorks Personal" by PC Dynamics and "Direct Access" by Fifth Generation Systems, in versions for both plain IBM-compatibles and those running Microsoft's Windows software. A tiny one-man company in North Wilkesboro, North Carolina, Pocket Change Software, offers a $20 program called Chastity to limit users' access to Windows.

A much better approach is offered by KidDesk, which installs a colorful picture of a desk that appears each time the computer comes on, completely obscuring the PC's familiar prompt for entering commands, or, on the Mac, the standard graphical work area.

On the main surface of the desk are icons or symbols, inserted by the parent, representing those programs to which a particular child has access. The child runs the programs by clicking on their icons with a mouse device, which is required. No other software or files can be used by the child.

A hidden "adult section" of the program, which can be protected by a password, allows grown-ups to leave KidDesk and use anything on the computer, and it lets them quickly and easily customize the child's desktop using commands unavailable to the child. No programming skills are required.

But KidDesk offers much more than controlled access. It's filled with a host of features to personalize and enrich a child's computing experience. The kids can pick from six desk styles, and add their names and a picture to each desk. Parents and kids can even record sounds and messages that can be played back by clicking on a kid's picture or an icon of a telephone, if the computer is equipped for audio.

There also are special kid-oriented "accessories" on the desktop, including a simple calculator, a talking clock, and a calendar that a child can customize with colorful "stickers" and print out.

Parents can establish separate desktops, with distinct sets of available programs, for each child in the family. KidDesk can even be customized for children with disabilities. A special "scanning" option slowly highlights each icon on the screen in turn, so that physically disabled kids have time to select choices using special devices. For learning disabled children, parents can turn off some features and icons to reduce confusion.

KidDesk is a terrific way not only to protect your files from the kids, but to give them a positive feeling of control over the machine, without constant nagging from you.

Apple's At Ease software is a much less ambitious product. It further simplifies the Mac's already famous easy-to-use features by presenting the user with just two customizable screens. One features large icons that launch selected programs when you click them, and the second features large icons that open particular documents when you click them. Programs and documents that you haven't deliberately made available through At Ease can be used only by those who know a password.

Apple is including At Ease with its line of low-cost Performa models of the Mac, and it can be bought separately for $55. But if your target is kids, I'd go with KidDesk for around half the price.

9/10/92

77
For Parents: Here's Educational Software That Gets High Marks

Many a parent's desperate search for educational software ends in disappointment. Much of what's called "educational" is either light on content or too dull to engage young minds used to Nintendo and Nickelodeon. So here's a sampling of some of the best kids' computer programs to cross my cluttered desk. This list isn't exhaustive, but I think your child will be entertained and educated by the software cited below.

The most interesting educational software I've seen recently is a series of programs called Knowledge Adventure Interactive Books, from a company of the same name based in La Crescenta, California.

These packages, for older grade-schoolers and above, are "interactive," meaning a child can roam through large bodies of information by simply selecting dates, places, and topics on a simple-to-use screen. Each selection brings up informative explanations of the subject, a colorful picture and even, in some cases, sound and animation, if your computer is equipped to handle it.

Topics are "linked" logically, so children can follow their own lines of questioning. This is the kind of software that has mainly been available only on CD-ROM disks, which require special disk drives. But Knowledge Adventure has discovered a way to compress a vast amount of data tightly enough to fit on regular disk drives.

So far, there are three of these $50–$60 packages, which run on IBM-compatible PCs. There's a general Knowledge Adventure program, another called Sports Adventure, and a third called Science Adventure, written by the late author Isaac Asimov. More titles are on the way, and the company aims to create an integrated library of computerized reference works, including titles written by other firms. Versions are also in the works for Apple Computer's Macintosh machines.

For younger kids, I like a $35 program called Kid Works 2, from Davidson & Associates of Torrance, California. A much-improved version of the original Kid Works, the new edition lets children write and illustrate original stories on screens that look like ruled school composition paper. It even reads their words back. The drawing module seems inspired by Kid Pix, Broderbund Software's terrific children's art program, with special effects and cheerful sounds. Kid Works 2 is currently available only for Macintosh, but an IBM-compatible version is promised.

Davidson also is about to ship an IBM-compatible program called "Zoo Keeper," in which kids ages six to eleven are challenged to rescue animals by making sure their zoo areas have the proper foods, temperatures, and other living conditions. Along the way, young players learn what animals need in order to survive.

I'm very impressed with a new series of interactive CD-ROM storybooks, called Living Books, from Broderbund of Novato, California. These are children's books transferred to the computer screen, with rich illustrations and text that match the originals. But there's a twist. The computer can read the story to the child, in English or Spanish, in a natural human voice. And the stories have been made interactive—when the child clicks on a part of a picture, wonderful animations occur.

Walt Disney Computer Software, of Burbank, California, is readying its own talking interactive-storybook program, Follow the Reader. This package lets kids ages five to eight construct miniadventures about Mickey Mouse and other Disney favorites from preselected sentences. Then, the software enacts the story, complete with dialogue in the characters' familiar voices. Expected to sell for $30 to $40, it doesn't require a CD-ROM drive.

Edmark, of Redmond, Washington, has a wonderful new preschool math program, called Millie's Math House. Loaded with colors and sounds, the $35 program guides kids through fun-filled activities designed to teach counting, recognition of shapes and patterns, and even simple problem-solving logic. It comes with an on-screen guide for parents, and the company—a longtime publisher of both printed and computerized educational materials—is offering parents a free booklet on choosing educational software.

Finally, there are two games in the genre of Broderbund's excellent *Carmen Sandiego* series. In these programs, kids assume the role of a detective or other investigator. They roam the world, or travel through time, seeking clues that will enable them to arrest a criminal or reach some other goal. Along the way, they must master geographical and historical facts.

Time Riders in American History, by Learning of Fremont, California, sends forth players to stop a villain from changing history to suit his evil purposes. In Nigel's World, from Lawrence Productions, of Galesburg, Michigan, the player becomes a photographer seeking a prize-winning photo using geographical clues.

Whatever you buy, remember that there's no electronic quick fix to education. Most educators agree that no amount of software, by itself, can turn your progeny into rocket scientists. There is no machine that can substitute, they advise, for good schools, hard work, and a supportive family.

9/17/92

78
Parental Guilt Sells Encyclopedias on CD-ROM, Too

Some people say the strongest force on earth is nuclear fusion. I say it's parental guilt, the endless worry that unless some benefit or other is made available to one's offspring, they won't succeed in life.

Parental guilt has long driven the sale of home computers. And it is a big reason for surging sales of a new type of software: electronic encyclopedias on CD-ROMs, the high-capacity computer disks that play multimedia educational software titles on special disk drives.

There are three leading CD-ROM encyclopedias: the *New Grolier Multimedia Encyclopedia*, *Compton's Interactive Encyclopedia*, and an entry from Microsoft called *Encarta*. Each packs the entire text of a traditional multivolume encyclopedia onto a single disk, augmented by pictures, audio clips, maps, animation, and short videos. Each costs about $300 at discount stores, though they sometimes come as part of a package when you buy a CD-ROM drive or a computer equipped with one.

Before comparing the three, it's worth considering the strengths and weaknesses of any electronic encyclopedia versus the familiar sets of books. By far the biggest advantage of electronic encyclopedias is their ability to rapidly search, across all volumes and articles, for topics you choose. This not only speeds the process of looking up material, but also digs out citations you may overlook in a book—for instance, a reference to Thomas Jefferson in an article on architecture.

A second advantage is the addition of audio, video, and animation. The ability to listen to a piece of music or see a film clip of the 1969 moon landing is especially appealing to today's kids. A third big plus is that you can move information directly from the encyclopedias into reports you're writing in a word-processing program. Finally, electronic encyclopedias cost much less than most paper competitors, if you don't count the cost of the hardware needed to use them.

But there are significant drawbacks as well. I compared the three CD-ROM products to the familiar $700 *World Book Encyclopedia* (which isn't available in multimedia form), and found most articles I checked were both longer and better-written in the *World Book.* The computer products also can't match the vividness and detail of color photos, maps, and tables in the *World Book.*

The electronic references require you to sit at a computer and stare at a screen—not the best way to read. And the ease with which electronic text can be copied whole threatens to diminish note-taking skills and increase plagiarism, despite warnings in the manuals and automatic tagging of some text with copyright lines (which can be erased).

Still, kids like these disks. My eighth-grader strongly prefers the computerized version. (It's "more of a real experience," he says.) So which one is best?

All three are adequate for school-age children, with thousands of articles on a wide range of subjects. But I found the Compton's text more geared to younger kids, and likely to be less satisfying as they grow up. *Grolier* was sometimes too adult-oriented, but often strikes a good balance between older and younger kids. *Encarta* is likewise written at a mid-range level.

Grolier's interface is a little clumsy, but it has a more versatile searching system and a nicer selection of videos than Compton's, including terrific newsreel footage of such events as the Hindenburg disaster and the London blitz. Both are available for IBM-compatible PCs and Macintosh computers.

Without a doubt the most promising entry is Microsoft's *Encarta.* As is typical of new Microsoft products, *Encarta* has both some wonderful features and major weaknesses the company must remedy in subsequent revisions.

Encarta has by far the most attractive and easiest user interface. It is the only one of the three in which pictures appear alongside the text; in the others, you must switch to a separate screen to view them, destroying any synergy between art and words. Its graphics and audio clips are far better than its rivals'. The manuals and help system are superb. *Encarta* also makes complicated searches easy with a "research wizard," an optional program-within-a-program that guides users step by step through the creation of a complex search request.

But *Encarta* has three main weaknesses. Its text comes from the Funk & Wagnalls supermarket encyclopedia, with short pieces on the computer industry added by Microsoft, including an audio clip of company chief Bill Gates reciting his corporate "vision." (There are also pieces—but no audio—on Gates rivals like Apple's John Sculley.)

Moreover, *Encarta* has no historical video clips, and few videos of any kind; it relies on still photos accompanied by audio and animations. *Encarta* is also painfully slow, even on a relatively powerful PC. For now, it works only on IBM-compatible PCs running Microsoft's Windows.

But *Encarta* has a promising future. Microsoft is hiring experienced encyclopedia editors to improve the text, and is working on adding videos and making *Encarta* faster. It also plans a Macintosh version.

You won't go wrong with any of these. If you must buy now, *Grolier* is a good choice. If you can wait, or are willing to buy now and upgrade to newer versions, *Encarta* is probably the way to go.

4/29/93

All three have improved, but Encarta *has gotten better fastest, adding content, an even cooler interface, and videos.*

79 Maybe You'll Admit You're Playing Games If They're This Clever

When asked in surveys what types of software programs they use frequently, computer users typically list sober stuff like word processors, or maybe spreadsheets. Well, I don't buy it. I think a lot of folks spend a lot of time playing games on their PCs, but just don't want to admit it. And, of course, that goes double for kids. They may do their homework on the machines, but the kids I know spend a heck of lot more time on games than on that electronic encyclopedia that helped their parents rationalize the purchase of the computer.

The trouble is, lots of games are pretty monotonous and/or violent—an endless series of similar screens in which some character you control goes around killing foes. It's tough to find more challenging and creative products.

So here's a rundown on four of the most interesting computer games for kids and adults that have crossed my desk—products that aren't based on simulated slayings and show considerable creativity. I've been playing these lately, purely for journalistic purposes, with the help of my game-savvy teenage son, who runs rings around me in this category. Each is of high quality, in our view. They won't bore you.

For little tykes, ages four to eight, I like an entry from Edmark of Redmond, Washington, called Thinkin' Things, available for IBM-compatibles and soon for Macintosh computers as well.

This is a collection of six different activities designed to entertain the kids while developing key educational skills, such as memory, pattern recognition, and drawing analogies. Some of the modules show colorful series of odd creatures and patterns, and then ask the player to repeat or extend them. Others create musical tunes kids try to re-create. Still others let kids create three-dimensional animations built out of spheres and other simple shapes, with accompanying music.

Slightly older kids, ages seven and up, will have a great time with Kid CAD, a program from Davidson & Associates, of Torrance, California, that runs on IBM-compatibles under Microsoft's Windows software.

In computer lingo, CAD means "computer-aided design," and usually refers to costly, complex software that lets architects and engineers render building plans accurately on a screen. Kid CAD puts some of that power in the hands of children, letting them create elaborate three-dimensional buildings in an urban, farm, or small-town setting. There are simple controls for adding a wide variety of features, ranging from foundations, wall and roof components, to furniture, people, paint, and decorative patterns, each accompanied by sound effects.

Kid CAD is basically the electronic equivalent of Tinkertoys or Legos. Obviously, there are advantages in such hands-on building toys that a computer simulation can't match. But if you've ever stepped on your kid's Legos while walking barefoot in the dark, you might prefer Kid CAD. The program also does things real building blocks can't. You can zoom and scroll through the designs, link components, print out pictures of them—even demolish the structures in various entertaining ways.

For grown-ups, the most fascinating recent game I've seen is called *Myst*. It's sold by Broderbund of Novato, California, but was created by a small outfit called Cyan Inc., which previously made such delightful, nonviolent games as Cosmic Osmo. In *Myst*, which requires a Mac with a CD-ROM player, you wander through fantasy worlds, attempting to solve a mystery whose very dimensions are unclear at first. Your weapon is ingenuity, not a ray gun. You don't have to "kill" anyone, and you don't "die" repeatedly. Yet it's anything but boring.

From the opening credits, it's clear that *Myst* sets a new standard for the visual and audio quality of games. It's more like a richly animated and scored motion picture than a typical computer game. There are thousands of beautiful images, over an hour of animation and video clips, and a very pleasing sound track that's nothing like the tinny tunes on game machines. You move through the fantasy world by just clicking the mouse. No commands need be memorized. At every turn, you must solve clever puzzles and interpret sophisticated clues. The whole thing is nonlinear—you can trace your own path through it, solving the puzzles in any order. *Myst* is an absorbing experience that lasts many hours.

A less fantastic but also impressive game for adults is *Who Killed Sam Rupert?*, by Creative Multimedia Corporation of Portland, Oregon. This one also comes on a CD-ROM, for both PCs and Macs, and relies heavily on videos and audio.

This game is like an interactive version of the old TV show *Dragnet*. You're given six hours to solve the murder of Rupert, who was found dead in the wine cellar of his restaurant. But, unlike earlier mystery games, this one uses actual photos and videos of actors to provide a realistic feel to the whole process.

You can zoom in on various parts of the crime scene photo—to read a wine label or check for fingerprints or do other forensic tests. You can play movies of the interrogations of prime suspects, and try to evaluate them from their expressions and tones of voice, as well as their words. There's even a press conference built in. I enjoyed the whole experience thoroughly.

So don't be ashamed to play games on your computer. But stop lying on those surveys, okay?

9/30/93

80
Toyland, Toyland, Software Girl and Boy Land

Here's a quartet of kids' programs I think fit the bill for most families. These titles aren't boring or violent, and don't require a CD-ROM drive. All are available in versions for both IBM-compatibles and Apple Computer's Macintosh machines.

Zurk's Learning Safari: This is a marvelous collection of skill-building games for preschoolers from a company called Soleil Software of Palo Alto, California. The package centers on animals and settings native to Africa. The most interesting is "Maya's Adventure," in which Maya the lion cub actually walks and turns as you move the mouse, encountering other animals, some of which help her find a path home through the tall grass. There are also alphabet games, jigsaw puzzles, a matching game, an on-screen animal picture book and a pair of clever hide-and-seek games. It comes with a nice booklet for parents that includes suggestions for added noncomputer activities and a story to read aloud.

Unfortunately, I can only recommend the Macintosh version of this terrific $60 program for average users. The IBM-compatible version (which doesn't require Windows) can be so tricky and frustrating to install, depending on your particular computer hardware, that I think it's best reserved for the technically adept. What a shame.

Creative Writer: The first entry by Microsoft into kids' software is a fanciful yet powerful word-processing program for children eight to fourteen with either Macs or IBMs running Windows. The emphasis here is on imagination and creativity. To achieve that, the actual word processor in Creative Writer is embedded in an entire fantasy world called Imaginopolis. A goofy-looking cartoon character named McZee leads users into a colorful "building" with floors housing a writing studio (the basic program), a Projects Workshop, an Idea Workshop, and a Library. There are lots of sounds and special effects.

The word processor itself has most of the functions of adult programs, including text that wraps around pictures, a limited choice of fonts and type sizes, a spellchecker, and a thesaurus. But there are also colorful background designs and borders, funny sounds, animations, jokes, and a system for turning words into "secret code."

There's a feature called the "Splot Machine" that creates thousands of "story starters"—nonsense sentences that prompt the young writer, such as: "The laughing anteater darted quickly into your desk." The Project Workshop holds step-by-step guides that create banners, cards, and "Moosepapers."

Using the $65 program is rather different from using, say, Microsoft Word. And it'll drive some grown-ups nuts, even though you can skip McZee and most of the "building." Menus and icons are colorful and arranged in short groups. To change a font, type size, or style, just "paint" over existing text after making a selection from the menu; in standard programs, you have to first highlight the words being changed.

Experienced computer users will note that Creative Writer borrows some features from outstanding predecessors, such as Broderbund Software's Kid Pix and Print Shop. But Microsoft has succeeded in creating something new, something that is an entire thinking environment for kids.

The Even More Incredible Machine: This is a fascinating $50 game for older children and adults, in which you solve puzzles by constructing animated Rube Goldberg–like machines out of parts that range from the mundane (pulleys, nails, and gears) to the silly (mice, dynamite, and trampolines).

For instance, in the easy first puzzle, you're asked to use three bowling balls to push a basketball through a hoop. You do it by dropping one onto a mouse, which runs around a little wheel, which you attach to a conveyor belt, and . . . you get the idea.

I found this program addictive and challenging, and I expect that it would appeal especially to children who like building things. The publisher, Dynamix, an arm of Sierra On-Line, of Coarsegold, California, has issued separate versions for IBMs running plain DOS and those that run Windows, and for Macintoshes.

3-D Dinosaur Adventure: Knowledge Adventure of La Crescenta, California, has rewritten its successful Dinosaur learning program to include a host of new multimedia features and restyled it to resemble the setting of the movie *Jurassic Park*. In particular, the program now features 3-D drawings and movies of dinosaurs that require those 1950s-style 3-D cardboard glasses (included) to see in all their glory. To the properly equipped viewer, the monsters seem to be leaping out of the PC screen.

In addition, the new version features a sort of virtual-reality feeling; you move the mouse and it seems you yourself are moving around in the "theme park" and even inside buildings. The program is loaded with facts and figures and pictures of dinosaurs, narration and several games. There's a separate CD-ROM version with more movie clips of moving dinosaur models.

Your children will enjoy using all four of these programs.

12/9/93

81
Computer Games Go Hollywood, for Better or Worse

The software industry is learning how to adopt Hollywood production values in multimedia software. That means computer owners will be able to choose entertainment and education titles that finally rise to TV production quality while offering the viewer a real interactive role.

Unfortunately, a few software companies are using those slick Hollywood techniques to produce story lines featuring Hollywood cultural values as well—especially gratuitous violence as a way of solving problems. And that means responsible parents may have to veto some of the multimedia titles with the best visual and audio effects on grounds of offensive content.

To help families sort it all out, here's a brief rundown on three of the earliest computer titles to display real TV qualities. One—*TuneLand*, by a start-up company called 7th Level—is a wonderful, wholesome interactive cartoon that uses the best animation I've ever seen on a computer. It makes a preschooler feel as if she's controlling the action in a Saturday-morning cartoon show. A second, *Wallobee Jack*, soon to be marketed by WordPerfect, is another TV-like animated feature that lets grade-schoolers solve a mystery.

The third, *Critical Path*, by MediaVision, is an action title for older kids and adults featuring a real actress and real video scenes that wastes great production techniques to tell a hackneyed tale featuring little but killing.

TuneLand stars a small bear called Lil' Howie, whose voice is provided by comedian Howie Mandel. The bear plays hide-and-seek in a series of richly illustrated and animated storybook settings—Old

MacDonald's farmyard, a train station, and more. The images and animations were hand-drawn and then transferred to the computer using a technique called anti-aliasing, which eliminates the jagged edges frequently found in computerized drawings.

The result is stunning TV-quality animation. The farm wife chasing around her kitchen after the three blind mice looks just like a scene out of a Warner Brothers cartoon. Children clicking on nearly any object in *TuneLand* are rewarded with action, sound, or music. The program contains forty or so full-length songs beautifully orchestrated in treatments ranging from classical to country to rock-and-roll. There's even a separate "jukebox" program that lets kids just play the songs, if they're tired of the animated adventure.

TuneLand is available at a price of under $50. Unfortunately, it only works on IBM-compatibles running Microsoft Windows and equipped with CD-ROM players. No Macintosh or disk-based version is planned.

WordPerfect's *Wallobee Jack* also is an animated cartoon, though less impressive and less extensive than *TuneLand*. Aimed at older kids, it follows a kangaroo named Wallobee Jack as he seeks to retrieve a famous Australian artifact before the villain, an evil crocodile, can get it. The player interacts with the game by trying to find hidden "hot spots" on the screen containing bombs that foil the villain or light bulbs that help the hero.

The game has a smart-aleck, cartoonish quality. The crocodile is afflicted with familiar devices like exploding cigars, and insults the player if she fails to foil him. Unfortunately, it gets a little too cute at times. A slick "host" interrupts at least once to try to sell the user a $15 Wallobee Jack T-shirt. And if you lose, and the crocodile grabs the artifact, he punishes you by rebooting your computer—a dangerous feature.

WordPerfect will start selling *Wallobee Jack* as part of its consumer Main Street line in March, for both PCs and Macs with CD-ROM drives. The title and others in the *Wallobee Jack* series were developed by Tune 1000, a Canadian company that has licensed them to WordPerfect.

Finally, there's *Critical Path* by MediaVision, a highly respected maker of multimedia hardware that is launching a new software line. *Critical Path* is the tale of a sort of macho woman, muscular and armed, who gets trapped in the factory complex of an evil madman in the aftermath of a nuclear war. She is constantly threatened with death and is constantly killing people to survive.

Technically, the title is brilliant—filmed at a special studio, using a real actress and skillfully melding video and animation. But it's a shame that a company with a good reputation has chosen to introduce such great technology in a title that glorifies violence. Not only is the theme trite and boring, it just piles on more violent entertainment at a time when parents are saying that enough is enough. And it echoes, however faintly, another Hollywood theme: that of the stalked woman, even if she is armed.

Some adults may like *Critical Path*, which is fine. It isn't gory, in the sense of showing blood and internal organs flying around. And I'm certainly not saying all interactive computer titles should be kids' cartoons or educational drills. Adventure stories, even those with a bit of violence, would be welcomed by most reasonable parents. But stories like *Critical Path*, with a major focus on violent action, are a problem for many of us.

Critical Path carries a warning label, and I'd like to add my own: don't buy it for a household with kids if you're concerned with the excess of violence in entertainment. I hope MediaVision will choose a better theme the next time it decides to use its hottest new technology.

1/20/94

82
Look Past the Hype Before You Buy the 3DO Game System

The problem with the gee-whiz approach to new high-tech products frequently favored by Wall Street analysts and some parts of the press is that it is driven mainly by the glamour of the new technologies themselves. These breathlessly positive reactions too often undervalue the more mundane issues of whether and when the new technologies will actually make a difference for consumers—providing benefits previously unavailable—and at what cost. Yet, in the end, those are the only questions that matter.

That's the flaw in much of the advance billing for the 3DO game-machine system, 1994's most heavily touted new gizmo for homes. Many of the glowing forecasts came from well-meaning folks who hadn't tried a 3DO player in a real home setting, as I have lately. After a couple of weeks of using a 3DO machine, I, too, am willing to admit the thing has potential for greatness. But I wouldn't advise anyone except well-heeled technology freaks or adult game addicts to run out and buy one any time soon. To my mind, the benefits 3DO delivers to families today are scant, especially considering its hefty $500 cost.

There's no problem with the hardware, which is based on technology developed by 3DO of Redwood City, California, and incorporated so far in only one player, Panasonic's REAL model. In our rec room, the 3DO showed itself capable of higher-quality, higher-speed animation and video than game machines from Sega and Nintendo and most standard PCs. My game-savvy boys, ages twelve and fifteen, rated it technically far above the Sega Genesis and the Macintosh and IBM-compatible PCs on which they've played. But, as with computers, it's the software that's key. If it's weak, predictable, or unsuitable for family use—in the eyes of the parents who pay for it—so is the game system that plays it.

And so far, to the eyes of this father, many of the handful of software programs available for 3DO (and even many of the new titles we tried out in prerelease versions) don't move the ball. With one impressive exception, what I saw were merely visually juiced-up variations of the same tired and often-violent genres now playable on much cheaper game machines, or copies of what's available on the multimedia personal computers parents are rushing to buy precisely so they can pry their kids away from game machines and bad TV shows.

The goal of 3DO is to deliver much better and more interesting entertainment and education programming than exists on game machines, and at a lower cost than that of a personal computer. The machine uses CD-type disks, not cartridges, and can play not only games but music CDs, Kodak photo CDs and, soon, movies on CDs—with a $200 attachment. It has a well-designed hand controller that even permits the use of headphones, and the player can accept add-on devices, including a keyboard, as they become available.

Unfortunately, the one game shipped with the Panasonic player, Crash 'N Burn by Crystal Dynamics, isn't an encouraging sign for 3DO. It's a road race, with armed cars that attack each other. Though visually impressive, it features a tired, violent theme nearly as old as the PC. It's the same with another highly praised 3DO title from the same publisher, called Total Eclipse. This is the old spaceship shoot-'em-up theme with better scenery.

Another Crystal Dynamics title, The Horde, shows promise because it uses some video clips with real actors and lets you build villages. But in the end, it's really about killing and wounding again—this time involving blob-like creatures who pillage the towns.

John Madden Football from Electronic Arts has videos of the colorful sportscaster, but otherwise seems a lot like other football simulators on other machines.

Much worse is the 3DO version of the notorious game Night Trap, from Digital Pictures. In it, a bunch of lovely teenage girls are stalked by masked men with grappling hooks in a spooky house. This violent, sexist theme is made more noxious by the 3DO's more realistic video and sound.

But we did see one terrific 3DO title, Twisted, by Electronic Arts, that showed how the machine's technology might be used to provide great interactive family entertainment beyond what I've seen on game machines and PCs. Despite its deviant-sounding name, Twisted is a fast-paced parody of a TV game show in which multiple players can compete by solving a variety of puzzles and challenges. It's packed with great video and audio, including an unctuous host and funny contestants, played by actors, who are controlled by the players. There's inventive content and lots of humor, though I always lose miserably to my offspring.

There are a number of other good titles out or planned for the system—though, unlike Twisted, they're not uniquely based on 3DO technology and are already available for personal computers. And the 3DO company is believed to be considering developing its own software offerings, to better show off the technology. It's also negotiating with more companies to build the machines, at lower prices, and working on making 3DO technologies available on personal computers, through an add-in circuit board.

If 3DO technology becomes a path for bringing unique and valuable content into the home, it'll make sense for many families to own one. But until then, wait.

3/10/94

3DO now costs less, and sales have picked up a bit. But it still lacks enough great, unique software and is still a minor factor in the market.

83
Ten Kids' CD-ROMs That Are Worth a Look

If you took all the CD-ROM software packages for kids and laid them end to end, you could probably circle Silicon Valley with glossy, shrink-wrapped boxes costing $39.95 each. Many, if not most, would be disappointing, but your kids would still want most of them for their birthdays.

There are so many of these titles now that it's impossible to keep up with them all. So here's a list of ten recent titles that I like, to help you figure out what to buy. Each costs under $50 at discount stores or by mail order. Most are for IBM-compatibles, but some also come in versions for Apple's Macintosh machines. Most will run in four megabytes of memory, the standard configuration, but all will do better in eight megabytes, and some require eight. Before buying any of them, check the specifications on the package to make sure they'll work on the computer used by the intended recipient.

First is a group of programs for preschoolers and elementary-school-age children:

Freddi Fish: This is a terrific, nonviolent mystery game, with fluid animation that looks like Saturday morning TV—only without the commercials. The idea is to guide Freddi and her pal through the undersea world in search of some missing seeds. Kids learn to gather clues and tools, and solve problems. The publisher is Humongous Entertainment of

Woodinville, Washington. One catch: it needs eight megabytes of memory.

The Farm: This "junior encyclopedia," also by Humongous, is like a digital field trip to a farm. Everything from the parts of a tractor to the animals themselves is pronounced and explained.

Thumbelina: At heart, this is just a book poured onto a screen—something I generally dislike. But the artwork, animation, and narration are so well done that the package, from Time Warner Interactive of Burbank, California, achieves a certain overall charm. It's aimed especially at little girls (though I could have done without the complimentary charm bracelet).

Harry and the Haunted House: This is another of the wonderful interactive story books from Living Books of Novato, California, which pioneered the genre. In this one, a group of kids explore a spooky house after their baseball lands inside. As always, the quality here is high, and each screen has a host of funny animations.

Arthur's Birthday: Yet another new title from Living Books, this story follows on the heels of the popular interactive *Arthur's Teacher Trouble*, also by author Marc Brown. If you can't find the newer one, you'll be just as pleased with the older one—indeed, with any of the Living Books. They're all great, in my view.

The Magic Schoolbus: This first in a planned series by Microsoft finds a group of kids roaming around inside the human body in a turbocharged schoolbus. Based on the popular books by Scholastic, the software is entertaining and educational, if not quite as impressive as some of the other titles in this list.

Zurk's Rainforest Lab: Little Soleil Software of Palo Alto, California, has produced a title that will educate kids about the creatures of the rain forest while entertaining them. This multilingual program centers on a village marketplace. Click on various people or shopping stalls, and you can jump to a series of engaging games or create a "photo album."

Then there are three cool titles for older kids and teenagers, all of which are also perfect for adults.

Blown Away: This is a challenging, exciting game with custom-made full-screen video footage and real actors, loosely based on the MGM movie. The object is to free a group of hostages held by a terrorist bomber, but you don't succeed by whipping out a machine gun or displaying the arcade-game reflexes of a sixth-grader. Instead you use brains and ingenuity to solve a series of tricky puzzles, which change each time you play. The game is designed by Imagination Pilots of Chicago and published by IVI of Eden Prairie, Minnesota. It requires eight megabytes of memory.

Cartoon History of the Universe: This clever, funny CD-ROM is based on the popular book by Larry Gonick and published by Putnam New Media. There aren't many bells and whistles, just hundreds of pages of history told in humorous cartoons and narrated by a "professor." In addition, there are three excellent games in which you explore the Pyramids, rebuild the Parthenon and traverse the maze of the Minotaur. Overall, it conveys more information more engagingly than most history classes do.

Vid Grid: This unusual program is a fast-paced visual game, much like those plastic puzzles where you slide around little tiles until all the numbers line up right. In this case, the puzzles are composed of nine full-length rock videos by artists like Aerosmith, Guns N' Roses, Peter Gabriel, Van Halen and the Red Hot Chili Peppers. The idea is to unscramble the videos, as they play, before they end. The CD-ROM, by Geffen Records and Jasmine Multimedia, is a lot of fun but works best if you have eight megabytes of memory rather than the four specified on the box.

So that's ten winners out of a sea of candidates. Given enough time and column space, I could probably come up with ten or twenty more, so don't worry if you pick something else. But I still say that gift-giving was simpler before computers came along to make our lives "easier."

11/17/94

Part VII
Other Stuff

Nearly all of the Personal Technology columns have been about computers, because they are the products that most confuse people and are in greatest demand. But once in a while, I've tried to cover other common technologies, like fax machines, fancy phones, and VCRs. And once, while I was on vacation, a pinch-hitter even penned an ode to the typewriter.

84

Ode to the Typewriter and (Gasp!) Those Who Still Use One

By Peter R. Kann

I once suggested that Walter Mossberg write a column for those of us who sometimes still use typewriters.

"But you are the last one," said Mr. Mossberg. The premise of this column is that I'm not.

Typewriter owners simply are intimidated, hiding our Royals in basements, furtively scrounging replacement ribbons from obscure stationery shops, flinching at the comments of our computer-age kids. ("Yo, Dad has a printer with a keyboard.")

Since I am actually on-line at the office, can almost match my five-year-old on his Mac, and am proud we produce *The Wall Street Journal* on computers, the aim here isn't to wage Luddite war on PCs, only to challenge P.C. views of the typewriter.

The classic manual typewriter manufactured from the 1870s to 1960s (not, mind you, electrics, Selectrics, and other doomed mutants of the 1970s) doesn't deserve to go the way of buggy whips. If radio can coexist with TV, matches with lighters, parents with teenagers, why not typewriters with computers?

Let's look at some merits of the manual:

Personality: Aficionados may debate the virtues of a Royal 10 versus an Underwood 5, but all agree that not only each model, but indeed each machine, has a distinct personality. Eccentricities—a resistant key, playful space bar, unruly margin—mirror our human foibles. With typewriters, from input to output, from the touch of your keys to the XXXXs on your paper, process and product are uniquely your own.

Independence: Typists, unlike computerized colleagues, aren't harnessed to electric currents or beholden to battery packs. We watch friends heading off on trips laden with laptops, modems, cables, batteries, plugs, adaptors, and alligator clips to hot-wire hotel phones. Some get arrested as spies by Third World customs agents. Others, having failed to lug along a heavy printer and then requiring hard copy, wind up using fax modems to send to hotel fax machines for exorbitant fees. Wouldn't a lightweight Olivetti Valentine typewriter serve more simply?

Versatility: While we're at it, try producing small notes, cards, or envelopes on a normal PC printer.

Durability: Classic manual typewriters are made of solid steel. Mine has withstood monsoons in New Guinea and sandstorms in Waziristan. Typewriters even survive airline baggage handlers.

Audibility: The comforting clack of the keys and rewarding ring of the carriage bell make typing a pleasing pastime, much like reading poetry aloud. Consider, there are now shareware computer programs on the market that seek to simulate the sounds of typewriter keys and bells. Better the real thing.

Health: Whoever heard of getting repetitive stress syndrome and other arcane ailments—or of having to sign up at the office for Ergonomics 101—because of a typewriter? The worst injury a typewriter can inflict is to drop on your toe.

Security: With a typewriter you can rest secure that no hacker will invade your memo or manuscript, no passing toddler will delete your document or diary. There's no trace data others can use to reconstruct documents you think you've expunged. And there's zero risk of pressing a wrong button and sending a memo about your boss to your boss.

Intimacy: Typed letters invariably are sent to a person. Computer correspondence, at the touch of a key, all too often goes to distribution lists—to scores of disinterested parties who have the misfortune to be "aliased" on line. The irony of our computer age is that never before have so many been hard-copied on so much that matters to them so little. Computers, it turns out, kill more trees than typewriters ever did.

Output: Mark Twain is reputed to be the first author to submit a typed manuscript to a publisher. This was in the 1870s and the title was *Tom Sawyer*. Has anyone yet written a better book on a computer?

Modesty: The typewriter is an honest instrument; it doesn't aspire to be human. There are no spellcheck programs and memory files. The typewriter doesn't pretend to spell when it cannot read, doesn't claim to remember when it cannot think. Typewriters are not in competition with their owners.

Procuring a typewriter: Keep in mind with typewriters, as with Bordeaux, that older is better. Production of all the fine manuals ended in the 1960s. Only Olivetti still produces some new plastic portables. So you are best off scouting garage sales for a vintage machine ($5 to $50) or finding a "reconditioned" model in the basement of an office supply store ($50 to $150). Test all keys, carriage return, and ribbon reverse. Be sure to bargain. Pick up extra ribbons when and where you find them.

My favorite is a handsome black Royal manufactured in the 1920s. It was bought from Lev Shapiro of Lincoln Center Business Machines in New York. Mr. Shapiro still sells, services, and loves typewriters.

For those with more academic interests, we recommend an out-of-print volume by Wilfred A. Beeching titled *Century of the Typewriter*. It provides a three-hundred-year history from Kytptographs and Chirographs to Clavier Imprimeurs and Writing Harpsichords, as well as detail on every classic manufactured model.

If, perchance, you are seeking to dispose of a typewriter, feel free to ship it (not c.o.d.) to Mr. Mossberg's t-mail address at *The Wall Street Journal*. Mr. Mossberg enjoys hearing from readers.

8/11/94

Peter Kann is the publisher of The Wall Street Journal *and the CEO of its parent firm, Dow Jones and Co. He wrote this column at my urging, becoming the only person other than myself to write Personal Technology. In an earlier career as a* Journal *reporter, he won a Pulitzer Prize for dispatches he filed from a war zone, presumably on the kind of typewriter he describes here.*

85

Here's Help in Finding the Essential Facts about Fax Machines

Fax machines are, at heart, simple to understand. They are best thought of as long-distance versions of that familiar office device, the photocopier.

Like copiers, fax machines accept original documents on paper, scan the documents with electronic sensors, and then spit out copies, or facsimiles. The difference, of course, is that the copy is sent to a distant fax machine, via special telephone circuitry built into both faxes.

But as fax machines have become ubiquitous, makers have offered so many features, in so many combinations, that shopping for a machine can be trying. Prices range from $300 or so to thousands of dollars. Ads are littered with terms such as "Group 3," "broadcast" and "fine mode."

The basic rule is this: Buy only the features you need. The simplest little fax machine may be enough for home use or low-volume professions. So analyze your likely needs and shun superfluous bells and whistles.

To help, here's a guide to some important features of fax machines.

First, let's clear away the underbrush. Fax ads are laden with certain buzzwords that you can ignore, because they apply to nearly every machine at every price. One is "Group 3" compatibility. This simply means the machine can send and receive according to the currently prevalent international standard. Another is the ability to handle both "normal" and "fine" output; this comes with Group 3 compatibility.

Then there is the claim that a machine can double as a copier.

Nearly every fax machine can do that, by "sending" a transmission to itself. But most make poor copiers, because they yield only one copy at a time and use waxy fax paper.

The rest of the key features can be divided into three categories: those that affect how you feed documents into the machines, those that affect how you receive faxes sent by others, and those that affect the telephone functions of the machine.

On the input end of the fax process, one feature is especially important: document feeding. The most basic machines require users to feed each page of a document by hand. That's fine for a college student faxing an occasional letter or research paper home. But even for most small businesses, it's essential to get a machine with an automatic feeder that lets you stack up at least a few pages and walk away.

On the receiving end, the biggest decision is whether a machine produces faxes on the familiar special fax paper or on regular paper. Most machines use rolls of the old-style greasy fax paper, and they cost less initially than plain-paper faxes. But fax paper curls and turns dark and brittle. It often must be photocopied if you want to keep it permanently, adding time and cost.

Plain-paper faxes using the same printing mechanism as copiers and laser printers are dropping rapidly in price. Some can be had for $1,700, with a strong array of other features bundled in. They also have lower per-page operating costs because they use standard office paper. But bear in mind that, like copiers and printers, plain-paper fax machines require the periodic purchase of supplies that old-fashioned fax machines don't need.

If you opt for standard fax paper and receive more than a dozen faxed pages a day, you should get a machine with an automatic paper cutter to separate faxes into cut pages. Otherwise, somebody has to snip the pages apart manually. And be sure to get a machine that can accept paper rolls long enough to meet your needs. Another useful feature is built-in memory, to store a page electronically if your paper roll runs out and then print it when you insert a new roll.

When you use the same phone line for regular calls and faxes, consider voice/fax switching. This feature enables the machine to recognize whether an incoming call is a voice or fax transmission. Otherwise, a human must answer the phone and decide. But to use such switching, you must make the fax machine's built-in phone your primary one for all incoming calls.

Finally, fax machines offer an array of dialing options to automate transmissions. Most offer some sort of speed dialing, where you can program in frequently called numbers and then dial them by pressing single buttons or entering two-digit codes. Some will redial busy numbers automatically; others can be set to transmit at a specified time.

Pricier machines offer "broadcasting": the ability to transmit a single outgoing fax to multiple recipients whose numbers have been programmed into the machine (this is the haven of "junk" faxers). Others can do "polling," or calling a group of fax machines to see whether they have material ready to send.

As with telephones, VCRs, and other high-tech gizmos, these programmable features may look nice on paper but can be difficult to operate using fax machines' limited keypads and screens. So, if you choose a complex machine, be sure to try before you buy.

2/6/92

Prices are much lower now, with plain-paper faxes available for around $600. But standard faxes are still much cheaper.

86 All-in-One Faxes Solve the Space Crunch, If Quality Isn't Everything

Despite the spread of computers into small businesses and homes, the fax machine remains a necessity for many people. Fax modems inside PCs are fine, but they can be complicated to use and only allow you to fax documents that are on a computer's screen, not hard copy such as a magazine article or other paper document. So the old fax machine is often still found right next to the personal computer.

The trouble with that is that it contributes to a space crunch in small offices. Many spare bedrooms and tiny business offices have a personal computer, a printer, a fax machine, and one of those small-volume copiers, all crammed so tightly together the places look like the scratch-and-dent table at an appliance store. And most of the fax machines out there still use those rolls of greasy, smelly paper, so you have to buy separate supplies for the fax, printer, and copier.

To solve the problem, electronics companies have long promised multifunction devices that would combine printers, faxes, and copiers in one box. Okidata introduced such a machine, a high-end product called the Doc-It, some time ago. But it hasn't taken the market by storm, partly because it cost too much and wasn't sold in enough stores. Now, Hewlett-Packard, Xerox, and others are trying to change the landscape with relatively low-priced (less than $1,000) multifunction machines.

My favorite is the HP OfficeJet, an $800 product that I've been trying out in my own home office, a spare bedroom more cramped than my office at the newspaper but just as messy. The OfficeJet looks like a large stand-alone fax machine, with the usual telephone keypad built in, but it's built around the guts of HP's popular DeskJet printers. It's kind of tall and boxy, weighs in at around twenty pounds and needs a fair piece of desktop space. But it consolidates a separate printer and fax machine. It can even replace a small copier—if you don't plan on making too many copies and don't care too much about the quality of the copies.

As a computer printer, the OfficeJet works pretty much like one of HP's basic monochrome inkjet printers, which work by spraying a fine mist of fast-drying ink onto the paper. It churns out most documents at two to three pages a minute, and the quality is very good—nearly as good as that of a laser printer. It handles letter, legal, and other paper sizes, as well as envelopes and transparencies. The machine is best suited for IBM-compatibles using Microsoft Windows, but it also works with older DOS programs. There isn't a specific version for Apple Macintosh computers, but a Canadian company called GDT Softworks sells a product called PowerPrint that connects the OfficeJet to Macs.

As a fax, the OfficeJet also does fine. It uses the same print mechanism as the printer portion of the device, so you receive faxes that are on real paper, not that waxy fax paper. It has a twenty-page document feeder, lets you program sixty-five numbers for speed dialing and can store around twenty-four pages of incoming faxes in its memory. The OfficeJet can receive faxes even when it's out of paper or ink or while you're printing a document from the computer. It just waits until you put in new ink or paper or until the computer is done using the OfficeJet and then prints out the faxes it has stored up. It can also send faxes while you're printing a computer document because the sending process doesn't use the print mechanism at all.

The copier function is the weakest part of the package. It can make up to ninety-nine copies of a document in one pass and can reduce legal-size documents to fit on letter-size paper. But since it works through the same scanning mechanism as the fax function, it can only produce copies with the resolution of an incoming fax—far less crisp than documents that the OfficeJet prints from the computer and not really up to top business standards. It's very much like the limited copying ability built into other fax machines.

The OfficeJet is also noisy—it makes a kind of ka-chunk sound when it's printing. And it only holds one hundred sheets of blank paper. But all in all, I like it and think it will be a welcome addition to many small offices.

I also took a brief look at a competing machine from Xerox, which is trying to break into the home market. The Xerox 3002 has the same basic features as the OfficeJet but with more bells and whistles and greater speed. Most important, its built-in copier uses the same high resolution as the printer, not the lower resolution typical of faxes, and it can collate documents. Xerox also offers an optional add-on kit that lets the machine scan hard copy into your computer and transmit faxes directly from a PC screen, two functions the HP lacks.

But the Xerox machine is expected to cost just under $1,000 in discount stores—$200 more than the OfficeJet. And the scanning add-on kit costs another $200 extra.

Worse, the ink on the Xerox printouts smeared easily in my tests when I accidentally rubbed a finger over them just after removing them from the machine. That's a very serious problem that HP and Canon have gotten under control in their inkjet printers by using special fast-drying ink. So I can't recommend the Xerox over the HP unless better copy quality is so high on your list you're willing to spend an extra $200 to get it and you're confident you'll never accidentally smear your printouts, faxes and copies. Me, I'm lucky if mine escape without coffee stains and bagel crumbs.

11/10/94

87 AT&T's VideoPhone Doesn't Measure Up to Its Price Tag

The other day, I called up my parents, and my two sons got on the line. Four hundred miles away, my mother leaned closer to her new telephone and said to them: "I'm glad you've got nice short haircuts." The newly shorn lads grinned back.

It was an unremarkable grandmother-to-grandson encounter, except that my mom could see those new haircuts over the phone, not just hear about them. For grandma and grandsons were talking over a pair of AT&T's $1,499 color video telephones, lent to us for a few weeks.

AT&T calls the VideoPhone 2500 the start of a new era of home communications. The company contends that America is ready to pay plenty for high-tech phones that will allow far-flung families to visit via video. But that prediction has been made, and left unfulfilled, more than once since AT&T first showed off a picture phone at the 1964 World's Fair.

My mother, beaming at her grandchildren, felt momentarily good about the new gizmo, as AT&T had hoped. But that wasn't her attitude when I had called the week before to let her know that AT&T was shipping her a VideoPhone 2500 so we could test it.

"I don't want it," she said helpfully. "It's an invasion of privacy. I don't want to have to look good whenever the phone rings." So I told her she could turn off the video at any time. "Oh, great," she cracked. "Then the other person will definitely know you look lousy."

My father didn't care about that. "It's progress," he said, recalling that he'd seen a prototype at the World's Fair. But my mom relented only after I assured her that her friends couldn't catch her on the videophone, because none owned videophones.

The phone is a handsome black desktop unit with a foldout video module on top. In the middle of this upright housing is a flat color screen like those on laptop computers. The screen is minuscule: only about two by two and a half inches in size. Sitting atop the screen in the housing is a small round camera lens, which can be blocked by sliding a privacy shield over it.

AT&T's VideoPhone is a prodigious technical achievement because it works over regular phone lines, not the special cables needed by business videophones. That means anybody can hook one up, and that video calls cost the same as regular voice-only calls. But this is also its greatest flaw, because regular phone lines lack the capacity to carry video images at the normal speed of thirty frames a second.

Though AT&T has used advanced compression technology to squeeze more video data into the phone lines, the VideoPhone can display no more than ten frames a second. So instead of smooth, full-motion video, the AT&T unit produces what amounts to a series of snapshots, a jerky slide show. If the person you're talking to blinks, the image of him with eyes closed will linger on the screen.

Even worse, the audio travels faster than the pictures. So it takes several seconds after hearing a sentence before you see the facial expression that accompanied it. Meanwhile, more audio has been received. This time lag makes for distorted conversations, because the words and body language are mismatched. I wouldn't want to rely on the VideoPhone to gauge a family member's mental state or negotiate a business deal.

Then there's the problem of privacy. My mother is still down on the VideoPhone for this reason, even after seeing the kids on it. My wife had the same reaction. People routinely use regular phones while in bed, or in other private settings. They can do other tasks, like cooking, while they talk, because there's no need to make eye contact. Video threatens to make phone calls full-time, formal work.

At least it won't be hard work to install the phones. Setup at both ends was a snap: we each just plugged the phone cord into a normal phone jack, and an electrical cord into a wall outlet (after wrestling with a huge accessory unit that goes on the floor).

Operating the thing is also easy, once you learn that calls begin only in audio. For the video to come on, both parties must push the big blue "video" button. There are also brightness and focus controls. And there's a self-viewer function you can use to check your appearance, in which your screen shows what your camera sees.

Using it takes some practice. In our test calls, we've been cut off a few times. We kept drifting out of camera range, cutting off chins and foreheads, adjusting the house lamps to curb glare and shadows.

I suppose the VideoPhone might be adequate for images that don't depend on synchronized conversation, like showing off the new baby or an antique vase. But it's too crude not only for most serious conversation but also for viewing business documents. When my father held up his local newspaper, all I could make out was a few words in huge type.

In the end, I decided that the video was so stilted the phone wasn't worth $1,500 to me. I know AT&T will sell a ton to users with special needs, such as hospitals and adoption agencies, and to technology fans who want whatever's new. But I doubt videophones will really take off until the pictures improve and prices fall.

When that day comes, please don't call my mother. She'll call you.

8/13/92

88
Simpler Programming of VCRs Is Possible with Two New Gadgets

The most familiar example of technology's failure to deliver on its promises is the difficulty people have in programming their videocassette recorders.

Typically, the process requires users to manipulate a long series of poorly labeled buttons or confusing "menus" that flash on the screen. Even setting the clock on the VCR can be an ordeal, so plenty of people just let their machines blink "12:00" in perpetuity.

These VCR owners may be confused and frustrated; but they aren't stupid. The stupidity lies elsewhere, in the absymal failure of VCR designers to provide a programming system—a "user interface"—that's obvious and unambiguous.

But bad design spawns innovation. For out of this mess a new class of products is emerging: special remote-control devices that aim to simplify VCR programming so anyone can do it, even without first setting the VCR's clock.

I've been trying out two such products. One, called VCR Plus, by Gemstar Development of Pasadena, California, has been sold nationally since 1991. A relatively simple and straightforward gadget, it's available for around $50 and uses those strange code numbers that you may have noticed in the television listings in your local newspaper or in *TV Guide* magazine. VCR Plus works with most VCRs and cable-TV boxes, and a version of VCR Plus is being built right into an increasing number of new-model recorders, eliminating the need to buy the add-on gadget.

The other product is a much more sophisticated and costly device, a $169 unit called VCR Voice Programmer, by Voice Powered Technology of Canoga Park, California. This one lets you control your VCR and your TV by simply talking into a built-in microphone. It lets you not only program the recorder verbally, but change channels, command the thing to play or rewind, and so forth. It also controls your TV. It's cool, but it's not so simple.

Both devices work by substituting their own simpler user interfaces for the ones built into your VCR. You do your programming directly on the add-on gadgets, both of which have tiny built-in screens. Then these controllers take over, sending the necessary commands to the VCR.

Of the two products, VCR Plus is not only much cheaper, it's also easier to use, and it's targeted directly at the problem of VCR programming.

Say you want to record the comedy *Murphy Brown* from 9:00 P.M. to 9:30 P.M. on Monday on Channel 9. With VCR Plus, you don't need to recall any of these details. You just look in the television listings, find the code number assigned for *Murphy Brown* on that night in your area, and enter it. You then tell VCR Plus how often you want it to tape the show (choosing from buttons marked "once," "weekly" or "daily") and you're done. All you need to remember to do is put a blank tape in the machine and lay the VCR Plus on top of your recorder.

In my test, the device worked perfectly every time, on two different VCRs. About the only hard part is configuring the VCR Plus. You have to enter a code number corresponding to your VCR and/or cable-TV box so the VCR Plus will know how to talk to it. And, because local cable-television systems use varying numbers for the same channels, you have to tell the device which numbers are used in your local area. This took me around twenty-five minutes, but it's a one-time job.

There are a few drawbacks. VCR Plus doesn't work with certain really old VCRs, such as those with wired remotes (though, despite what the manual says, it does work with many older VCRs whose remotes lack number keys). It adds still another remote control to your repertoire. And your local newspaper may only provide the codes for a limited number of shows (like mine, *The Washington Post*).

This last hassle isn't a problem for VCR Voice Programmer, because it doesn't use the code numbers. That gadget still requires you to enter start and stop times, and channel numbers. But it lets you do so with voice commands. For the example above, you'd speak the time and channel numbers into the device when prompted to do so on its little screen. That isn't as easy as just punching in a code number, but it's more fun. And you can use such voice commands to control most of the other functions of your VCR and TV, including changing channels. There are also regular buttons.

But VCR Voice Programmer is harder to configure. You have to train it to recognize your voice and to emulate your existing remote controls. I had to go through both processes twice in my tests, after my initial efforts caused my VCR to turn on fast forward when I said, "Stop!" It seems the room was too noisy when I did my first voice training. But once I had spent about ninety minutes getting it set up, VCR Voice Programmer did fine.

The voice recognition is impressive; it can even store the voices of several family members. But I suspect the Voice Programmer, which costs as much as an audio CD player, will mainly prove attractive to people who have to own all the neat new gadgets and can afford to collect them.

For the rest of us poor, befuddled VCR owners, the simple little VCR Plus is a better choice.

9/24/92

Index

About the Author

Walt Mossberg is the author and creator of the weekly Personal Technology column in *The Wall Street Journal.* Since it was launched in October 1991, the Thursday column has become one of the most popular features the *Journal* has ever introduced, as well as one of the most influential technology columns in any publication. For his work on the Personal Technology column, Mr. Mossberg was nominated for a Pulitzer Prize in 1993 and became the first person ever to win two journalism awards in one year from the Software Publishers Association. In 1995, he won a National Headliners Award for his columns, and was cited by *Marketing Computers Magazine* as the most influential computer journalist in the nation.

Mr. Mossberg has been a reporter and editor at the *Journal* since 1970. He is based in the *Journal*'s Washington, D.C., office, where he spent eighteen years covering national and international affairs before starting the column.